The Evaluation of Land Resources

The Evaluation of Land Resources

Donald A Davidson   University of Stirling

Longman
Scientific &
Technical

Copublished in the United States with
John Wiley & Sons, Inc., New York

Longman Scientific & Technical,
Longman Group UK Ltd,
Longman House, Burnt Mill, Harlow,
Essex CM20 2JE, England
and Associated Companies throughout the world.

Copublished in the United States with
John Wiley & Sons, Inc., 605 Third Avenue, New York, NY 10158

© Longman Group UK Limited 1980, 1992

First published in the Topics in Applied Geography Series in 1980
Second Edition 1992

British Library Cataloguing in Publication Data
A catalogue record for this book is available
from the British Library

Library of Congress Cataloging-in-Publication Data
A catalogue record for this book is
available from the Library of Congress

ISBN 0–582–02399–8

Set by 8 in 9½/ 12pt Ehrhardt Medium
Printed in Malaysia by CL

Contents

1

Land Resources and Land Use Planning Issues   1

2

Land Resource Surveys   19

3

Soil Surveys   38

4

Land Capability   57

5

Methodology of Land Evaluation

6

Soil Survey Interpretation

7

Land Resource Information Systems

8

Modelling of Land Resources

9

Conclusion

Preface

This book is a revised and enlarged edition of *Soils and Land Use Planning*, which was published in 1980. The original book evolved from courses taught at St David's University College, Lampeter, and at the University of Strathclyde, Glasgow. The dominant theme was to demonstrate how soil survey information can be interpreted in a form helpful to land use planning. The book was published at a time of rapidly evolving methodology in land evaluation. The FAO *Framework for Land Evaluation* had been published in 1976 and many organizations were in the process of adopting its approach. The 1970s were also a decade of considerable interest in the interpretation of soil survey and other environmental data for land use. This was expressed in a proliferation of land capability schemes which resulted from a need to produce maps which could be understood by non-specialists. Another important factor was new guidelines or legislation in some countries designed to protect high quality agricultural land from other uses; this necessitated the adoption of land classification schemes.

Attitudes to land evaluation are very different at the beginning of the last decade of the twentieth century to those which prevailed when *Soils and Land Use Planning* was written. In western Europe, the main factor for such change is agricultural overproduction. The need to extend or retain areas for agriculture is not so evident; in contrast increasing emphasis is being given to finding non-agricultural uses for farmland. In contrast, there are still many areas of the world where there is a desperate need to match food production with population requirements. In such areas land resource evaluation and policy implementation will continue to provide a considerable challenge.

Since the publication of *Soils and Land Use Planning*, the applied science of land evaluation has been transformed through the use of techniques culled from information technology, in particular geographical information systems (GIS) and modelling. This new edition explores such new opportunities. The underlying concept is that better decisions are likely to be made about land use and land management if the best available land resource information is presented in the manner most appropriate to defined issues. There is an increasing trend to require predictions of land use patterns, impacts and performance under different policy or management options; the production of such estimates requires land evaluation involving the integration of GIS, yield prediction and policy or management scenarios. In the earlier book, *Soils and Land Use Planning*, the emphasis was on presenting soil information in the most helpful form to land use planning; such a concern is still central to this new edition, but particular emphasis is given to answering 'what if' type questions.

Little attention is given in this new edition to issues of degradation of the land resource base though the concept of sustainable land use systems is fundamental throughout. *Soil Erosion and Conservation* by R. P. C. Morgan (1986) is viewed as a companion volume. In writing this book I have been very much helped by the provision of papers and reports from many scientists. I have benefited from a collaborative land evaluation research project with the Soil Science Institute of Athens and in particular I wish to thank Dr S. P. Theocharopoulos. I am very grateful to Roy Morgan, who reviewed a draft copy of this book. Thanks are due also to Bill Jamieson and Mary Smith, cartographers in the Department of Environmental Science, who have drawn the diagrams, and to John McArthur and Sandra Winterbottom, who helped with providing GIS processing and output. I acknowledge with affection all the support of Caroline, who found time to correct and improve my English, and I hope that the publication of this book will explain to Louise, Lorna and Alan why I have spent so much time in my study rather than being with them.

Donald A. Davidson
University of Stirling
August 1991

Acknowledgements

We are grateful to the following for permission to reproduce copyright material:

Agricultural Institute of Canada and the author, Dr. G. Wall for Table 3.2 (Patterson & Wall, 1982); Blackwell Scientific Publications Ltd. for Figs 4.3 (Rudeforth, 1975), 4.6 (Davidson, 1989), 6.8 (Bouma *et al.*, 1986), 7.10 (Burrough 1989), Tables 3.3 (Ragg & Henderson, 1980) & 4.4 (Davidson, 1989); CAB International for Fig. 8.4 (Allan Jones & O'Toole, 1987); CSIRO (Division of Soils) for Fig. 6.3 & Table 6.3 (Murtha & Reid, 1976); CSIRO (Division of Water Resources) for Figs 2.6 (Purdie, 1984) & 6.7a & b (Booth & Saunders, 1985); Elsevier Applied Science Publishers Ltd. for Table 5.7 (Gbadegesin, 1987); Elsevier/Geo Abstracts for Tables 2.1 (Bellocchio & Magaldi, 1987), 4.3 (Burnham *et al.*, 1987), 5.4 & 5.5 (Chinene & Shitumbanuma, 1988) & 6.5 (Dent & Scammell, 1981); Food & Agriculture Organization of the United Nations for Figs 1.3 (Higgins *et al.*, 1982), 2.2 & 2.3 (FAO, 1978a), 5.1 & 5.3 (FAO, 1976), Tables 1.1 (Alexandratos, 1988), 1.2 (Higgins *et al.*, 1982), 5.1 (Kanyanda, 1988), 5.2 (FAO, 1975), 5.3 (FAO, 1984a) & 6.4 (FAO, 1985); Forestry Commission (Edinburgh) for Fig. 6.6 (Hamilton & Christie, 1971); the Controller of Her Majesty's Stationery Office for Fig. 1.4 (Scottish Development Department, 1987b); Institute of Terrestrial Ecology for Fig. 7.3 (Davidson & Jones, 1988); International Institute of Aerospace Survey and Earth Sciences (ITC) for Fig, 5.2a & b (Bouma & van Lanen, 1987) & Table 5.6 (Kalima & Veldkamp, 1987); The Macauley Land Use Research Institute for Figs 2.4 (Bibby *et al.*, 1982), 4.4 (Soil Survey of Scotland, 1982) & Table 4.2 (Bibby, 1990); Macmillan Publishing Company for Fig. 4.1 (Brady, 1984) Copyright © 1990 by Macmillan Publishing Company; Natural Resources Institute for Fig. 6.5 (Water Development Department, Cyprus, 1982); the author, B. Rizzo for Fig. 2.5 (Rizzo, 1990); Soil & Water Conservation Society for Figs 1.5 (Lee, 1984), 7.9 (Nielson *et al.*, 1990) & Table 6.2 (Bartelli, 1962); Strathclyde Regional Council (Dept. of Physical Planning) for Fig. 4.7; The Winard Staring Centre for Integrated Land, Soil & Water Research (DLO) for Figs 4.5 (Vink & van Zuilen, 1974), 6.2a–f (Dekkers *et al.*., 1972) & Table 6.1 (Haans, 1978).

Whilst every effort has been made to trace the owners of copyright material, in a few cases this has proved impossible and we take this opportunity to offer our apologies to any copyright holders whose rights we may have unwittingly infringed.

1

Land Resources and Land Use Planning Issues

1.1 Introduction

The 1980s was a decade of dramatic change in
the evaluation of land resources, a trend which is
being further accelerated in the 1990s. Until the
1980s, considerable emphasis was placed upon
carrying out different types of land resource
surveys. The main aim of national geological and
soil surveys was to produce maps and related
memoirs, the view being that such resource data
could be interpreted and applied to different land
use planning and management issues. Of course
there are many examples of approaches which were
specifically developed in order that such land
resource data could be presented in a form suited
to non-specialist use and perhaps the land use
capability schemes are the best known ones. But
despite innovative research on land capability
assessment and soil survey interpretation during the
1960s and 1970s, there has been a tendency for
inventory resource reports such as soil, geological
or land system surveys to gather dust on shelves

rather than to be used.

A customer-orientated approach has become
increasingly common whereby geological and soil
survey institutes to varying extents have had to
finance their activities through contract funding.
One benefit from this change has been the move
towards the integration of land resource surveys
and land evaluation with the processes of land use
planning and management. The continuing need to
define and thus protect prime agricultural land has
led to the development in Britain during the 1980s
of more refined systems of land classification. Soil
surveyors have found themselves in public inquiries
when arguments exist over land quality in
connection with proposed developments which will
result in the permanent loss of land from
agriculture. Another area of increasing involvement
by land resource specialists is environmental impact
assessment. This can range from attempting to
predict change in water quality and yield following
afforestation schemes to assessing the impact of
different forestry patterns on landscape quality.
The gradual adoption of government schemes
designed to maintain or enhance environmental
quality has resulted in the need to monitor the
effects of such policies. Thus in Britain, certain
areas have been designated as 'environmentally
sensitive'. Farmers in such localities can receive
grants to pursue less intensive forms of land
management and to retain field boundaries.
Monitoring schemes will become increasingly
important as a means of determining the success of
particular policies designed to encourage particular
land management strategies. In essence, finance is
being made available for such monitoring whilst
expenditure on routine soil or geological survey is
less easy to justify.

Technological developments since the
mid-1980s in geographical information systems
(GIS) have had considerable impact on the
methods of input, processing and output of spatially
referenced data. The major attractions of such
systems are

1 the ease of updating and correcting mapped data

2 the ability to produce output in the precise form
required by clients

3 the capacity to integrate datasets from a wide

range of sources including digitized maps and remote sensing imagery

4 the potential for mapping change through monitoring programmes

5 the capability to integrate with modelling whereby outputs can be produced in the form of landscape simulations under different policy scenarios, or in terms of predicted crop or financial yields under different management strategies.

Thus information technology as applied to land resource analysis is given particular emphasis in this book.

Another methodological development initiated in the 1980s has been the increasing application of modelling techniques. The term 'modelling' is open to a wide range of interpretations, but in essence a model can be considered as some form of abstraction or simplification of the real world. Thus spatial patterns and processes can be investigated in order to quantify relationships between component variables. Such relationships can then be used as the basis for predicting change under a variety of management, planning policy or environmental scenarios. In summary, the prediction of change and the ability to map the results using an integrated GIS are proving to be the current research frontier in land evaluation.

The 1980s were distinguished by the increasing application of computer technology and a greater emphasis on shaping the results from projects to particular circumstances and planning needs. Such developments built upon the major methodological advance of the *Framework for Land Evaluation* (FAO 1976) and geological and soil survey traditions in many countries. There is the danger of technology becoming the main driving force in the further development of land evaluation. The writer freely admits to the fascination of operating a GIS whereby different layers of information on a map can be zoomed into and modified, or watching the emergence of a digital terrain model with superimposed land use distributions on a computer terminal. Use of such systems should nevertheless be driven by practical needs, though use of a good GIS opens up new possibilities of data processing and presentation. A book which has *evaluation* in its title and gives

computer techniques particular emphasis, ought to begin by reviewing the land use planning issues which should drive the methodological and technological advances in land evaluation. Of course such a theme warrants a book of its own, but for introductory purposes, an adequate overview can be obtained by discussing land use planning issues at scales ranging from the global to the local.

1.2 Global scale: issues of food

There is no more fundamental a question in land evaluation than an assessment of the ability of the earth to provide proper nutrition for its human population in the years and decades to come. According to the 'medium' projection of the United Nations, world population is expected to grow at 1.6 per cent between 1985 and 2000 to nearly 6.1 billion with 4.8 billion in the developing countries. On a global scale, agriculture according to Alexandratos (1988) has the proven potential to increase food supplies faster than the growth of population, a pattern to be expected for the foreseeable future. Thomas Malthus in 1798 first drew attention to the tendency of people to increase in numbers at a geometric rate in contrast to the arithmetic rate of increase in food production. His pessimistic predictions were not realized because of technological, economic and sociological changes as well as the opening up of new agricultural areas in North America and Australia, and the gradual introduction of birth control. His views have come to the fore again in recent decades resulting from a renewed concern with population trends, especially in particular parts of the world where there also exist serious problems in providing adequate and reliable food supplies. However, it is important to recognize that food situations in particular countries can alter quite dramatically. During the 1970s many Asian countries seemed to be heading for massive food deficits while during the 1980s food production and security have massively improved in India and China. In 1984 China and India had a net import of 10 million tonnes of cereals; by 1985 these two countries became net exporters to the extent of about 3 million tonnes (Alexandratos 1988). China and India have the capacity to become substantial exporters of cereals, but this is unlikely to occur because of higher per caput domestic consumption and as a result of poor world cereal prices. In contrast many African countries have an escalating problem of feeding their increasing populations while their agricultural growth rates are very low. The effect of high population growth is to accelerate problems of land degradation through cultivation of marginal lands, soil erosion, deforestation and overgrazing. Furthermore, variability in crop yields becomes more marked as more marginal areas are utilized and as farmers are less able to improve land management techniques. There exists this tragic paradox of severe food shortages in the midst of global abundance (Weitz 1986). In western Europe there is gross overproduction of cereals and dairy products, a situation also present in North America. It is a global obscenity that 400–500 million people suffer chronic undernutrition while a further billion are subject to periodic undernutrition. It is far beyond the scope of this book to enter into an analysis of this complex issue, but it is important to stress that any estimate of food production potential can be made only if global land resource data exist along with information on the growing requirements of particular crops.

It is only since 1978 that soil maps covering the whole world based on soil surveys have existed. Prior to then, estimates of the potential arable area of the world were very varied reflecting the inadequate database. Grigg (1970) quotes studies dating from 1937 to 1958 which compare as percentages the global potential arable area with the arable area in use; the values range from 13 per cent to 375 per cent. In a review of the potential arable areas of the world, Kellogg and Orvedal (1969) conclude that almost one-half of the soils in the world which have good physical and biological potential are already in use and they visualize soil surveys playing an important role in increasing productivity from such areas. In addition, according to their analysis, the area of arable cultivation could be increased from 1.4 billion hectares to c. 3.2 billion hectares and this extra 1.8 billion hectares

would not require additional irrigation beyond the existing wells and streams. Over one-half of this additional area lies in the tropics. This prediction by Kellogg and Orvedal is based on examination of major soil types and their distributions. Revelle (1976) in another analysis of global potential arable land concludes that 3.2 billion hectares of land could be cropped without irrigation while this could be increased to 4.2 billion hectares if irrigation systems were used. An optimistic value of 7.0 billion hectares for potential arable land use is given by Pawley (1971). Buringh (1985) considers that some 12 per cent of the earth's surface (at present grassland and forest) has potential for crop production. He believes that all land reserves on the earth will be lost within a hundred years with reserves of highly productive land being lost within twenty-five years. Such a pessimistic view is very much countered by his opinion that the earth could increase its output of food by a factor of ten using known technology. As already stated, the marked variation in these estimates is in part due to a poor global soil and climatic database, as well as to differences in assumptions about management level, agricultural investment, economics of particular farming systems and the financial ability of farmers to buy fertilizers.

For the globe as a whole, about 770 million hectares are cropped at an intensity of 78 per cent which means that the annual harvested area is about 600 million hectares (Alexandratos 1988). According to this FAO report, the expansion of arable land along with increases in cropping intensities will account for about 40 per cent of the growth in production. In order to achieve required production levels for the year 2000, an increase in arable land of 83 million hectares is required. At any one time, not all arable land is in production, and if a cropping intensity of 84 per cent is attained, then an extension of 115 million hectares is necessary. Another crucial issue in such predictions is land loss through urbanization, industrialization, recreation, transportation and land degradation. Examples will be given in Chapter 4 of land loss in Canada where urbanization consumes a disproportionate amount of good quality land. In the United States of America, erosion rates on 25 per cent of the arable areas are higher than the natural rates of soil formation. Globally between 4 million and 7 million hectares of cropland are taken out of production each year and according to Larson (1986), the rate is likely to increase and an annual loss of 10 million hectares is predicted for 2000. The additional dimension is the lowering in soil productivity by 20 per cent in developing countries (Dudal 1987). According to FAO, despite such land losses there is still on a global basis a net annual addition to arable land though increasing problems may become evident in some developing countries (Alexandratos 1988). Some scientists consider that future increases in food production can be achieved by increasing the productivity of existing cropland. Larson (1986: 222) argues that

> protection of already cultivated soils should take precedence over development of potentially arable soils. First, presently cultivated soils are generally of higher productive potential, and management technology for the cultivated soils is generally better understood and available. Second, presently cultivated soils are located closer to the food needs. Third, clearing of forested lands for cultivation is expensive. And fourth, clearing of forests may cause extreme environmental damage.

This technological solution to future food supplies is very appealing, but economic, social, demographic and political factors necessitate a considerable expansion of the current agricultural frontier in certain developing countries, for example Brazil. As already stated, FAO have concluded that a large new area will need to be in cultivation by 2000 and this organization undertook during 1976–78 a major project to locate potential agricultural lands. The aim was to provide 'a more precise assessment of the production potential of the world's land resources, and so provide the physical database necessary for planning future agricultural development' (Dudal 1978: 315). The research was based on the identification and delimitation of major agro-ecological zones to provide data on the rainfed production potential of the developing world's land resources. The

FAO/Unesco 1:5,000,000 Soil Map of the World provided the soil information and the focus of the project was on determining crop potentials through matching at two input levels the climatic and soil requirements of the eleven main global crops: wheat, paddy rice, maize, pearl millet, sorghum, soybean, cotton, phaseolus bean, white potato, sweet potato and cassava, with the climatic and soil inventories. Matching of the crop climatic requirements with the climatic inventory was done in a quantitative manner by first determining if the crop temperature requirements could be met; second, ascertaining if the length of growing period was sufficient; and third, calculating potential net biomass and yield of crops. Maps at a continental scale were produced showing grades of land suitability for different crops.

The agro-ecological zones project was concerned with developing areas of the world and reports have been published for Africa (FAO 1978a), South-west Asia (FAO 1978b), South-east Asia (FAO 1980) and South and Central America (FAO 1981). Figure 1.1 illustrates the results for south-west Asia where the analysis was restricted to rainfed wheat since this crop is grown on over 75 per cent of the total cultivated area. It is thus the sole crop of significance in all the included countries (from Turkey through the Middle East to Afghanistan). The report proposes that 23.5 million hectares of land can be considered suitable for wheat; this compares with reported harvests of 19.8 million hectares in 1976 and 21.6 million hectares (excluding Kuwait, Oman and Quatar) in 1986 (FAO 1987). It is also noted that the total 'arable' land in this region is 50.9 million hectares, implying that less than half the total arable area is under wheat at any one time. The report explains this by pointing out that wheat is grown in areas with annual precipitation considered too low. Such cropping may be successful if two or more years of fallow precede cultivation to allow some accumulation of soil moisture storage. But the general result from the agro-ecological analysis for south-west Asia is that there is no reserve of land suited to the expansion of rainfed cropping of wheat. Indeed, the overall impression is of the present over-extension of arable activities into areas of unreliable moisture supply.

Summary results for all the developing countries are given in Table 1.1. These figures indicate a potential increase of almost 280 per cent on the existing arable area in the developing world though there are striking differences between countries. There appears little scope for extension of arable land in the Near East, a situation repeated in Asia though Indonesia and, to lesser extents, Burma and Malaysia have potential. The results highlight the scope for extension by an order of about times four in sub-Saharan Africa and Latin America. The country with the greatest potential is Brazil where 82.3 million hectares are currently arable and this could be increased to 504.3 million hectares. Of course there is great concern about the consequences of such extensive deforestation as already mentioned.

The agro-ecological zones project thus identifies substantial land reserves, but these are concentrated in particular countries such as Brazil and Zaïre. These potential new arable lands all pose serious problems in terms of development, such as poor soils or marginal rainfall. The view of FAO is that between 1982/4 and 2000 about two-thirds of the increase in arable lands will be by expansion of irrigation, especially in Asia and in India in particular (Alexandratos 1988). Expansion

in the Near East and North Africa can also be achieved only by more irrigation given the marginality of rainfed crops as already indicated.

The obvious follow-up to the agro-ecological zones project was an analysis to determine potential population supporting capacities of lands in the developing world and a report with this title has been published (Higgins et al 1982). The task faced by this team was to determine if the agro-ecological zone crop potential estimates could be converted into estimates of potential population supporting capacities, and if so, then to compare these population potential estimates with present and projected population figures to identify critical

Table 1.1 Actual and potential areas of arable land in the developing world, based on the results of the Agro-ecological Zones Project with some adjustments

	Arable land	
	In use	Potential
	(million ha)	(million ha)
Africa (sub-Saharan)	201.3	815.7
Near East/North Africa	91.7	94.7
Asia (excluding China)	280.0	342.8
Latin America	194.8	889.6

(source: Alexandratos 1988: 317–20)

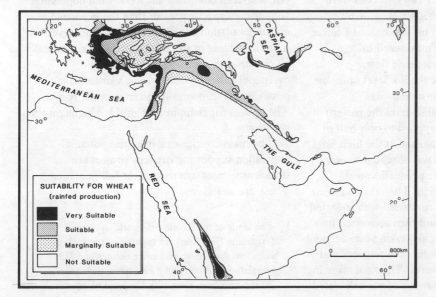

Figure 1.1 Land suitability for rainfed production of wheat in south-west Asia (based on FAO 1978b)

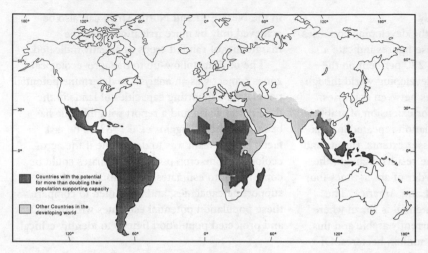

Figure 1.2 Countries in the developing world which have the capability at the intermediate input level of more than doubling their agricultural output between 1975 and 2000 (based on Higgins et al 1982)

Countries with the potential for more than doubling their population supporting capacity

Other Countries in the developing world

areas where land resources would be insufficient to meet food needs. In the potential population supporting capacities project, the first step was the identification of an optimum agro-climatic yield potential for every crop that could be grown in a particular area. Allowance had to be made for multiple cropping when this was possible. Next, consideration was given to soil conditions since these modify agro-climatic potentials. The effect of soil erosion on lowering productivity was then incorporated into the calculations. Allowances were made for seed requirements as well as wastage. Crop options for component 100 km^2 cells were determined and then a decision was made on a particular crop for each cell on the basis of a linear programming model which maximized calorie production under three input levels (low, intermediate and high). For the low level of inputs, the pattern of presently grown crops was maintained; at the intermediate level the pattern of presently grown crops was applied to only half of the potentially cultivable area, and at the high level of inputs all cultivated land was allocated to crops providing the highest calorie production with minimum protein requirement. The rainfed calorie production potentials were combined with irrigated calorie production figures and then converted into population supporting capacities taking into account country specific data on calorie requirements and demographic age/sex structures. The final stage in the project involved a comparison of the calculated

population capacities with the 1975 population and that predicted for 2000. Results for the developing world are shown in Figure 1.2 which illustrates those countries which have the potential to more than double their population supporting capacities between 1975 and 2000 at the intermediate input level. Table 1.2 gives results for south-west Asia and Figure 1.3 shows the spatial patterns in potential carrying capacity at the intermediate level of input. When the figures for potential supporting capacity are compared with the predicted population density for 2000, then only one (Turkey) out of sixteen countries has a potential population supporting capacity greater than the predicted actual population density at the low input level. Thus according to this ecological analysis, virtually all countries in south-west Asia will be overpopulated. Of course, such a situation is possible only through oil earnings in the region. The figures for Bahrain in Table 1.2 highlight this situation.

The main conclusions from the potential population supporting capacity project are sufficiently important to warrant full quotation. These are as follows.

1   The lands of the developing world *as a whole* (excluding East Asia) are capable of producing sufficient food to sustain twice their year 1975 population and one and a half times their year 2000 population, even with low level of inputs.

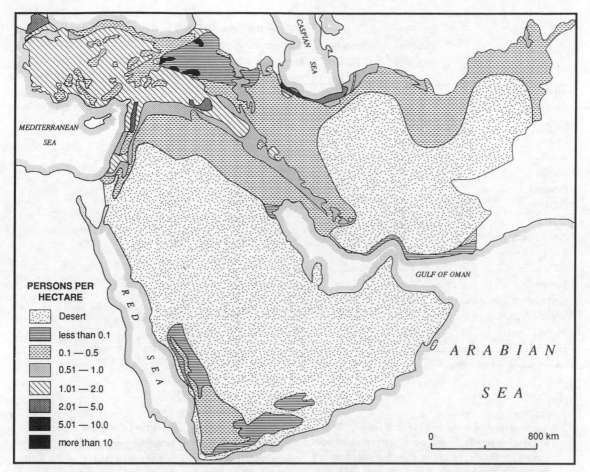

Figure 1.3 Potential population supporting capacities (average densities) assuming intermediate levels of input (Higgins et al 1982)

PERSONS PER
HECTARE

Desert
less than 0.1
0.1 — 0.5
0.51 — 1.0
1.01 — 2.0
2.01 — 5.0
5.01 — 10.0
more than 10

With application of intermediate level of inputs to all cultivable areas, these lands would be able to meet the food needs of more than four times their projected population of 2000 AD. These aggregated developing world findings presuppose massive and unrestricted movement of surplus potential food production and labour within and between all five regions.

2 At the other extreme, assuming no movement of surplus potential food production and labour between *individual-country length of growing period zones*, 2453 million hectares – 38 per cent of the total land area – are unable to produce sufficient food for their 1975 populations with low inputs. In these zones, no fewer than 1165 million people – 60 per cent of the total – were living on land resources able to sustain only 602 million people.

3 A more realistic assumption is that of movement of surplus potential food production *within countries*. On this basis, fifty-four countries (out of the total of 117 studied) have insufficient land resources to meet the food needs of their 1975 populations with low level of inputs. The number of critical countries would rise to sixty-four by the year 2000 AD.

4 Of these critical countries, for the year 2000, twenty-eight would need to raise their inputs to at least intermediate level, on *all* their potentially cultivable land, if they are to meet food requirements from their own land resources. A further seventeen would need to raise inputs to the high level to attain food self-sufficiency. Nineteen countries will be unable to meet their food needs, from national land resources, even with high level of inputs.

	Pop density 1975	Pop density 2000	Potential population supporting capacity		
			low inputs	inter inputs	high inputs
Afghanistan	0.30	0.57	0.24	0.29	0.38
Bahrain	4.27	8.97	<0.01	<0.01	<0.01
Iran	0.20	0.40	0.25	0.31	0.40
Iraq	0.25	0.56	0.21	0.41	0.68
Israel	1.67	2.72	0.85	1.11	1.37
Jordan	0.28	0.60	0.09	0.14	0.16
Kuwait	0.63	1.98	<0.01	<0.01	0.01
Lebanon	2.69	4.70	1.07	1.43	1.57
Quatar	0.08	0.20	<0.01	<0.01	<0.01
Saudia Arabia	0.03	0.07	0.01	0.01	0.03
Syria	0.40	0.88	0.54	0.84	1.17
Oman	0.04	0.08	<0.01	<0.01	<0.01
Turkey	0.52	0.90	1.21	1.58	2.07
United Arab Emirates	0.07	0.20	0.02	0.02	0.02
Yemen Arab Rep	0.27	0.51	0.18	0.24	0.46
Yemen Dem	0.06	0.12	0.04	0.04	0.07

Table 1.2 Population supporting capacities as expressed in population densities (persons per hectare) for south-west Asian countries at three input levels

(source: Higgins et al 1982: 135)

5   South-west Asia is the most critical region. With low level of inputs, fifteen out of sixteen countries cannot feed their present or expected populations from their own lands. In Africa, the year 2000 populations of twenty-nine (out of fifty-one) countries would exceed the physical potential population supporting capacity of their entire land resources with low level of inputs.

6   Preliminary land degradation assessments indicate that, unless conservation measures are introduced on all cultivable land, 544 million hectares of potentially productive rainfed cropland – more than one-sixth of the total – could be lost.

(source: Higgins et al 1982: vii)

Global land resources require to be continually reassessed with respect to the adequate provision of food in response to better environmental resource data, the improvement of yield prediction models, changing population needs and impacts of environmental change on land resources. As already discussed, the Agro-ecological Zones Project of FAO was possible because of the publication of the 1:5,000,000 FAO/Unesco Soil Map of the World as well as the compilation of climatic statistics at the continental level. The results formed the basis to estimating the population supporting capacities of lands in the developing world. The results as already indicated are of considerable importance though it must be stressed that they should be considered as a first approximation. Spatial generalizations had to be made for component 10×10 km cells, and furthermore, the quality of the database was necessarily very varied. This led to an international programme to establish a 1:1,000,000 level digital soil resources map of the world with an associated database system. The aim is to collate and correlate national and regional geographical soil databases and to put them on a comparable basis in order that a better soil map of the world can be produced. This project to develop a World Soils and Terrain

Digital Database (SOTER) is in progress though will take ten to twenty years to fully establish (Baumgardner and van de Weg 1988; Sombroek and Colenbrander 1990). The results will be input to a GIS which will allow ease of update and correction of soil information. A need is perceived of providing a global spatially referenced database to assist with the assessment of agricultural production potential, the identification of alternative and sustainable land use systems, for evaluating the buffering capacity of soils with reference to pollutants and for global change investigations. The database of SOTER is designed to be compatible with the United Nations Environment Programme (UNEP) Global Resources Information Database (GRID) as well as FAO's information system which also links many databases.

Systems such as SOTER are now possible given the availability of powerful GIS and associated relational databases. Such software developments along with the ever increasing power of computers means that the technology now exists for a global resources information system as advocated by Billingsley and Urena (1984). They argue that through networking, efficient remote access is now possible to multiple distributed databases to thus make global scale research and monitoring feasible. Such monitoring is heavily dependent upon the processing of remotely sensed data. In this section, particular emphasis is given to the issue of food production at the global scale, but there are other issues of increasing concern such as global carbon dioxide and methane cycles, acid rain and pollution dispersion, biochemical cycling, deforestation, desertification and climatic change. Billingsley and Urena (1984) stress the key point that any attempt at modelling and simulation of these processes at the global scale, requires an adequate global database. The provision of such a database is central to a programme called GRID (global resource information database) which evolved from GEMS (global environmental monitoring system). GEMS was established in 1974 by UNEP as a result of the 1972 Stockholm Conference on the Human Environment. The aims of GRID are to co-ordinate and make available using GIS

environmental datasets as collected by GEMS (UNEP 1990). The headquarters of GRID are in Nairobi while a node in Geneva is primarily concerned with data capture, monitoring, modelling, analysis and distribution. Another regional node is in Bangkok and additional ones are planned. One of the first GRID projects was concerned with assessing the population of African elephants. On the basis of elephant survey data from limited areas, correlations were established between elephant density and such variables as degree of vegetation protection, presence of tsetse flies, vegetation type, human population density, average annual rainfall, and per capita gross domestic product and growth rate. From such correlations it was thus possible to predict elephant densities in unsurveyed areas. Other examples of GRID projects include an evaluation of coastal sites for aquaculture in Costa Rica, predicting the effects of a higher sea levels in the Nile delta, developing an environmental database for Uganda to produce assessments of soil erosion hazard and land suitability for particular crops. Examples of global datasets held by GRID are elevation, soils, soil degradation, vegetation, cultivation intensity, natural wetlands, precipitation and temperature anomalies and ozone distribution. As examples of datasets held at the regional level, GRID has data for Africa on vegetation, rainfall, wet days, wind speed, population density, albedo, tsetse fly, elephant range and density, endangered species and protected areas. The overall objective is that every country, especially in the developing world, will have its own GRID centre serving national needs but also have access to regional and global databases (Gynne 1990). The condition of such provision is that any participating country also contributes national data for inclusion in GEMS.

The development of global resource information systems is possible because of available technology in terms of handling, processing, transmitting and interfacing different spatial databases. One crucial issue is that land resource data must apply to land mapping units. In turn such units can be defined only in terms of the dominant taxonomic class of land or soil. Thus the validity of transferring experience and results from one area to another is dependent upon the careful application of detailed classification systems, such as the US *Soil Taxonomy* (Soil Survey Staff 1975). This was the background to the Benchmark Soils Project which was initiated by the University of Hawaii in 1974 (Swindale 1978). The first objective was to establish a network of benchmark soils in the tropics belonging to common soil families as defined in the US *Soil Taxonomy*. The broader aim was to assist the co-operating countries in formulating agricultural development plans through a scientific appraisal of the potential of upland areas for intensive food production. Sites belonging to three families located in Cameroon, Indonesia, the Philippines and Hawaii were used to test the assumption that a methodology could be developed to transfer crop and management technology from one tropical region to another on the basis of soil classification. A related project was mounted by the University of Puerto Rico with sites in Puerto Rico and Brazil. The Benchmark Soils Project, which was completed by 1983, was succeeded by the establishment of an International Benchmark Sites Network for Agrotechnology Transfer (IBSNAT). The aim of this project is to identify the critical relationships between land characteristics and crop requirements and thus facilitate the exchange of agrotechnological production methodologies using a network approach. The first part of the IBSNAT project focuses on the identification of minimum datasets while the second phase concentrates on the use of the database in order to calibrate models which predict crop yield under a range of environmental and management conditions. The direction of the IBSNAT project is very much towards the development of dynamic interactive systems of datasets and crop production models.

The major global issue concerning land resources is the continuing ability of the world to feed its growing population. The results of the agro-ecological zone and potential population supporting capacity projects demonstrate that at the global scale agricultural production can be increased through higher yields and use of greater arable areas though serious deficiencies will continue to exist in particular regions. Schemes such as IBSNAT thus assume particular

importance since they encourage the transfer of experience from one area to another. Better systems of land management must play a vital role in improving agricultural output from those areas with serious food deficits.

1.3   Land resource issues within the European Community (EC)

In a review of trends in the use of land within the EC, G. H. Moss (1987) describes three major impacts on the land resource base. First, there is land loss resulting from urbanization and industrialization. Nearly 7 per cent of the land in the EC has been lost to such uses with The Netherlands heading the national league at 15 per cent. Though such figures may seem acceptable, it must be remembered that the effect of urbanization and industrialization is not limited to direct land loss. Agriculture and forestry have particular problems in the urban–rural fringe. In an analysis of future European Community land use demands, Lee (1987) estimates for the then ten members of the EC that 0.8 million hectares or about 0.8 per cent of the currently utilized arable area will be lost by the year 2000 to urbanization, industrialization and transport developments.

The second major issue is the growth of pollution on soil and vegetation quality. Such pollution varies in scale from the EC level down to sites where toxic emissions from chemical processing plants may have an effect on local vegetation and soils. The third broad issue is the adverse impact of agricultural practices on soil quality. Of course there are many instances within the EC of considerable land improvement through drainage, water control, stone clearance and fertilizer application. However, much current concern is over the effect of heavy agricultural machinery on soil compaction. Related to this has been the loss of diversity in leys and reduction in livestock on arable farms which in turn has led to reduced levels of soil organic matter. Structural problems are more evident, especially in areas of high rainfall. The increase in winter cereals such as in Britain is also leading to an acceleration of soil erosion (Frost and Speirs 1984). G. H. Moss (1987) highlights potential problems which may arise through the use of sewage sludge as a fertilizer which may contain trace or heavy metals as well as organic pollutants. Public concern exists over the transfer of these pollutants by water and vegetation through food chains, ultimately to human consumers.

These three issues within the EC of urbanization, pollution and agricultural impact are applicable to many other parts of the world and are topics of considerable international concern. In this book, particular focus is given to the evaluation of land resources, again a current issue within the EC. This is particularly relevant given the problem of agricultural overproduction within the EC. Over 20 per cent of the value of the total agricultural production is spent on subsidies and maintenance of excess cereals, meat, sugar beet and dairy products; on the other hand there is an increasing demand for oil seeds, protein crops, fruits and timber (Verheye 1986). Substantial changes in land use have occurred within the EC during recent decades. Over the period 1969–71 to 1983, there was a decline in 6 million hectares utilized agricultural area (UAA) to a total of 136 million hectares in 1983 (Lee 1987). Such a net overall reduction masks increases in woodland, oil seed crops, annual green fodder (especially green maize), and temporary grasses and grazing; reductions were most marked in permanent green fodder crops followed by root crops and cereals.

The management of agricultural change at the level of the EC is possible only through the Common Agricultural Policy (CAP). It is increasingly evident that the high levels of subsidy cannot be supported and various policies, for example milk quota, have been introduced to begin to tackle the problem of overproduction. Policy formulation should not be governed solely by economic or political considerations, but should incorporate the results from land evaluation (Verheye 1986). The approach which is currently being pursued is very similar in methodology to the agro-ecological zones project. The core to the

approach is matching of crop requirements with land attributes to determine degree of suitability. Use is being made of the 1:1,000,000 EC Soil Map along with an agro-climatic inventory.

Results from evaluating the land base of EC-10 for grassland and arable uses are given by Lee (1987). For grassland, assessment of moisture availability, poaching susceptibility and accessibility to machinery allowed the definition of five suitability classes. He reported that 28 per cent of EC-10 was classed in the first two categories, The Netherlands on a national basis having the greatest extent (74 per cent). The suitability for arable use was based on wetness, moisture availability, slope, boulders, rock outcrops, soil workability or texture and structural properties affecting tilth. Lee (1987) defined three classes of land suited to arable use and a fourth unsuitable class. France has 50 per cent of the total EC-10 class 1 arable land and 29 per cent of the class 2 arable land. Lee also notes that for the EC-10 area, the extent of classes 1 and 2 arable land is 8 per cent more than the existing arable area.

Such first estimates of land suitability need to be translated into agricultural output and then related to agricultural policy, changing patterns of agriculture, and market demand. Lee (1987) reports that EC grain production has increased 60 per cent since 1960 and is now 7 per cent more than is needed. Increases in yield account for such improvements. If current agricultural policies are unchanged, he quotes an EC report which suggests an EC cereal surplus of 58 million tonnes by the year 2000. This could be reduced to 38 million tonnes if the import of cereal substitutes was curtailed; this surplus production comes from 6.7 million hectares of land under cereals. Areas with a yield disadvantage such as southern France, northern Britain, Italy and Greece are most likely to experience the greatest reduction in cereal cropping. A 5 million hectare reduction in grassland is envisaged by Lee (1987). An expansion of 4 million hectares in protein crops (rapeseed, peas, beans, lupins) is anticipated with these crops being primarily used for feed protein. Such expansion is dependent upon substantial EC policy changes. Predictions on additional forestry areas are equally dependent upon policy issues and Lee (1987) estimates an additional 4 million hectares by the year 2000.

As was discussed in section 1.1, increasing attention is being given at the global scale to systems which allow easy access to transfer of land resource data, for example the SOTER and GRID projects. A similar programme has been underway in the EC since 1985, the CORINE project (Wiggins et al 1986; Wiggins et al 1987; Briggs and Martin 1988). The aim is to develop a GIS with an associated database to assist with the formulation of policy. In the first instance priority is given to digitizing the 1:1,000,000 soil map of the EC and Madsen (1989) reports on progress towards building a soil profile and analytical database connected to the soil map. Briggs et al (1989) describe a project designed to assess soil erosion risk in Mediterranean areas of the EC; the necessary data on climate, soils, topography and vegetation cover were input to the CORINE database. These authors describe considerable problems associated with variations in the projections of soil maps, but nevertheless they are able to present a potential soil erosion risk map for Crete.

It is interesting to compare the results of land evaluation at the global scale with those at the EC scale. At the former, prime emphasis is on identifying agricultural potential in terms of expanding the agricultural area and increasing output from existing areas, the overall objective being to improve world food production. At the EC scale, the issue is one of agricultural surplus and the results of land evaluation are being incorporated into various land use policies. The consequence is the increasing concentration of different types of agriculture in the most favoured areas. As an example, France is likely to become even more the prime area of cereal production. The corollary is that alternative land uses have to be found for marginal localities.

1.4 Land resource issues at the national level

Since there is no global government, land use planning backed by legislation at that scale is impossible. FAO acts as the key data-collecting centre and provides continuous reviews of the world food situation; FAO is also very much involved with agricultural development projects in various parts of the world. As discussed in section 1.3, the EC is the first level of national groupings where policies have a direct effect on land use. For agricultural products much effort is being made to balance demand and supply within the EC and revision of the Common Agricultural Policy (CAP) is a topic of continuing political concern. But it is at the national scale that a land use planning policy supported by legislation is first possible. This is discussed in this section with reference to Britain and North America.

Britain

In Britain there is a long tradition of some form of control over land use. The first Planning Act was passed in 1909, though its prime concern was with public health and housing. Further Acts followed in 1931 and 1932, but it was not until 1947 that comprehensive Acts were passed. These Town and Country Planning Acts (one for England and Wales and one for Scotland) imposed a statutory planning structure so that most forms of development had to receive planning permission from local authorities. Integral to these Acts was the zoning of land used for agriculture and forestry. Various amendments were made to these Acts which were consolidated into the Town and Country Planning Act for England and Wales in 1971 followed by an Amendment Act in 1972. A separate Act for Scotland was passed in 1972. According to the 1947 Acts, authorities had to produce development plans which contained proposals on the use of land over a twenty-year period. Land was zoned for specific purposes, for example for urban, industrial, recreational and agricultural development and other community uses. The 1971 and 1972 Acts provide a more positive approach to planning with the introduction of structure plans. These deal with strategic issues and policies for the development and the use of land. In addition detailed proposals for specific locations are presented in local plans. The procedure for such structure plans to become planning policy for specific areas is laid down fully within the Acts; before adoption, the plans must be available for public inspection and a method of objecting to any proposals is given in the Acts. In England and Wales the Ministry of Agriculture, Fisheries and Food, and in Scotland the Scottish Office Agriculture and Fisheries Department, are consulted about such structure plans so that every attempt is made to conserve the best land for agriculture. Day-to-day planning is achieved by development control. This is when individual development proposals, for example extensions to private houses or the construction of new factories, are examined by the planning authorities. A variety of factors has to be taken into account including the policy statements in the strategic plan before planning permission can be granted. Planning authorities in England and Wales are obliged under the statute to consult the Ministry of Agriculture, Fisheries and Food when planning applications affect agriculture on areas greater than 5 hectares. No such statutory requirement applies in Scotland, though the Secretary of State has issued a directive that planning authorities should consult the Scottish Office Agriculture and Fisheries Department when areas greater than 5 hectares and of grades A+ and A (or LCA classes 1, 2 and 3 division 1 in the new system) are being considered for non-agricultural development.

A report by the Centre for Agricultural Strategy (1976) identifies several unsatisfactory aspects of British planning procedures in relation to agriculture and forestry. According to their view 'there is insufficient consideration of the future consequences of land use changes in the context of national policies for agriculture, forestry and urban activities' (1976: 18). They identify the problems of making the correct planning decisions at the local level in terms of national priorities. Another

unsatisfactory feature of the planning process in Britain noted in the report is that the involvement in the planning process of those concerned with agriculture and forestry is inadequate. Indeed, the prime function of this report was to focus attention on the very high priority which should be given to food and timber production in Britain; in addition the report proposes 'that everything possible should be done both to prevent the unnecessary loss of land from agriculture and forestry and to stimulate the potential output per unit area from the land remaining in use for these purposes' (1976: 16). Such a view with respect to agriculture is outdated given the agricultural surplus problem of the EC discussed in section 1.3. Taking land out of agriculture is now a priority which is expressed in the schemes for farm diversification, set-aside and farm woodland. Farmers in environmentally sensitive areas (ESAs) can receive grants if they pursue more traditional and less intensive systems of land management.

A longstanding issue is the loss of good agricultural land to urbanization and industrialization. As already indicated, planning policy is to limit such development to poorer quality land wherever possible. In the past this seems to have worked quite well for England and Wales according to Best (1973). In Scotland, in the older scheme, land was classed into one of seven categories (A+, A, B+, B, B−, C and D) by the former Department of Agriculture and Fisheries. In the previous edition of this book, figures were given which demonstrated the disproportionate loss of good agricultural land during the 1970s. For example, 2.8 per cent of agricultural land in Scotland is in classes A+ and A while the percentage losses through land transfer from these top classes were 17.5 per cent for 1976–7, 29.7 per cent for 1975–6 and 25.0 per cent for 1974–5. In the early 1980s the situation seems to have improved (Figure 1.4) and in part this must be explained by the better incorporation of national policy into structure and local plans. Other factors relate to the changing demands for land for housing and industry. In 1987 a new land capability classification system was adopted in Scotland, and the details of this scheme will be discussed in

Chapter 3. Prime land is now defined as comprising classes 1, 2 and 3.1. Revised national planning guidelines have been issued (Scottish Development Department 1987a). The key point is the continuing presumption against the development of prime agricultural land. Such a policy is maintained because despite the issue of agricultural overproduction, areas of prime land are of very limited extent and require protection wherever possible. In contrast, on non-prime land, policy is now towards diversification of the rural economy both on and off farms.

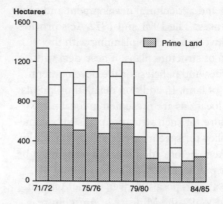

Figure 1.4 Loss of prime agricultural land in Scotland from 1971 to 1985 (source: Scottish Development Department 1987b)

North America

The main land resource issues of continuing concern in North America are land loss and land degradation. In an assessment of land degradation of agricultural lands in Canada, Coote et al (1981) conclude that many soils are degrading as a result of one or more of the following processes: soil erosion by wind or water, soil structural damage and fertility loss as a result of intensive tillage, and soil salinization, acidification and pollution. Erosion by water is a problem throughout Canada, but is particularly marked in parts of Ontario, Quebec, Alberta, British Columbia and in potato fields in New Brunswick and Prince Edward Island. The effects of intensive cultivation on soil quality are found throughout Canada with particular emphasis on sand and clay soils. Salinization is a problem of increasing magnitude and extent, especially in the prairie provinces where increased summer-fallow and changed land use patterns are the causes. The

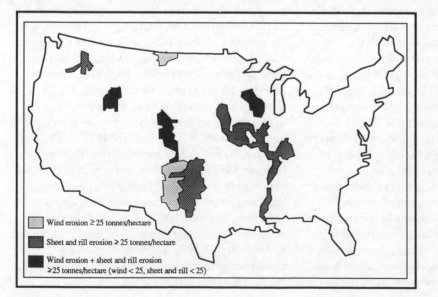

Figure 1.5 Major land resource areas (MLRAs) in the United States where the erosion rate is equal to or more than 25 tonnes per hectare; only MLRAs with at least 30 per cent of federal rural land in cropland are shown (source: Lee 1984: 227)

result is the raising of water-tables to mean that salts are precipitated at higher levels in the soil.

In the United States, the 1982 National Resources Inventory assembled data on land quality, potential cropland, conservation treatment needs, pastureland and rangeland condition, land use and soil erosion; Lee (1984) summarizes the results. Erosion rates were compared to soil loss tolerance values (T) which are the maximum average annual soil losses which are sustainable without lowering long-term productivity. In the United States these values range from 2.5 to 12.5 tonnes per hectare. Estimates from the National Resources Inventory indicate that about 44 per cent of all cropland is eroding at rates greater than the appropriate T value. Virtually all pastureland and forestland has erosion rates at or below the T value while about 11 per cent of rangeland areas are eroding at rates over twice the T value. Assessments of erosion were made for what were termed major land resource areas (MLRAs). Such units were defined in terms of particular combinations of soils, climate, water resources and land uses. The fourteen MLRAs which have average erosion rates over 25 tonnes per hectare and have cultivated cropland for 30 per cent or more of all rural land are shown in Figure 1.5. The map highlights those cropland areas in the United States with the most severe problems of erosion. Wind erosion is particularly serious in North Dakota, Montana, Kansas, New Mexico, Oklahoma and Texas while serious water erosion occurs in Idaho, Oregon, Washington, Iowa, Missouri, Indiana and Illinois.

In North America the other major land resource issue which continues to generate debate and controversy is land loss to non-agricultural uses. In countries like Canada and the USA there is growing concern at the national level about the loss of good agricultural land. In the USA until the early 1970s, there was the widespread belief that there was no need for concern about such losses given the mistaken perception about the almost infinite untapped land resources of the country. Furthermore, there was the belief that continual increases in output were possible by the application of more fertilizers, and the introduction of new

crop varieties and more efficient land management techniques (Clawson 1972). In Canada, only about 15 per cent of the country has some potential for agriculture and less than 0.5 per cent can be considered to have prime soils in prime temperate climates (Nowland 1978). In Canada about 20,000 hectares of land are lost to urbanization each year and the point that Nowland stresses is that most of this loss is taking place in the very limited areas of good land, a situation rather similar to Scotland. Land is graded by the Canada Land Inventory (CLI) into seven classes (Chapter 3) and Nowland notes that over half of Canada's class 1 agricultural land and one-third of the class 2 land is within 80 km of Canada's twenty-three metropolitan areas. Manning (1987) expresses this in another way by pointing out that 46 per cent of the value of Canadian agricultural production came in 1981 from areas within this 80 km zone. Manning further emphasizes the significance of this spatial concentration by pointing out that 40 per cent of Canada's gross national product and 25 per cent of its jobs are dependent upon the land resource.

In Canada varying action has been taken at the Provincial level to try to arrest the loss of good agricultural land. As an example, the Government of Ontario produced a Green Paper on *Planning for Agriculture: Food Land Guidelines*. The underlying objectives of the paper are to preserve better land for agriculture and to ensure the economic feasibility of using the best land for agricultural production. Since this is a Green Paper, the aim is to produce a set of guidelines to assist planning authorities at subprovincial scales in making decisions over agricultural land. The key task is the identification of high capability agricultural resource lands which the Green Paper considers to include

1   all lands which have a high capability for producing speciality crops (eg peaches, grapes, apples, tobacco, vegetables)

2   all lands where soil classes 1, 2, 3 and 4 predominate as defined in the Canada Land Inventory

3   additional areas where farms exhibit characteristics of ongoing viable agriculture

4 additional areas where local market conditions ensure agricultural viability where it might not otherwise exist.

Following their identification, these high capability agricultural areas have to be given a priority rating – for example speciality crop areas and lands of class 1 should be given top priority. After such a rating procedure, there must be an evaluation of alternative land uses. Areas designated for top agricultural priority must be mapped and given strong agricultural protection. On land in the second agricultural designation, some non-agricultural activities may be allowed. The Green Paper provides a discussion on agricultural policies, code of practice, compatible uses and severances for the highest priority agricultural designation. Clearly urban development, for example, is excluded from such areas.

The overall objective of the Ontario Green Paper is to give a policy directive at the local, county or regional level so that the better agricultural areas are protected. The objective is highly commendable, but in practice a serious limitation is that land use decisions are made at the subprovincial level. Decisions at such a level may be made bearing local factors particularly in mind and without close reference to the agricultural needs of the state or indeed of the country as a whole. The Green Paper also lacks enforcement provision, and as Williams and Pohl (1987) note, it has been invoked on an inconsistent basis with the greatest effect being in areas under the least pressure from urban expansion and with relatively less favourable soils and climates.

Although the loss of prime agricultural land to urbanization is serious, of even greater concern is the loss of unique lands. These are areas, usually of very limited extent, which have particular climatic and soil conditions which make them highly suited to specific crops. One of the best examples in Canada is the Niagara fruit belt which occurs along the south shore of Lake Ontario from Hamilton to the Niagara River and produces most of Canada's peaches and grapes as well as large quantities of apples, pears, plums, cherries, small fruits and vegetables. The loss of this unique area is described by Krueger (1977) who summarizes the problem in stating that between 1951 and 1971 there was a reduction of 3760 hectares of orchards corresponding to a 30 per cent decline in twenty years. The greatest decreases occurred near the cities and along the roads. The essential conflict is that the area is also well located for industrial and urban development. Krueger reviews the attempts at controlling such sprawl, but he concludes that 'it is hard to be optimistic about the chances of saving a significant portion of the Niagara fruitlands' (1977: 147).

Another speciality cropland area under attack is the Okanagan Valley in British Columbia (Krueger and Maguire 1985). Apples are the main crop with grapes also being important. Although the population total in the Okanagan Valley is low (under 200,000 in 1981), a growth rate of 55 per cent occurred between 1971 and 1981. Settlement is located on the best land with low density sprawl further extending on to such land. A major highway has encouraged such development through the centre of the fruit growing soils. The best orchard lands provide excellent sites for housing with many people keen to grow their own fruit and vegetables. Increasing pressure for building plots has pushed up land prices to cause serious problems for farmers to buy more land for fruit growing. Krueger and Maguire (1985) report that the average price of a hectare in 1971 was $7400 and this had risen to about $50,000 by 1981. In addition there are increasing problems to fruit growers caused by urbanization through vandalism, crop theft and traffic congestion. Krueger and Maguire (1985) review land use control in the Okanagan Valley at the municipal, regional and provincial levels. At the municipal level, the conclusion is that there is a lack of commitment to agricultural land preservation through poor rural planning. At the regional level, planning is the responsibility of Regional Districts and ought to operate through planning controls over urban development. Krueger and Maguire (1985) conclude that there has been ineffective control over haphazard low density sprawl. At the provincial level, British Columbia has established Agricultural Land Reserves (ALRs), the main aim being to protect agricultural land. These ALRs were identified on the basis of land capability classification by the Canada Land Inventory. Integral to the scheme was financial support to farmers should market returns fall below production costs. The ALR scheme was introduced in the Okanagan Valley in 1974. The success of the ALR scheme is open to debate, but Krueger and Maguire (1985) point out that there was a greater urban-related land loss between 1976 and 1981 than between 1966 and 1976. Nevertheless, these authors claim that the rate of land loss has been slowed and they view the ALR programme as a bold and innovative attempt at protecting agricultural land. They conclude their paper by noting a decline in commitment within British Columbia to the ALR scheme and 'it is difficult to be optimistic about the long-term future of the Okanagan Valley fruit-growing industry, and concomitantly, about success in preserving the prime agricultural lands of the Okanagan Valley' (Krueger and Maguire 1985: 299).

In the United States there is similar need to preserve agricultural land. The National Resources Inventory found that between 1967 and 1982, built-up area and rural transportation uses increased by about 5.3 million hectares (Lee 1984). The more serious matter is that such losses take place in a disproportionate manner on the best land. As in Canada, many cities are located in areas of good land; Furuseth and Pierce (1982) summarize the situation by commenting that 28 per cent of prime land lies within 160 kilometres of the 100 largest urban centres in the United States. One response by state planning authorities has been the creation of Agricultural Districts, a topic reviewed by Volkman (1987). The creation of these districts is voluntary and the main objectives are to preserve land for future agricultural production and to control the spread of urban land uses. Integral to the scheme is the protection of the family farm. Volkman reports that forty-nine states have some form of agricultural land preservation programme and nine have laws for Agricultural Districts. California was the first and there farmers can agree to limit the use of their land to agriculture for a given number of years. In return farmers receive

various financial benefits as well as protection under right-to-farm policies. The usual lower limit for an Agricultural District is 40 hectares, but in California this is 8 hectares if the soil classes are either I or II and if more than $2000 are generated through sale of farm products. In an assessment of the scheme's success in California, Volkman concludes that not all prime land has been protected but there has been a slow down in such losses. She considers the programme in New York as the most comprehensive with 3.4 million hectares in Districts. One of the main problems with Agricultural Districts is that since they are voluntary, farmers do not opt for them in the most sensitive areas, namely the urban fringe. The voluntary approach also means that the resultant parcels need not necessarily be contiguous. Despite such limitations, Volkman (1987: 30) concludes that Agricultural Districts have 'shown great promise as a way to slow intrusive development and protect farming'.

This chapter has attempted to outline the wide spectrum of issues associated with the management and conservation of land resources. Particular emphasis has been given to the maintenance of the agricultural land base and to options for increasing food production. During the 1980s the dominant theme in the European Community, Canada and the United States was agricultural overproduction, an issue which has continued into the 1990s. This is leading to a dramatic reappraisal of land resources which are marginal to particular types of agriculture. A pattern of increasing polarization can be identified between those areas particularly suited to particular crops and those more marginal areas where land use diversification is now encouraged. Land lost to urbanization or industrialization is usually irretrievable and it is important that planning policies ensure the retention of good agricultural land. Examples of policies which have had varying success have been quoted in this chapter. Agricultural surpluses have been increasingly evident during the 1980s, but there are many difficulties associated with prediction of future land needs in terms of agricultural production. One trend which is beginning to be evident is the increasing growth of industrial crops. Examples are sunflowers for industrial oils and maize to produce ethyl alcohol for use as a fuel. Also, it must not be forgotten that in many parts of the developing world, the continued increase in food output is of paramount significance. Thus the evaluation of land resources, both in the developed and developing world, is of ever increasing importance. Much emphasis is given in this book to the techniques of land evaluation, but these can be applied only if base land resource surveys have first been carried out. Attention turns in the next chapter to methods of land resource survey.

2

Land Resource Surveys

Any assessment or evaluation of land resources is possible only if there has been the collection of basic land resource data. Much current research is concerned with such themes as computerized techniques of land evaluation, the application of geographical information system (GIS) technology, and modelling. It is easy to overlook the fundamental point that the results from such analyses are only as good as the original data. In this chapter, attention is focused on methods of land resource survey.

The subject of land classification is inevitably a key one in land resource surveys. Land classification is only the starting-point in land resource analysis. It is not just a question of knowing where areas are which meet a defined range of ecological thresholds. Increasingly questions are being posed about such issues as carrying capacity, productivity, environmental sensitivity and environmental impact. As an example, afforestation is on the increase in Scotland and questions are being raised about the

consequences on soil and water quality as well as on adjacent farmland. To answer such questions, knowledge and understanding are necessary on the ecosystem dynamics not only of the relevant forests, but also of the adjacent areas. The continued and increased use of the ecological approach to land resource survey is dependent upon being able to predict the outcome of different land management strategies.

It is possible to devise schemes of land evaluation or classification only if the information to be assessed is precisely defined. The concept of land has been the subject of constant discussion since the first schemes of land classification were produced. In fact land is interpreted in a wide variety of ways according to outlook. It can be viewed as embracing all the characteristics of the physical environment – the atmosphere, soil, geology, hydrology and flora and fauna. It may be considered as three-dimensional space within which humans live. Other interpretations take land as a consumer good or commodity, as location, as property or as a form of capital. An ecological view is also possible whereby land is equated with nature and is thus defined in terms of ecosystems. In the discussions convened by the FAO in 1972 concerned with developing a land evaluation framework, much consideration was given to defining land (Brinkman and Smyth 1973). The ultimate definition which emerged from these FAO studies is worth full quotation:

> Land: an area of the earth's surface, the charac-
> teristics of which embrace all reasonably stable, or
> predictably cyclic, attributes of the biosphere
> vertically above and below this area including those
> of the atmosphere, the soil and underlying geology,
> the hydrology, the plant and animal populations,
> and the results of past and present human activity,
> to the extent that these attributes exert a significant
> influence on present and future uses of the land by
> man.
>
> (FAO 1976: 67)

In essence land is thus viewed as *areas* composed of physical environmental characteristics which are or may be of importance to human use. In a scientific sense this definition is far from satisfactory since an assessment of relevant characteristics is necessary before land can be defined. Thus two land evaluation researchers, for example, commissioned to investigate a particular area, could disagree from the beginning about the data which ought to be collected. Perhaps it is inappropriate to try to define *land* in a scientific way, though R. P. Moss (1978) suggests that a theoretical definition in terms of the function of land in the particular ecological system should ultimately be achieved. However, the FAO statement as quoted does provide clear guidance on how land can be interpreted. The key point is that land is taken to mean the assemblage of all environmental variables which influence land use. Since land uses vary and change, land also requires to be approached in a dynamic ecological manner.

The FAO definition of land as quoted above includes reference to climate, soil, geology, hydrology, flora and fauna, and the effects of human activity. It then follows that land resource surveys must assemble data on one or more of these topics and two broad approaches are possible. The first involves the survey of a particular aspect of land, for example geology or soils. The second approach can be described as ecological since the main objective is the identification of homogeneous ecological areas where there is a grouping of differing land attributes to give a distinctive environment for land use.

2.1 Land resource inventories

Methods of land resource survey can be introduced by describing the approach which has been adopted in New Zealand. The national land resource survey in New Zealand is geared to assisting the National Water and Soil Conservation Organization in its responsibilities for developing catchments and promoting sustainable land use. The New Zealand Land Resource Inventory (NZLRI), initiated in 1972, has two key objectives: first, the provision of nationally consistent erosion and land use capability standards, and second, the provision of a national land resource base for regional and national planning (Eyles 1986). The main aim of the NZLRI is land evaluation at the national, regional

and district level. The inventory is used to assist with developing general land use strategies; an example of land assessment for horticulture in Taranaki is provided by Fletcher (1982). The results from the NZLRI are published as a series of Land Resource Inventory Worksheets at a scale of 1:63,360 with newer ones at 1:50,000; associated documentation accompanies the Worksheets. Fundamental to the approach is the mapping of land management units which are first characterized in terms of their physical resource attributes, and second, evaluated for land use capability; the mapping system is illustrated in Figure 2.1. About 90,000 mapping units have been delimited, ranging from twenty to several hundred hectares.

Information on the physical resource attributes for each mapping unit is given as an inventory code, in particular for rock type, soil unit, slope class, erosion type and degree, and vegetation type. The delineation of the mapping units is based on those attributes which are considered to be of permanent relevance to land use, namely slope, rock type and soil. Subdivisions are made according to vegetation and/or erosion if this is possible at the mapping scale. It is vitally important that every attempt is made to encourage the use of land resource surveys and this can be aided by the provision of easy-to-follow and well-presented booklets. In New Zealand an excellent publication 'Our Land Resources' was produced by the Water and Soil Division, Ministry of Works and Development (1979) and this not only gives a simple description of the land inventory, but also presents a wide range of land use examples which benefit from an input of land resource data. Greater detail on the erosion classification is provided by Eyles (1985).

The second part of the NZLRI is a land use capability assessment whereby each mapping unit is evaluated in terms of its capacity for sustained productive use bearing in mind physical limitations, management requirements and soil conservation needs. In other words an *interpretation* is made of the physical information as given in the inventory code, but also taking into account other factors such as climate. In essence, land capability assessment involves the grading of land according

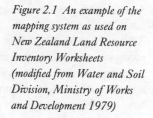

Figure 2.1 An example of the mapping system as used on New Zealand Land Resource Inventory Worksheets (modified from Water and Soil Division, Ministry of Works and Development 1979)

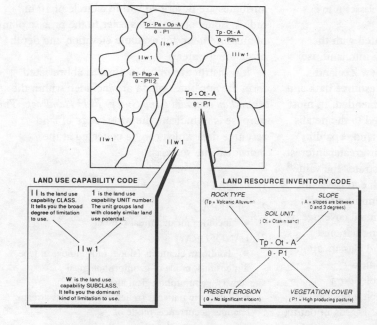

to degree of limitation into classes ranging from I to VIII, with subdivisions into subclasses to indicate the dominant limitation, and further subdivision into units on the basis of areas requiring similar management and conservation. Thus a mapping unit on the 1:50,000 Worksheet, as illustrated in Figure 2.1, could have in addition to the codes for rock, soil, slope, erosion and vegetation, another code such as IIw2 indicating land capability Class II, wetness (w) as the dominant limitation representing the Subclass, and a code of 2 indicating a particular Unit. In the extended legend to the map, information for each mapping unit is given on present land use as well as on potential grazing carrying capacity, potential cropping and forestry, and fertilizer requirements for pasture for sheep and cattle.

Eyles (1986) identifies three phases of development for the NZLRI. The first period was from 1972 to 1979 when the first edition mapping was done. The second period from 1979 to 1985 was one of consolidation with attention being given, for example, to the development of computer mapping systems and to preparation for an updating programme for the Worksheets and for remapping at the 1:50,000 scale. The third phase began in

1986 and has focused on this updating and re-mapping, and the use of a geographical information system (GIS) for the input, editing, processing and output of land resource data. Increasing emphasis is being given to the provision of derivative information and one example is the Vegetative Cover Map of New Zealand at a scale of 1:1,000,000 prepared from the vegetation data in the NZLRI (Newsome 1987). Another development in this third phase has been a system for assessing urban land use capability (Jessen 1987). The cost-effectiveness of urban land use capability surveys in advance of urban development is increasingly being realized and the New Zealand scheme describes how such surveys can be carried out at scales ranging from 1:25,000 to 1:1,000. In outline, the New Zealand urban land use capability scheme necessitates the collection of four types of information:

1   data on rock type, soil landform, erosion, drainage, land cover/land use

2   subdivision of landscapes into mapping units which display similar physical features

3   interpretation of the types and degrees of constraint posed to urban development in each mapping unit

4 an overall capability assessment in classes A to E.

There are many difficulties associated with the incorporation of land resource data into land use management and planning. The New Zealand approach of publishing both land resource data and land capability assessments is commended. In most instances planners are not interested in the details of soil types, but an assessment of land capability class and land use potential is of far greater interest to them. Thus the NZLRI demonstrates the value of producing results in forms which can be easily used by non-specialists. Another important point about the NZLRI is that it has national coverage. Major difficulties arise in persuading national planning authorities to accept a land classification scheme as the basis for planning unless comprehensive map cover is available. New Zealand is fortunate in being in such a position so that current effort can be directed towards updating and enhancing the existing land resources inventory by making increasing use of GIS technology.

In Australia there is a tradition of carrying out integrated surveys whereby a wide range of land resource data are assembled during one survey. The best known technique is identification of land systems which are usually identified at 1:250,000 or smaller. At the other end of the scale, at the site level, there is also need to devise methods for collecting land resource data in a consistent manner. There are many different handbooks on geological, vegetation and soil surveys, but in Australia, a handbook has been prepared to facilitate the description of landform, vegetation, land surface, and soil and substrate material (McDonald et al 1984). The field observations are for descriptions of *sites* and not for mapping units as with the New Zealand scheme. A site is defined as 'a small area of land considered to be representative of the landform, vegetation, land surface and other land features associated with the soil observation' (McDonald et al 1984: 4). The extent of a site is taken to vary according to particular attributes. For example, landform elements are described within a circle of 20 m radius while landform pattern is done over a circle of 300 m radius. Vegetation is investigated within 400 m^2 while most land surface attributes are described within a circle of 10 m radius. Some observations refer to the precise point of measurement, for example elevation and depth of standing water.

It is instructive to list in a much abbreviated form the attributes which are included within the *Australian Soil and Land Survey Field Handbook*. The purpose is to indicate the wide range of land resource data which can be collected at the individual site scale.

1 LOCATION

2 GENERAL
   • includes mean annual rainfall

3 LANDFORM
   • landform elements (slope, morphological type, dimensions, mode of geomorphological activity, geomorphological agent)
   • landform patterns (relief, modal slope, stream channel occurrence, mode of geomorphological activity, geomorphological agent, status of geomorphological activity, component landform elements)

4 VEGETATION
   • if rainforest, record for tallest stratum: complexity, leaf size, height, crown cover, emergents, composition, rainforest species present, sclerophyll species present
   • if non-rainforest, record for at least the tallest stratum and preferably for all strata: growth form, height, crown cover, emergents, species present

5 LAND SURFACE
   • record slope, aspect, elevation, drainage height, disturbance of site, microrelief, erosion, aggradation, inundation, surface coarse fragments, rock outcrop, depth of standing water, run-off

6 SOIL PROFILE
   • record horizons, depth of horizons, depth of regolith, colour, mottles, field texture, coarse fragments, structure, fabric, cutans, voids, soil water status, consistence, condition of surface soil when dry, pans, segregations of pedogenic origin, effervescence of carbonate in fine earth, field pH, roots, boundaries between horizons, internal drainage

7   SUBSTRATE MATERIAL
- record properties of substrate: grain size, porosity, special features, mineral composition, strength, alteration
- record lithology.

The aim of carrying out a land resource survey is to provide an inventory which can be interpreted for a wide variety of land use purposes. The collection, processing and publication of land resource data are expensive operations and can be justified only through the results proving to be of assistance. One distinct trend in recent years has been that land resource surveys have been giving increasing priority to produce results in forms which can be easily used by non-specialists; furthermore, greater attention has been given to the quality of the predictions being made about land attributes. In terms of land use matters, the overall objective concerning land resource surveys is the provision of data or land resource assessments about *areas*. Thus if some form of land resource survey is adopted based on sites such as the Australian one described above, then spatial interpolation is necessary in order to provide information on land mapping units. Field-based approaches must necessarily focus on collection of information at sites and then extrapolation to larger areas. This forms the longstanding core to traditional geological and soil surveys. Considerable use is made of aerial photographs and other forms of remote sensing imagery to aid selection of sites and mapping of units. In the ecological approach to land resource inventories, prime focus is given to the identification of *areas*, with site investigations being used to provide additional data as well as assisting with revisions to boundaries of land mapping units.

2.2   Agro-climatic surveys

The importance of climatic characteristics in influencing land use potential requires no emphasis. As with soil profile data, climatic data are obtained from sample points – meteorological stations. Spatial interpolation is then necessary in order to produce maps of individual variables such as average annual rainfall or average number of days above 4°C. When the need is to characterize areas in terms of a number of climatic attributes, then use has to be made of a climatic classification, a topic of longstanding importance in climatology. Early work is very much associated with W. Koeppen, a biologist, who was primarily concerned with the relationship between climate and vegetation. His first climatic classification as published in 1900 was largely based on vegetation zones, but a revised one in 1918 incorporated temperature, rainfall as well as seasonal characteristics.

The climatologist C. W. Thornthwaite (1948) criticized the Koeppen system for not being based on temperature and precipitation measures in relation to plant requirements. He introduced two measures, the first being precipitation effectiveness which depends on precipitation and evaporation. Monthly precipitation is divided by monthly evaporation and summed for a year to give the P-E index. The second measure is the temperature efficiency index which is obtained by adding the mean monthly temperatures above 0°C. In his second classification, Thornthwaite introduced the concept of potential evapotranspiration which is the amount of water that would be evaporated from soil and transpired by plants if it were present in sufficient abundance. This potential evapotranspiration index (PE) can be calculated from either measuring the evaporation from an area of short stemmed green crop of uniform height with moisture being maintained by irrigation, or from using formulae as provided by Thornthwaite or Penman. According to a revised Thornthwaite method, PE is calculated on a monthly basis using temperature data with adjustments being made for the number of daylight hours (Shaw 1988). This is done as follows:

$$PE_m = 16N_m(10t_m/I)^a$$

where PE = potential evapotranspiration (mm)
   m = months 1,2,3 . . . 12
   N_m = monthly adjustment factor related to hours of daylight

I = annual heat index ($I = \Sigma \ (t_m/5)^{1.5}$
   for m = 1 . . . 12)

t_m = monthly mean temperature

a = $0.49 + 1.791 \times 10^{-2}I - 7.71 \times 10^{-5}I^2 + 6.75 \times 10^{-7}I^3$

Thornthwaite's approach to calculating potential evapotranspiration is entirely empirical. It is not based on knowledge of the component processes associated with evapotranspiration. For example, no account is taken of the influence of vegetation. Thus there are distinct merits in using a method for predicting potential evapotranspiration based on models of heat transfer between leaves and the atmosphere and on water movement within plants. Such an approach has been pioneered by Penman (1948; 1962) and Monteith (1973). For the Penman approach, data are necessary on duration of sunshine as an indicator of radiation, mean air temperature, mean air humidity and mean wind speed as influencing heat and vapour losses from surfaces. In the compilation of an agro-climatic databank for England and Wales, Jones and Thomasson (1985) report about 100 meterological stations for which adequate data are available to calculate potential evapotranspiration using the Penman equation. As a result they were able to calculate and map potential soil water deficits by subtracting potential evapotranspiration from rainfall data. In many countries with limited meteorological data, alternatives to the Penman approach are necessary for predicting potential evapotranspiration. As an example, Joshua (1987) proposes for Sri Lanka the use of the following equation as originally devised by Hargreaves (1985):

PE = $0.0023 \times Ra(T + 17.8) \times TD$

where PE = potential evapotranspiration

Ra = extraterrestrial radiation (obtained from latitude)

T = mean temperature

TD = difference between mean maximum and mean minimum temperatures.

Despite these innovative approaches by Thornthwaite and Penman in the 1940s, attention swung away in subsequent decades from climatic classification issues. However, it is interesting to observe that the development of land classification schemes since the late 1960s has led to further refinement of climatic classification, but with different objectives. As already mentioned, the original focus was on the characterization of natural regions based on climate–vegetation interactions. More recent efforts have been far more specific in that the aim has been to characterize climatic attributes of direct relevance to crops. The nature of such *agro-climatic* assessments can be introduced by giving a number of examples ranging from the global to regional scales.

Agro-climates at the global scale

In Chapter 1, reference was made to the Agro-ecological Zones project of FAO which has as its aim a first approximation of the production potential of the world's land resources. The starting-point in such a land evaluation exercise is the definition of climatic and soil requirements for the different crops. In the Agro-ecological Zones project, inventories of crops were prepared based on their climatic requirements for both photosynthesis and phenology. Then it was necessary to assemble an agro-climatic inventory with particular emphasis on the attributes of land relevant to the defined climatic requirements. Particular emphasis was given to water availability and temperature as initial factors in determining crop suitability for rainfed agriculture. The combination of available water and adequate temperature for crop growth is expressed in *the growing period*. For the Agro-ecological Zones project, the growing period is taken as the continuous period from the time when rainfall is greater than half the potential evapotranspiration until the time when rainfall is less than the full potential evapotranspiration, plus a number of days required to evaporate an assumed 100 mm of soil moisture reserve when available (FAO 1978a). The objective of defining the beginning of the growing season in this way is largely to eliminate the problem caused by 'false start of rains'. The end of

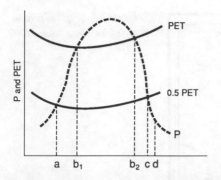

Figure 2.2 An illustration of the growing period as defined by FAO (1978a).
PET potential evapotranspiration
P precipitation
a beginning of rains and growing period
b₁ and b₂ start and end of humid period respectively
c end of rains and rainy season
d end of growing period
(source: FAO 1978a: 36)

the growing period extends beyond the rainy season to varying extents with crops extracting water from soil moisture reserves. The definition assumes a general figure of 100 mm storage water being available to crops. An example of a normal growing period is shown in Figure 2.2. An intermediate growing period exists when the average monthly precipitation is between the full and 0.5 average monthly potential evapotranspiration. For the African study it was concluded that crop growth is severely restricted when the 24 hour (daily) mean temperature falls below 6.5°C. Thus the period during which temperature falls below 6.5°C is subtracted from the growing period as determined from water availability. Data from more than seventy meteorological stations in Africa were obtained and the length of the growing season was computed. Isolines of growing periods of values of 0, 75, 90, 120, 150, 180, 240, 270, 300, 330 and 365 days were interpolated indicating growing period zones of 0–74 days, 75–89 days, 90–119 days, etc (Figure 2.3). Such a map is an excellent example of an agro-climatic inventory designed to be relevant to a particular crops.

Agro-climates at the national scale

Many countries have developed systems of land capability classification to aid land use planning and land management. The common approach is to devise a method of grading land according to degree of limitation posed by climatic, relief and soil characteristics. Thus some form of agro-climatic assessment is integral to such land classification. For example, a land use capability classification was introduced in Britain by Bibby and Mackney (1969); in this system climatic characteristics are incorporated in a quantitative manner to define three climatic groups. This is done on the basis of the water balance and temperature during the period April to September. In particular, figures for the following factors are obtained for this period:

R: average rainfall (mm)
PT: average potential transpiration (mm)
T(x): long-term average of mean daily maximum temperature.

Three climatic groups can thus be defined:

Group I
    $R - PT < 100$ mm and $T(x) > 15°C$
(no, or only slight climatic limitations imposed on crop growth).

Group II
    $R - PT < 300$ mm and $T(x) > 14°C$ but excluding group I
(moderately unfavourable climate which restricts choice of crops).

Group III
    $R - PT > 300$ mm or $T(x) < 14°C$
(moderately severe to extremely severe climate which further limits the range of crops).

In addition, assessments of climatic conditions in Scotland were based on accumulated temperature and potential water deficit (Birse and Dry 1970) and on exposure and accumulated frost (Birse and Robertson 1970).

The scheme of Bibby and Mackney (1969) was the national one for Britain during the 1970s and

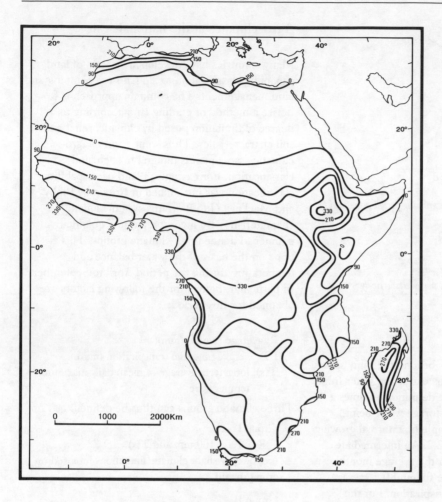

Figure 2.3 Length of growing periods in Africa (source: FAO 1978a: 40)

early 1980s. A new scheme was published by Bibby et al (1982) and this has been adopted for Scotland while different ones are in use in England and Wales (Ministry of Agriculture, Fisheries and Food 1988). It is instructive to outline the agro-climatic components of these schemes.

In the Scottish scheme, the two key climatic variables are the maximum potential soil moisture deficit and accumulated temperature. The maximum potential soil moisture deficit is defined as the theoretical deficit achievable under short grass covering soil which is assumed to have a large store of available water (Bibby et al 1982). It is a measure of the maximum deficit between rainfall and evaporation. For the temperature statistic, accumulated day-degrees above 0°C are calculated and the lower quartile value is selected. The

maximum potential soil moisture deficit and accumulated temperature values are plotted on a diagram as shown in Figure 2.4. In the handbook a large number of stations are plotted on this diagram and thus in classifying a site, use can be made of the nearest and most comparable station. The resultant land capability class and division is the highest possible; downgrading may be necessary on the basis of exposure, relief and soil considerations. In the English and Welsh scheme, again two key climatic variables are used – average annual rainfall as a measure of overall wetness, and accumulated temperature as a measure of warmth (Ministry of Agriculture, Fisheries and Food 1988). Accumulated temperature is calculated above 0°C for the period January to June since this is the critical growth period for most crops; furthermore

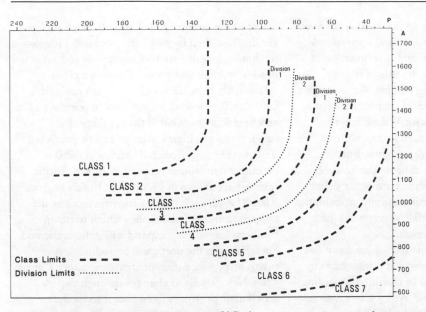

Figure 2.4 Land capability classes and divisions in relation to maximum potential soil moisture deficit (P) and accumulated temperature (T) (source: Bibby et al 1982: 22)

limited crop growth is possible down to 0°C. As with the Scottish system, use is made of a plot of the two climatic variables to provide the first approximation of land capability classes. The Soil Survey of England and Wales identified the importance of being able to integrate agro-climatic data with their national soil inventory. This necessitated the prediction of agro-climatic values on a regular grid framework, either at 10 km or 5 km intervals. Jones and Thomasson (1985) explain how regression equations were used to predict accumulated temperature on the basis of elevation and grid reference.

In temperate countries such as Britain, accumulated temperature during the growing season is a critical agro-climatic control. In contrast, for Mediterranean areas, the prime agro-climatic control is usually available water. An example of agro-climatic assessment in Puglia, Italy can be given for the growth of tomatoes based on the work of Bellocchio and Magaldi (1987). They considered that the mean temperature during the growing season is not limiting to the growth of tomatoes since the region has more than 135 days with mean temperatures over 15°C. Thus their agro-climatic suitability for tomatoes was based on estimates of water deficit on the assumption of an available water holding capacity of 200 mm. The agro-climatic classes, termed cropwater

requirement classes, are given in Table 2.1. Bellocchio and Magaldi (1987) were thus able to map these agro-climatic classes for south-east Italy. The results are of particular interest because they indicate the irrigation water required for the successful growth of tomatoes. It needs to be stressed that consideration also has to be given to soil and topographic conditions to assess the overall suitability of the region for tomatoes as illustrated by Ferrari and Magaldi (1989).

For an example in a developing world country, brief mention can be made of the agro-climatic classification as used in Malaysia (Ghazalli and Nieuwolt 1982; Sooryanarayana 1985). Of critical importance in Malaysia is the likely duration of dry months. A month is considered as dry when the

Table 2.1 Agro-climatic classification for tomatoes in Puglia, Italy

Cropwater requirement class	Water deficit (mm)	Per cent of maximum production obtainable without irrigation
W1	0–150	80–100
W2	150–275	60–80
W3	275–400	40–60
W4	>400	<40

(source: Bellocchio and Magaldi 1987: 44)

agricultural rainfall index is less than 40, a situation when soil moisture stress occurs and corresponds approximately to a mean monthly precipitation of 100 mm. The length of the dry season is determined according to the number of consecutive dry months with a frequency of occurrence of at least one year in five. Thus for Malaysia, agro-climatic zones were determined according to frequency and duration of dry seasons. Further division of these zones was done on the basis of rainfall variability causing short term water deficits of less than a month's duration and the probabilities of occurrence of heavy rainfall, strong wind gusts and periods of heavy cloudiness.

Although the focus in this section has been on the assessment of agro-climates, it is important to stress that climates can also be classified according to other criteria, for example, ecology. In Canada, the Ecoregions Working Group (1989) have defined and mapped ecoclimatic regions for the

whole of the country at 1:7,500,00. Such regions are distinguished by particular ecological responses to climate, as expressed by vegetation and reflected in soils, wildlife and water. There is a close relationship between ecoclimatic and ecological land classifications. The practical importance of an ecoclimatic assessment is that ecological implications of climatic change can be predicted. The present and predicted extents in 2050 of ecoclimatic provinces (groupings of ecoclimatic regions) are shown in Figure 2.5. In this analysis by Rizzo (1990), such ecoclimatic provinces as the temperate and grassland ones which occur in southern Canada will expand while the arctic and boreal ones in the north will be reduced. A subarctic province disappears from eastern Canada while Newfoundland changes through two ecoclimatic provinces from boreal to moderate temperate. In western Canada, a new pattern of ecoclimatic provinces emerges, including two new

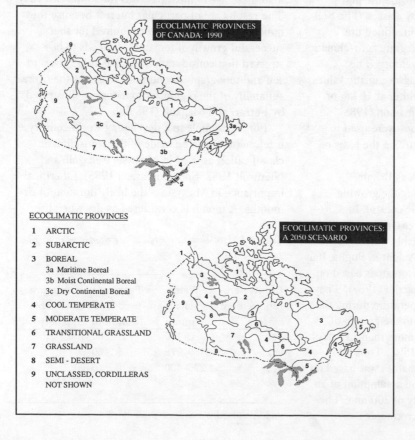

Figure 2.5 Ecoclimatic provinces in Canada for 1990 and as predicted for 2050 (source: Rizzo 1990: 5)

ECOCLIMATIC PROVINCES

1   ARCTIC
2   SUBARCTIC
3   BOREAL
   3a Maritime Boreal
   3b Moist Continental Boreal
   3c Dry Continental Boreal
4   COOL TEMPERATE
5   MODERATE TEMPERATE
6   TRANSITIONAL GRASSLAND
7   GRASSLAND
8   SEMI - DESERT
9   UNCLASSED, CORDILLERAS
    NOT SHOWN

units, transitional grassland and semi-desert. Rizzo (1990) indicates some of the ecological implications of such climatic change; substantial alteration in habitat patterns would occur with consequences for migration patterns. A major change in forest cover of Canada is also predicted with tree-lines moving northwards. As Rizzo (1990) stresses, these predictions are the results from one modelling exercise and further research will yield other outcomes.

2.3   Landscape approach to land resource survey

The *landscape approach* involves the delimitation and characterization of land mapping units on the basis of distinct ecological complexes being expressed in landscape patterns. The land systems approach is the best known landscape approach for providing a rapid inventory of land resources. This approach was used as far back as 1933 in Michigan (Cooke and Doornkamp 1974), but credit is usually given to the Commonwealth Scientific and Industrial Organization (CSIRO) in Australia for pioneering the technique in the 1940s to assess the agricultural and pastoral potential of northern Australia. The first area to be mapped was the Katherine–Darwin region in 1946 and this study by Christian and Stewart (1952) has come to be the model for many others. Since this first survey, about 2 million square kilometers of Australia and most of Papua New Guinea have been covered.

The land systems approach, also called integrated survey, is fully described by Christian and Stewart (1968). To a large extent the method is based on the interpretation of aerial photographs and areas with a recurring pattern of topography, soils and vegetation are mapped as individual land systems. The central concept is that in specific areas all the environmental characteristics (topography, soils, vegetation, geology and geomorphology and climate) will interrelate, resulting in distinctive patterns on aerial photographs. The approach is described as integrated because the method depends on identifying distinctive areas resultant upon the

integration of environmental variables; the survey is also executed by a team of scientists (for example, a geomorphologist, geologist, pedologist, ecologist and an agriculturalist). The resultant maps showing the distribution of land systems are produced on scales varying from 1:250,000 to 1:1,000,000 and it can be recognized immediately that the land systems approach is essentially a reconnaissance assessment of natural resources. For the planning of agricultural development, such surveys are able to identify areas of little or no potential, but more detailed investigations are required in areas which seem to offer scope for development.

A report on an area which has been surveyed by the land systems approach contains not only a land system map, but also other maps, for example of geology or geomorphology; the properties of individual land systems are summarized in tables giving information on the geology, topography, major soils, major vegetation communities, characteristics of agricultural importance and comments on agricultural potentialities. The nature of the land system is also illustrated by the presentation of a schematized cross-section or block diagram for each one. Such diagrams and tables permit the description of the components of land systems, that is land units which clearly display a greater deal of internal homogeneity than land systems. As an example, Purdie (1984) describes the land systems of Simpson Desert in the general region where the Northern Territory, Queensland and South Australia adjoin. It is an area of 200,000 square kilometres consisting mainly of sand dunes. The analysis of aerial photographs and Landsat images aided by field survey resulted in thirty-two land systems being defined and delimited. Land systems are summarized in the form of cross-sections with information given on component land units for landform type, soils and vegetation; an example of one system as mapped in the Simpson Desert is shown in Figure 2.6. The overall objective of the report is to provide an inventory of the land resources with particular emphasis being given to vegetation species. The study by Scott et al (1985) provides an example of a resource inventory using similar methodology, but at a more detailed scale; this project deals with Chimbu Province in

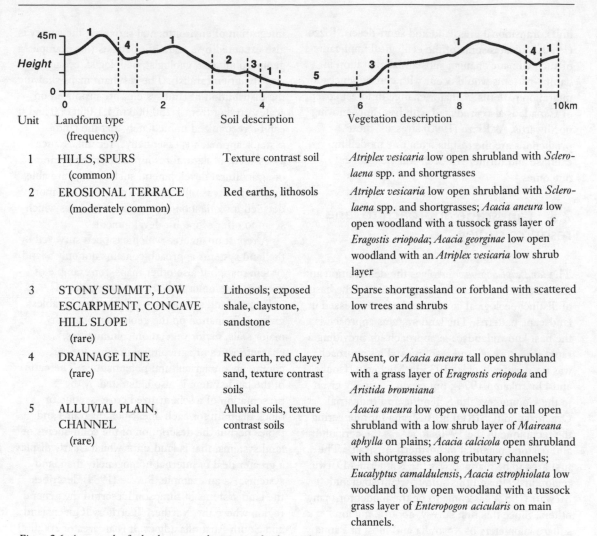

Unit	Landform type (frequency)	Soil description	Vegetation description
1	HILLS, SPURS (common)	Texture contrast soil	*Atriplex vesicaria* low open shrubland with *Sclerolaena* spp. and shortgrasses
2	EROSIONAL TERRACE (moderately common)	Red earths, lithosols	*Atriplex vesicaria* low open shrubland with *Sclerolaena* spp. and shortgrasses; *Acacia aneura* low open woodland with a tussock grass layer of *Eragostis eriopoda*; *Acacia georginae* low open woodland with an *Atriplex vesicaria* low shrub layer
3	STONY SUMMIT, LOW ESCARPMENT, CONCAVE HILL SLOPE (rare)	Lithosols; exposed shale, claystone, sandstone	Sparse shortgrassland or forbland with scattered low trees and shrubs
4	DRAINAGE LINE (rare)	Red earth, red clayey sand, texture contrast soils	Absent, or *Acacia aneura* tall open shrubland with a grass layer of *Eragrostis eriopoda* and *Aristida browniana*
5	ALLUVIAL PLAIN, CHANNEL (rare)	Alluvial soils, texture contrast soils	*Acacia aneura* low open woodland or tall open shrubland with a low shrub layer of *Maireana aphylla* on plains; *Acacia calcicola* open shrubland with shortgrasses along tributary channels; *Eucalyptus camaldulensis*, *Acacia estrophiolata* low woodland to low open woodland with a tussock grass layer of *Enteropogon acicularis* on main channels.

Figure 2.6 An example of a land system and component land units for an area of steep-sided hills, dissected spurs and associated valleys in the Simpson Desert, central Australia (source: Purdie 1984: 40)

the central highlands of mainland Papua New Guinea and covers an area of 6,200 square kilometres. Interpretation of aerial photographs for this tropical region had to be limited to the topography with the exclusion of patterns due to vegetation. Dense forest covers much of the region. Mapping was done at 1:50,000 and was based on interpretation of aerial photographs. The broadest categories are land types which are subdivided into land units and in turn into sub-land units. Maps at 1:100,000 accompany the report and these show the distribution of land units. Details of the land units and their component sub-land units are given in the main report; of note is the systematic description of topography, drainage, climate, geology, landform, surface water patterns and soil characteristics. As with the Simpson Desert survey, the main aim is to provide an inventory of the land resources. The intention is that such an inventory can provide the basis for subsequent land assessments.

Organizations other than CSIRO have also applied the land systems approach to land resource assessment. The former Land Resources Division of the Ministry of Overseas Development undertook such surveys as part of British foreign aid or under contract. Projects involving a land systems analysis have been carried out in such countries as Lesotho (Bawden and Carroll 1968), north-east Nigeria (Bawden et al 1972), Zambia (Mansfield et al 1975–6), and Ethiopia (King and Birchall 1975). These surveys are very much of a reconnaissance nature; where the need is for more detailed land resource assessment, recourse is made to soil survey procedures. These soil data, combined with vegetation and climatic information, allow land use capability maps to be produced. For example, in the Belize study (Jenkin et al 1976), land is classed as to whether it is suitable for arable use (further subdivided into four classes), conditionally suitable for arable land (further subdivided into two classes), and unsuitable for arable use (further subdivided into two classes). The results are presented on maps at a scale of 1:100,000.

Reference must also be made to research on terrain classification and evaluation by an Oxford team (Webster and Beckett 1970). This work was sponsored in the first instance by the Military Engineering Experimental Establishment (MEXE), later to be called the Military Vehicles Experimental Establishment (MVEE), since the military need was for the development of a fast method which could predict the trafficability of terrain for army vehicles. The method in the original study focused on the identification and mapping from aerial photographs of land facets at scales of 1:10,000 to 1:50,000. A facet 'is a part of the landscape, usually with simple form, on a particular rock or superficial deposit, and with soil and water regime that are either uniform over the whole of the facet or if not, vary in a simple and consistent way' (Webster and Beckett 1970: 54). Land facets are grouped together to produce land systems which are mapped at scales in the range 1:250,000 to 1:1,000,000. The close similarity between the CSIRO and MEXE land system as well as between the respective land units and land facets should be immediately clear. The Oxford team tested their method to determine whether it would permit the classification of all the terrain in their area, if mapped facets were internally homogeneous in terms of specific variables, and if

photo interpreters would produce similar results. Overall, the outcome of this investigation was satisfactory which led the Oxford method to be applied in surveys in such countries as Uganda, Swaziland, Kenya and parts of southern Africa. King (1970) has also carried out research to determine if land systems can be investigated in a quantitative manner. He established by statistical analysis a large number of correlations between geomorphic, soil and land system data for an area in Zambia. Another study has investigated whether the land system-facet classification could provide a basis for the acquisition of information on soil and land capability (Lawrance et al 1977). The general approach proved to be applicable, though land facets were found to be rather complex and had to be subdivided into land elements.

Without doubt there has been much improvement in land resource surveys using the land system approach since the pioneering works in the 1940s and 1950s. A distinct trend has been towards making aerial photo interpretation more objective through being more specific about relevant land attributes. Nevertheless, some fundamental objections are still voiced about the method. For example, R. P. Moss (1978) argues that such land resource reports contain much data of dubious or irrelevant value through trying to describe so many characteristics. This criticism may well be valid for some of the old surveys while more recent ones are more specific in objective and approach. As an example, a study in Malaysia exemplifies the Oxford method as applied to terrain evaluation for highway engineering (Lawrance 1972; 1978). This project, carried out by the Overseas Unit of the Transport and Road Research Laboratory, had the objectives of testing the Oxford method in a humid tropical environment and of examining the variability of soil properties of relevance to engineering within mapped units. A map at a scale of 1:250,000 shows the distribution of land systems within the study area; the accompanying report contains information in tabular form about the component land facets. Attention is focused on their topography and the nature of their soils from an engineering standpoint. In particular, information is given on such properties as particle size, liquid and plastic limits, linear shrinkage, maximum safe angles for excavations, rock strength, and suitability for fill. Block diagrams, topographic sections and annotated stereo triplets indicate the spatial pattern of land facets within land systems. The results demonstrate how a road engineer at the early stage of planning a new road could benefit from the results of a land systems analysis.

The development of the land systems approach in Australia was motivated by the need to produce quickly reconnaissance level land resource inventories, especially for undeveloped areas. A similar requirement has been identified for Canada and an ecological approach similar to the land systems technique has been adopted. A method for ecological land classification has been devised (Environmental Conservation Service Task Force 1981). Again it is an integrated or holistic approach to land classification and each component mapped area is deemed to be distinct in terms of a particular assemblage of geological, landform, soil, vegetation, climatic, wildlife, water, and human factors. The approach can be applied at any of the scales listed below:

ECOPROVINCE (1:5,000,000)
An area of the earth's surface characterized by major assemblages of structural or surface forms, faunal realms, vegetation, hydrological, soil and climatic zones.

ECOREGION (1:1,000,000–1:5,000,000)
A part of an ecoprovince characterized by distinctive ecological responses to climate as expressed by the development of soils, water, fauna, etc.

ECODISTRICT (1:250,000–1:1,000,000)
A part of an ecoregion throughout which there is a recurring assemblage of terrain, soils and vegetation.

ECOSECTION (1:50,000–1:250,000)
A part of an ecodistrict throughout which there is a recurring assemblage of terrain, soils and vegetation.

ECOSITE (1:10,000–1:50,000)
A part of an ecosection in which there is a relative uniformity of parent material, soil, hydrology and vegetation.

ECOELEMENT (1:10,000)
A part of an ecosite displaying uniform soil, topographical, vegetative and hydrological characteristics.

Note: the scale varies according to the diversity of the landscape under survey.

(source: Hirvonen 1984: 8)

To this hierarchy can be added ecozones which have been mapped for the whole of Canada; a report by Wiken (1986) gives details of the fifteen terrestrial ecozones which are defined as areas of the earth's surface representative of large and very generalized ecological units characterized by interactive and adjusting abiotic and biotic factors. As an example of ecological land survey at a different scale, Hirvonen (1984) describes the Atlantic region at the ecoregion level.

An interesting application of ecological land classification is given by Gilbert et al (1985) for Quebec. For this province, the mapping of ecodistricts and ecoregions formed the starting-point for assessing the sensitivity of ecosystems to acid precipitation. These authors state that for studies involving multiple parameters such as acid precipitation, an integrated ecological approach is essential. The approach was based on the concept that ecosystem sensitivity is inversely related to the potential of soils and bedrock to reduce acidic inputs. An assessment was made of the potential acidity reducing capacity of each ecodistrict based on soil texture and depth. Coarse textured and shallow soils have the least buffering capacity while fine textured and deep clays have the greatest. A map at a scale of 1:2,500,000 shows for Quebec the potential of soils and bedrock to reduce acidity.

The methods and objectives of the Canadian system of ecological land classification are specified in the report by the Environmental Conservation Service Task Force (1981). An initial impression may be that the approach lacks quantitative guidelines and much interpretation is necessary to apply the approach. Nevertheless, it is claimed that the procedure provides a standardized approach to ecosystem characterization and the resultant units can be evaluated in ecological terms for land use management. M. R. Moss (1985) argues that a major limitation of many ecological land classifications is the inability to produce data on relative values. He believes that a greater focus on processes within land units is required and he demonstrates such an approach by assessing energy and moisture inputs. His analysis is concerned with data on ecoregions and ecodistricts for Manitoba and Ontario. It is instructive to summarize his analytical method to demonstrate how ecological land classification can lead to land productivity assessments.

STEP 1
Calculate potential evapotranspiration using the Thornthwaite method.

STEP 2
Calculate potential net primary productivity; this is a function of the actual evapotranspiration. It indicates potential biomass production.

STEP 3
Calculate potential organic decay and decomposition rates; again this is a function of actual evapotranspiration. Organic matter which is generated by photosynthesis must ultimately decay if it is not consumed in higher order trophic levels.

STEP 4
Calculate a soil performance index. Use can be made of correlations between land capability classes and agricultural or forestry yields in order to derive scorings for the classes. Weightings have to be applied in order to take into account the extents of different land capability classes.

STEP 5
Calculate average potential net primary productivity. This takes account of the different proportions of potential net primary productivity (step 2) which occur within each ecodistrict.

STEP 6
Calculate the adjusted potential primary productivity value by multiplying the average potential net primary productivity (step 5) by the soil performance index (step 4). This adjustment is included in order to reflect the varying effect of land capability on biomass production.

Details of the method are given by M. R. Moss (1985) who summarizes his results through

mapping adjusted potential primary productivity values by ecodistricts. He proposes that such maps can be used for assessing carrying capacity of wildlife or extensive forms of agriculture. But the most important application in Canada is for forestry in terms of predicting yields and aiding management decisions.

A landscape ecological approach to the assessment of land resources in Greece is described by Nakos (1983). The first aim in this survey is to describe, classify, map and evaluate land resources in upland areas in order to provide base information for assisting land use and management decisions. Land mapping units at a scale of 1:50,000 are identified on the basis of information extracted from existing vegetation, geology and topographic maps, from the interpretation of aerial photographs and from field survey. For each mapping unit, a code is provided to give information on the following criteria: regional climate, degree of vegetation alteration by humans, landform type, soil depth, erosion class, slope and aspect. Such 1:50,000 maps are gradually being provided for the whole of Greece and constitute an important land resource database. Interpretative maps in the form of land capability maps for forestry are also published. Christodoulou and Nakos (1990) explain how the mapping units of the land resource system can be evaluated under different scenarios, for example, with priority given to agriculture followed by forestry, rangeland and land protection uses. The suitability of the mapping units in terms of these different scenarios could then be assessed with maps and tables being produced to indicate required land use changes. Such analysis will become much easier and more versatile with the adoption of a geographical information system, the next stage with this land resource project in Greece.

2.4 Parametric approach to ecological land classification

A parametric approach to ecological land classification is fundamentally different from the

the integrated technique. In the latter, areas on the earth's surface with distinctive ecosystems are identified in the first instance as entities. Thus lines are drawn on aerial photographs to delimit areas deemed to be ecologically homogeneous. With the parametric approach, layers of information are built up on component attributes such as climate, soils and vegetation and then an ecological classification is adopted. As an example, this is the approach adopted for an ecological land classification in the United States (Driscoll et al 1984); one advantage of such an approach is that the ecological land classes can be disaggregated into the component attributes if specific data on soils or vegetation are required. The advantages of a parametric approach become particularly evident when use is made of a geographical information system. Data on the component variables can be stored and processed in ways appropriate to users' needs. The older approach is to consider ecological land classifications, or indeed any form of spatial classification, as essential for the management of data. The use of GIS outdates such a view given the capabilities of processing spatial data in forms directly relevant to users. This will be discussed in Chapter 7, but for present purposes it is important to discuss examples of parametric approaches whereby component variables are combined to classify land.

The Agro-ecological Zones (AEZ) Project of FAO has already been introduced and it serves as a very useful example of the parametric approach to ecological land classification. The general methodology of the evaluation procedure is summarized by the following steps:

1   Review and refinement of the proposals of the evaluation in conjunction with identification of the basic data and assumptions to be used.

2   Selection of alternative land uses (crops, levels of inputs, etc) for consideration.

3   Determination of the climatic and soil requirements of the selected alternative land uses.

4   Compilation of an inventory of the land (climate and soil) and mapping units (agro-ecological zones) with respect to 3.

5   Matching of the requirements 3 with the land inventory 4 and calculation of anticipated production potential in the different agro-ecological zones recognized.

6   Estimation of production costs, and identification of the various suitability classes to be employed and their differentiating parameters.

7   Classification of the land into various suitability classes for the selected alternative land uses, and presentation of results.

(from FAO 1978a)

The first step involves an overall assessment of the project with particular regard to basic assumptions and availability of information. The AEZ Project decided to focus on rainfed potential and furthermore, to limit itself to eleven major crops (see p. 4). These were further considered at two levels – a low one similar to traditional systems of shifting cultivation or bush fallow rotation, and a high one involving mechanical cultivation under capital intensive management practices.

The third step was probably the most difficult and important in that the climatic and soil requirements of the eleven crops had to be determined. For climatic requirements, particular attention was paid to rainfall, soil moisture and temperature. Importance was given to calculating the growing period when water availability and temperature conditions permit crop growth. In essence, this is a season when rainfall is in excess of evapotranspiration and temperatures are above a critical thresholds, for example 6.5°C for winter wheat. Consideration was also given to the photosynthetic requirements of the different crops. Five photosynthetic pathways are defined and the crops are assigned to these different groups. In terms of soil requirements, a list was compiled of all properties which were considered to have an effect on the success of the crops. Properties such as soil depth, texture, salinity, etc, were then subdivided in order to define optimum soil conditions.

Following on from the identification of climatic and soil requirements was step 4, whereby data on climate and soil characteristics were collected. The climatic data input has already been described in section 2.2 and the results for Africa in terms of growing periods were shown in Figure 2.3. The soil data were derived from the 1:5,000,000 FAO/UNESCO Soil Map of the World. The agro-climatic regions were then superimposed over the soil map in order to define agro-ecological zones. The determination of climatic and soil requirements in step 3 and the production of an agro-ecological zones inventory in step 4 then permitted the matching process to operate in step 5. By this process the requirements of the specific crops are matched with the actual nature of the agro-ecological zones in order to produce a suitability assessment. Matching of the climatic crop requirements with the climatic inventory is done in a quantitative manner by first determining if the crop temperature requirements can be met; second, ascertaining if the length of growing season is sufficient; and third, calculating potential net biomass and yield of crops. For the matching of soil requirements of crops with the nature of specific soils, a more qualitative approach is necessary because of the lack of models and data relating soils classified according to the FAO/UNESCO legend and crop yields. On the basis of experience and personal judgement, the FAO team for Africa were able to grade soils according to suitability for crops. Thus a soil which imposed no constraints on a specific crop would have been classed as S1 while a soil which imposed some limitations would have been S2.

The final steps in the methodology of the AEZ Project are the estimation of production costs and the definition of suitability classes (step 6) and the assignment of agro-ecological zones to these suitability classes for the eleven crops at the two input levels (step 7). In step 7 the anticipated yields from step 5 may be reduced in order to take into account rainfall variability, excess moisture or losses due to pests, diseases and weeds. The results are described as agro-climatically attainable yields. At the end of the land evaluation process, areas are categorized as being very suitable, suitable, marginally suitable or not suitable for each crop at the two input levels.

The AEZ Project had as its focus the assessment of land resources of developing countries. The approach has also been applied at the national level as demonstrated in Bangladesh (FAO 1988). In this study the overall aim was to present a broad but comprehensive overview of the physical environment in relation to actual and potential land use. The hope was to provide the basis for the more rational planning, development and conservation of the country's land resources. A map of agro-ecological regions was produced by the successive overlay of physiographic and agro-climatic attributes.

Physiographic attributes are taken as the basis for defining and delimiting agro-ecological regions. By physiography is meant the combination of parent materials from which soils have formed and landscape types. The results are in essence geomorphological units and as an example, the Ganges river floodplain of 24,508 km^2 is the most extensive. This unit is subdivided into three regions, the active Ganges floodplain, the high Ganges river floodplain and the low Ganges river floodplain. A total of thirty such physiographic regions, which are also described as agro-ecological regions, are mapped at a scale of 1:750,000; in turn these are subdivided into agro-ecological subregions. Information on the general soil types as well as soil textures within each agro-ecological region or subregion is given in the legend to the map. This has the merit of indicating the variation in soils within these regions or subregions.

Agro-climatic information is also superimposed on the 1:750,000 map of Bangladesh. In such a country, temperatures are suitable for crop production throughout the year and thus the natural length of growing period is determined by moisture supply. On the map are plotted four agro-climatic variables:

1   average length of the pre-kharif period when rainfed soil moisture supply is intermittent and uncertain

2   average lengths of the rainfed kharif and rabi growing periods

3 average number of days in a year with minimum temperatures below 15°C and certain other temperature limits of importance for major rabi crops grown in Bangladesh

4 average number of days in a year with maximum summer temperatures higher than 40°C.

The legend also lists for agro-ecological regions and subregions the occurrence of different degrees of flooding. For example, highland is defined as normally above flood levels while lowland is normally flooded up to between 180 and 300 cm during the flood season.

Even from this outline, it can be appreciated that the resultant agro-ecological map showing all these attributes of physiography, soils, inundation classes and agro-climatic variables is very complicated. Such map complexity presents a user with considerable difficulty. To facilitate use, reference needs to be made to the accompanying report where details are given for agro-ecological regions and subregions. Of particular relevance to agriculture are the comments on development constraints as well as on agricultural possibilities.

As another example in the developing world, Joshua (1987) describes the method which was used to subdivide Sri Lanka into twenty-four agro-ecological regions. In the first instance the country was divided into wet, intermediate and dry zones based on rainfall, forest type and agricultural land use. The resultant areas were subdivided according to elevation and soils to produce the twenty-four agro-ecological regions which are considered homogeneous in respect of soil, landform and rainfall pattern. The results have been used for planning land use in development projects as well as for giving recommendations on appropriate agricultural practices for specific regions. Refinements in the method of climatic assessment are planned in order to incorporate potential evapotranspiration.

A rather different approach to agro-ecological classification is given by Scholz (1987) for Sumatra and Costa Rica. As an initial stage he delimited the occurrence of broad agro-ecological zones. Then the distributions of different crops were mapped using dots corresponding to 1000 ha for Sumatra

and 100 ha for Costa Rica. Much effort was spent on locating these dots on the actual areas where the crops were grown. It was then possible to overlay the crop distributions over the agro-ecological zones in order to calculate basic agricultural data for such zones rather than for administrative regions. Crop combinations were also defined so that the occurrence of farming systems in the different ecological zones could be determined. The areas of land within the agro-ecological zones were calculated for the different farming systems. Model farm profiles were then devised in order to assist with integrated rural development.

The Institute of Terrestrial Ecology (ITE) in the UK has developed a system of ecological land classification (Bunce et al 1981). One of the early ITE projects focused on Cumbria where concern was with devising an ecological land evaluation in order to provide a framework for comparing different demands on rural land. A 1 km² grid was superimposed over Cumbria and the presence or absence of 186 map derived attributes was recorded for each cell. Indicator species analysis was then used in order to identify groupings of grid cells with similar attributes. As a result, sixteen land classes were defined and mapped for Cumbria (Smith 1982). To aid interpretation of these land classes, grid cells were sampled in order to compare, for example, observed and predicted vegetation. It was then possible to apply linear programming using the land classification and sample data in order to optimize, for example, the production of timber, milk and meat, subject to one or more constraints. It was thus possible to produce maps showing land use changes as proposed by the optimization models.

The ITE land classification approach has been adopted by the Planning department of Highland Regional Council in Scotland in order to develop a rural land use information system (Claridge 1988). Such an approach has proved particularly effective given the size (25,000 km²) and ecological diversity of this region. In the first instance, the database for each kilometre square was restricted to only those attributes needed for assigning cells to the ITE land classes. The database has subsequently been extended to include information on other aspects, for example nature conservation designations and land capability for agriculture. The Planning Department of Highland Regional Council use the system to produce single factor maps, for example for peat and existing woodland, and also to appraise land use potential. As an example, much current interest focuses in Highland region on the extension of forestry. The assessment of forestry potential was tackled in two stages. In the first, the ecological suitability of land was assessed through considering altitude, exposure and land use constraints, for example agricultural land. In the second, an economic appraisal was made in order to compare agricultural and forestry enterprises. The experience of Highland Regional Council demonstrates the value of linking ecological land classification with a database system. The results have proved of value in aiding strategic land use planning.

The essential advantage of an ecological approach to land classification lies in the summation of environmental attributes relevant to land use and management. This is expressed in the United States in the delineation of major land resource areas (MLRAs) designed to be useful for state, interstate, regional and national planning. Douglas et al (1988) argue that the approach can be extended down to the local level with the objective of giving advice on agronomic and tillage practices. Their approach is a simple parametric one through the successive overlay of soil and climatic distributions. For their study area in north central Oregon, depth is considered the key soil variable and a distinction is made between areas with depths more than and less than 1 m. Threshold values for average annual precipitation are next given. With precipitation over 400 mm per year, annual cropping is deemed to be a safe operation regardless of soil depth. If the annual average is between 350 and 400 mm per year, then annual cropping is possible on seven out of ten years if soil depth is greater than 1 m. In areas of deep soils with an average annual precipitation of between 250 and 350 mm, the cropping of wheat is possible if use is made of two winters' supply of water. Summer fallow thus becomes necessary. With average annual precipitation below 250 mm, irrigation is usually necessary for cropping. The other climatic variable is a measure of heat input, expressed in total growing days between 1 January and 31 May. Thus growing degree days are the sums of daily degree days for the five month period calculated as follows:

degree days $= 0.5$ (daily maximum $+$ daily minimum) $-$ base temperature

The base temperature was taken as 0°C. Critical thresholds were selected at 1000 and 700 total growing degree days. The overlay of soil depth, precipitation and growing days resulted in the delineation of six agronomic zones in north central Oregon. The results are used to assist with agronomic models and the extension of conservation tillage results. The ecological classification which is carefully related to agronomic criteria thus serves as an efficient mechanism for the transfer of management experience.

3

Soil Surveys

The tasks of a soil survey are the description, classification, analysis and mapping of soils and most countries have organizations charged with carrying out such studies. The focus of soil surveys traditionally has been towards agriculture, and thus soil is usually taken to be the natural medium within which plants will grow. However, the definition of soil as the plant rooting medium is rather limited and there is the question of the minimum depth of a soil. Plants obviously vary in their maximum rooting depths – another problem for defining soil precisely using the rooting zone concept. Soil information is being used increasingly for non-agricultural purposes, yet another reason for not using this approach to defining soil. A more scientific definition can be suggested if soil is viewed as the result of soil-forming (pedogenic) processes which give it distinctive properties. A formal definition has been proposed by Joffe (1949) and has been slightly modified by Birkeland (1984: 3): 'a soil is described as a natural body consisting of layers or horizons of mineral and/or organic

constituents of variable thicknesses, which differ from the parent material in their morphological, physical, chemical, and mineralogical properties and their biological characteristics.' In the investigation of soils, this means that the parent material ought always to be recognized and described; the uppermost part of this material and the overlying layers constitute the soil.

3.1   Soil survey procedures

The starting-point for most soil studies is site examination which involves site and profile description. The profile is composed usually of several horizons which are approximately parallel layers characterized by distinctive colour as well as by structure, texture, consistence, and chemical, biological and mineralogical composition. Even within a soil pit of 1 m width, marked variations in depth of horizons can occur and this stresses the three-dimensional nature of soil. The two-dimensional unit of study is a soil profile, while the smallest three-dimensional unit is called a *pedon*. A pedon is the smallest volume which can be considered a soil and the surface extent varies from about 1 to 10 m². For mapping soils it is clearly impossible to indicate variation in individual pedons; instead similar pedons have to be grouped into *polypedons* and these form the basis of soil mapping. The aim of a soil survey must be to recognize mapping units or polypedons made up of pedons which are comparatively similar in terms of horizon types and sequences, soil properties and parent material. Soil maps at 1:50,000 or 1:25,000 usually show the distribution of soil series which are named after a local type-site. A soil series is a group of soils with similar profiles developed on similar parent materials and is thus a *taxonomic unit*. On soil maps, soil series are used as *mapping units* and it is important to appreciate the difference between these two units. Within an area mapped as one soil series, instances of other soil series will be encountered but the intention is that these will be of far less spatial extent than the named series. Webster (1981) suggests that it is not reasonable to expect more than 60 per cent of the soil in any one mapping unit to belong to the type of profile which the unit is supposed to exhibit. Guidance on soil survey procedures is provided by Dent and Young (1981), Hodgson (1978), Western (1978), Clarke (1971), Breimer et al (1986), Soil Survey Staff (1960) and McRae (1988). The reader is also encouraged to study any soil memoir since such a book always summarizes the methods used in that particular soil survey.

Prior to any soil survey, the surveyor will study the climate, geology, geomorphology, vegetation, land use and land use history of the area. This will deepen the surveyor's feel for the area by the examination of aerial photographs and possibly also satellite imagery. Most soil maps have been produced by the interpretative approach to sampling. In essence this involves the surveyor in identifying landscape units which would appear to be homogeneous in terms of soils. This is done by the recognition of morphological, geomorphological and vegetational units in the landscape. For example, the surveyor might recognize a recurring set of slope units in a valley and this would lead to the delimitation of these units and to sampling. The close association between soils and morphology is of prime assistance, not only for subdividing the landscape into areas for soil sampling but also for ultimately guiding the mapping of the soils. This methodology is described as the free approach to soil survey. Surveyors must also be closely influenced in their subdivision of the landscape by variations in other environmental characteristics. In this regard aerial photographs are particularly useful since differences in tone and textures directly indicate variations in vegetation, drainage conditions and soils. As surveyors become increasingly familiar with their area, greater and greater use is made of aerial photographs for guiding field sampling and for drawing in the boundaries between soil series. Guides on the use of aerial photographs in soil surveys are provided by Caroll et al (1977) and White (1977).

Central to the free survey approach is the selection by the surveyor of sites at which soil profiles are described and sampled. This is essentially a stratified sampling design since the landscape is subdivided into mapping units which

are then sampled. Other sampling techniques are random sampling, systematic sampling, unaligned sampling and unequal sampling (Webster and Oliver 1990). As an example of a systematic design, Rudeforth and Bradley (1972) sampled on a 1 km grid interval the soils of west and central Pembrokeshire in West Wales. At each of their c. 1000 grid intersections, they examined the soil. Such an approach proved particularly useful for computer mapping and for processing of the data to provide different forms of land assessment. Mew and Ball (1972) compared the results from a grid sampling scheme, also in Wales, with those from a free survey using aerial photograph interpretation. They concluded that the advantages of grid sampling were not clear-cut in moderately large-scale (1:10,000) soil surveys of complex areas. Instead they supported the efficiency of sampling being based on aerial photograph interpretation. Grid sampling seems best for broad regional or national cover or at the other end of the scale when investigation is concerned with soil properties at the experimental plot or field level. As an example of the former, the Soil Surveys in England and Wales and Scotland are compiling a national soil inventory based on sampling points on a 5 km grid. What is beginning to be appreciated is that the nature of the sampling design as well as sampling intensity ought to take into account spatial variability.

The other aspect of sampling is intensity and soil surveys have to give their surveyors guidance on this matter. Required intensity is influenced by a variety of factors including scale of the map to be published, objectives of the survey, required accuracy of the results, landscape complexity in terms of soil variability and the financial resources of the survey organization. A very rough guide to sampling intensity is given by Webster (1981) who suggests 5.00 observations per cm^2 of map though he appreciates that judicious use of other information combined with the nature of the area may make less than 5.00 observations per cm^2 perfectly adequate. In Britain experienced surveyors make about 30–60 soil observations per km^2 (Beckett 1978) which is equivalent to 1.88 to 3.75 observations per cm^2.

Irrespective of sampling design and intensity, it

is essential that there are standard procedures for describing soils to ensure that observations by different surveyors are comparable. This means that every national Soil Survey has to instruct its surveyors to use a particular field manual. Computerization of profile descriptions demands standardization of approaches both nationally and internationally. As an example, the Soil Survey of England and Wales uses the *Soil Survey Field Handbook* compiled and edited by Hodgson (1974). In summary, the full description of a site and soil using this method would produce data under the headings listed below. Many of the terms are defined in the glossary (Appendix 1); full definitions of all terms are given in the *Soil Survey Field Handbook* (Hodgson 1974).

1   *General and site description*
    grid reference
    elevation
    slope (value, aspect and form)
    soil erosion and deposition
    rock outcrops (extent of exposed bedrock)
    land use
    surface form (form, condition, thickness of litter
        horizon)
    bedrock (lithology, structure, hardness, colour)

2   *Profile description (for each horizon)*
    lower depth
    colour (moist soil, ped face, air-dry, rubbed and
        main mottles)
    organic matter status
    particle-size class
    stones (size, abundance, shape, lithology)
    soil-water state
    ped (size, shape, grade)
    voids (packing density, porosity class, fissures,
        macropores)
    consistence (soil strength, ped strength, failure,
        cementation, stickiness, plasticity)
    roots (size, abundance, nature)
    nature of O (peaty) horizon
    nodules (composition and nature, abundance,
        shape)
    coats (kind, abundance)
    horizon boundary (distinctiveness, form)
    horizon notation
    sample number.

The field data combined with results from laboratory analysis allow the soil surveyor, after some experience, to assign each site to a soil series. Greater consistency in results can be achieved if use is made of a detailed flowchart along with defined quantitative criteria; such an approach is demonstrated for the identification of soil series in England and Wales by Clayden and Hollis (1984). On the basis of aerial photo interpretation and field observation, the surveyor would then draw the boundaries between soil mapping units. As already stressed, such mapping units will contain more than one series, but one should be dominant, otherwise units are mapped as complexes. Soil mapping is only possible if a classification system is used. There are methods of numerical taxonomy whereby statistical procedures are followed in order to identify which profiles are most similar to each other (Webster and Oliver 1990). Such techniques are not used in routine soil survey; instead soil surveys use some defined hierarchical system with the best known being the US *Soil Taxonomy* (Soil Survey Staff 1975). Thomas et al (1979) have produced a useful range of flow diagrams to aid the implementation of *Soil Taxonomy*. Comprehensive reviews of soil classification are provided by Butler (1980) and Finkl (1982). As a specific example, the soil classification system for England and Wales (Avery 1980) has the following levels:

Major group (eg lithomorphic soils, brown soils,
    podzolic soils, pelosols, etc)
Group (eg rankers, rendzinas, brown calcareous
    earths, brown podzolic soils, stagnopodzols, etc)
Subgroup (eg humic ranker, brown rendzina, gleyic
    brown calcareous earth, paleo-argillic brown
    podzolic soil, ironpan stagnopodzol, etc)
Soil series (named after type sites, eg Hanslope series,
    Stretham series, etc)

It has been assumed so far that soil maps result primarily from detailed soil survey work. Soil maps, of course, vary in scale, and level of generalization. Maps in the scale range from 1:10,000 to 1:2,500 or more require *intensive* surveys following FAO practice as described by Webster (1981); the scale range 1:25,000 to 1:10,000 requires *detailed* survey

Table 3.1 Minimum-size delineation values on actual ground scale for a number of map scales (minimum-size delineations for all published maps being 0.4 cm²)

Map scale	Minimum-size delineation on ground scale (ha)
1:5,000,000	100,750
1:1,000,000	4,030
1:500,000	1,008
1:250,000	252
1:200,000	161
1:100,000	40.3
1:50,000	10.1
1:25,000	2.52
1:20,000	1.61
1:10,000	0.40

(from Eswaran et al 1977: 41)

intensity while the next range up to 1:100,000 needs *semi-detailed* survey. Scales smaller than 1:100,000 are based on *reconnaissance* survey. Maps of 1:25,000 and larger use phases of soil series as well as soil series as the mapping units. Phases cannot be shown in the scale range 1:25,000 to 1:100,000 when soil series and associations of soil series provide the mapping units. At scales smaller than 1:100,000, groups, major groups or some type of physiographic assemblage are the mapping units. As published map scales become smaller, so the minimum size of a particular mapping unit which can be shown increases (Table 3.1).

The old view of soil survey institutes was that their prime responsibility was the publication of soil maps and supporting data. A similar attitude prevailed with respect to geological surveys. In the past soil survey teams were able to concentrate for considerable periods of time on the mapping of individual map sheets. Of course there had to be standardization of approach to profile description, soil classification and site selection with profile descriptions being recorded on forms which could be later stored in box files. Variations between surveyors necessarily occurred in terms of site selection, profile description, soil classification and delimitation of mapping units, though priority was always given to checks through regional correlation.

In other words, the boundaries on adjacent soil maps had to fit together! During the 1970s and 1980s the major changes in the techniques of soil survey can be listed as the greater standardization in nomenclature and profile description, use of more refined soil classification schemes, greater emphasis on standardization of approach to sampling intensity and use of better schemes for data recording. Of particular interest in this book is this last development.

Free format recording cards were replaced in the first instance by cards upon which codes were noted. These codes were fully defined as in the *Soil Survey Field Handbook* for England and Wales (Hodgson 1974). The obvious merit of such an approach was that results from different surveyors were more consistent and that computer input, processing and retrieval became possible. A variation in approach is described by Ragg (1977) who used a voice-tape recorder in the field with tapes later being transcribed to forms using numerical codes. The introduction of computer compatible forms made it possible for the Soil Survey of England and Wales to launch its Soil Information System in 1979. In the United States, soil surveyors enter morphological data and observations on a special Soil Conservation Service Form using specified codes. Mausbach and Stubbendiek (1987) describe the advantages in using a microcomputer for the processing, storage and output of the results. They describe how pedon description data can be retrieved in either a narrative descriptive format or as tabular output of coded horizon data. In similar vein, Kukachka (1987) argues that use of a microcomputer in a soil survey field office increases productivity and provides better quality control over data collected during soil survey. Transcription errors can occur between the initial coding and later computer input; such problems can be reduced if information is input in the field. This is now standard practice, for example, in the Soil Survey of Scotland. Field computers are pre-programmed with a database system and the surveyor directly inputs information on all relevant attributes (Clarke et al 1986).

Some readers may wish clarification about the meaning of a database management system

(DBMS) and this can be illustrated by mentioning how the references in this book have been processed. At the early stage of preparing this book, a bibliography was compiled. The old approach would have been to use reference cards, but a DBMS offers far greater flexibility and efficiency. Each reference was input to a DBMS with codes for keywords, codes for where the references were stored, and a code for the section of the book where the reference was of particular relevance. Thus in writing this chapter on soil survey, all relevant references could be listed and their locations in box files indicated. Once input, it is very easy to correct or update references and a bibliography for this book could be produced at any time by moving the selected references into a word-processing file. When both field and analytical data from a soil survey are input into a DBMS, it becomes a simple matter, for example, to extract certain information for a particular area or soil series as demonstrated by Davidson and Jones (1985).

There is no doubt that the use of a DBMS offers considerable advantages, especially to national soil survey institutes which have to handle considerable volumes of data. The task of soil surveys in countries blessed with a long tradition of mapping will increasingly be towards the updating of their land resource database; this is feasible given the editing versatility of a DBMS. A research issue of much current activity is the integration of DBMS with geographical information systems (GIS), a topic of considerable relevance to soil survey.

3.2   Presentation and update of soil survey reports

The results of a soil survey are presented in a map and associated report or memoir. The ease with which the map can be used depends upon the cartographic quality and the clarity of information in the legend. Many soil surveys in the United States publish their maps in the form of vertical aerial photographs over which the soils are plotted. A high degree of landscape realism is thus achieved

and users find it easy to orientate themselves when the field and land use patterns are evident. Soil map legends vary from those which are very easy to understand by the non-pedologist to legends which are highly complex and use many technical terms. Sombroek and van de Weg (1980) argue that the information on a soil map must be readily available to the non-specialist. They stress the advantages in providing information on landforms as the first entry, geological units as the second entry, and soils as the third entry. Based on their experience in Kenya, they list the following characteristics as being described for each soil:

drainage conditions, depth (effective depth), colour (moist conditions), mottling if present, consistence (moist conditions, deleted for shallow soils), cal-careousness if present, salinity, sodicity if present, stoniness if present, rockiness if present, cracking if present, texture; other characteristics can be added as relevant.

An example from a sample legend is given below:

COASTAL PLAIN (slopes in general less than 5 per cent)

PL   Soils developed on coral limestone with sand admixtures (coral reef)

   PL1   □ well drained, deep to very deep, red to yellowish red, very friable, fairly rocky, loamy sand to sandy loam
                    (ferralic ARENOSOLS)

   PL2   □ well drained, deep to very deep, dark red to reddish brown, friable, sandy clay loam to sandy clay, underlying 20 to 50 cm of loamy sand
                    (rhodic FERRALSOLS)

(source: Sombroek and van de Weg 1980: 15)

One consequence of this approach is that legends to soil maps become very lengthy. A soil map user usually requires particular information about a specified area. An alternative approach is to restrict the legend to a simple listing of mapping units and then in the separate handbook or memoir, to provide tables on the attributes of the different units. The advantages of this are becoming more evident with the use of computerized databases.

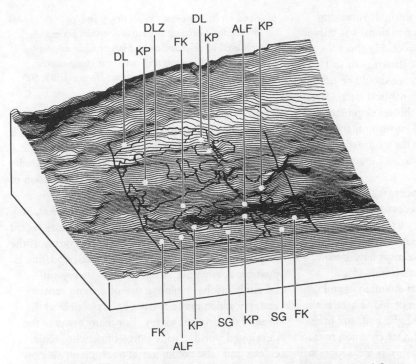

Figure labels: DL, KP, DLZ, FK, DL, KP, KP, ALF, KP (top row); FK, KP, ALF, SG, KP, SG, FK (bottom row)

Figure 3.1 DTM of the Gargunnock area with superimposed soil mapping units; names of units: Darleith (DL), Darleith Skeletal (DLZ), Kippen (KP), Fourmerk (FK), Stirling (SG), Falkirk (FK), alluvial fan (ALF)

The mapping unit (eg soil series) thus becomes the key into the relevant part of the database from which further relevant data or evaluations can be extracted.

The information on soil maps can also be presented in more visually acceptable forms. An obvious technique is the superimposition of soil mapping units over digital terrain models (DTMs). A DTM is a three-dimensional representation of the relief in an area and powerful geographic information systems have the capability of producing these from digitized contour data. Using methods of spatial interpolation, heights of points on a grid frame can be extracted from contour patterns. Three-dimensional views of landscapes can thus be generated and viewed from different heights and positions. Digitized information on soil mapping can thus be superimposed over this DTM and the great merit of such an approach is that soil landscape patterns are much more evident than with conventional soil maps. An example is shown in Figure 3.1 for an area round the village of Gargunnock, about 10 km to the west of Stirling in central Scotland. The Stirling Soil Series (SG), a poorly drained alluvial soil, occurs on the lowermost and flat area; brown forest soils as expressed in the Falkirk Soil Series (FK), the Kippen Soil Series (KP) and the Darleith Soil Series (DL) predominate in the middle and lower slopes.

DTMs have another use in soil survey as shown by Klingebiel et al (1987). Soil pattern is intimately related to slope, aspect and elevation which are computed in order to generate a DTM. Klingebiel et al (1987) demonstrate for an area in Wyoming how a premap based on slope, aspect and elevation criteria was very similar to a soil map produced by traditional means. Their results suggest that one major benefit of using DTM-derived data will be to improve the quality of soil maps.

The publication of substantial soil survey memoirs to accompany individual soil maps is becoming less common. This is due to the costs of such publications; furthermore, such publications while providing excellent land resource inventories of particular areas, often fail to present succinct, easy to comprehend information for non-specialists. Another criticism is that soil surveys often took many years to produce a memoir following the publication of the soil map. The increasing use of computerized data-handling methods is making redundant the publication of traditional soil survey memoirs. There is value in producing short handbooks as guides to particular areas or soil mapping units, but otherwise use should be made of GIS to extract spatial and analytical data. One unfortunate consequence of this development is that increasingly users of soil survey in many countries will have to pay for the information as soil survey institutes introduce charges for access to their databases.

An issue of increasing concern is the extent to which soil survey update is necessary. For Scotland, which had a strong soil survey tradition, 1:63,360 or 1:50,000 and 1:250,000 maps are available for the whole of the country. The maps have been published over thirty-two years (1964–86); inevitably there will have been evolution of soil survey techniques over such a period. There is the danger in believing that once published, soil maps do not require to be updated. One common reason for new soil maps being published is the adoption of an improved soil taxonomy. Brown (1985) argues that update may be necessary for one or more of the following reasons:

1 need for soil information that extends to a greater depth than in existing reports (eg information on soil morphology to the 2 m depth or greater, where information may be available currently only to the 1 m depth)

2 need for soil interpretations for land uses that were not considered in earlier reports (eg septic tanks, hazardous waste disposal sites, hydric soils, etc)

3 need for aerial photo base maps that reflect recent changes in landscapes and cultural features (eg man-made adjustments of coastlines, re-routing of roads, major urban expansion, mining and reclamation, etc)

4 need for maps that reflect significant recent changes in the soils themselves (eg mining, reclamation, subsidence, erosion, etc)

5 need for base maps with improved cartographic control and/or more useful scales, to ensure compatibility with other mapped information that is to be used in geographic information systems

6 need for improvement in accuracy and/or precision of existing soil survey reports (as may be achieved by re-mapping at a larger scale and/or by reassessing and reporting map unit composition).

(source: Brown 1985: 92)

There is a wide range of possibilities for producing updates of existing soil surveys. The simplest approach is the addition to the database of profile and analytical data for sites which are investigated for various reasons subsequent to the publication of the original report. A decision to change map scales, for example from 1:63,360 to 1:50,000, may give an opportunity for corrections or a more recent soil classification to be introduced. Of course, if the map information is contained in a GIS, updating is possible at any time. A full field re-survey will certainly involve extensive use of remote sensing imagery which may not have been possible at the time of the original survey. For many areas in the developed world, a wide range of panchromatic, colour and false colour aerial photography is now available. The traditional approach has been to draw on boundaries between proposed soil mapping units and then to transfer these by optical means to a base map. The use of digitizing cameras can now automate such a process; by the use of a video camera, an annotated photo can be converted into digital form and then rectified in order to be superimposed over a map base. Such operations can be performed with integrated image analysis-GIS. The next stage is to determine the extent to which image analysis of digitized aerial photographs can identify land surface features relevant to soil attributes. Harrison et al (1987) report such an investigation for a study area in Idaho. Colour photographs at a scale of 1:4,800 were digitized and the results of two types of image analysis were compared in terms of predicting soil drainage classes. The authors concluded that such techniques offered advantages through improving map quality and in speed of operation. They suggest that colour infrared imagery will offer further possibilities for such predictions. The analysis of images derived from satellites has also been shown to yield data on particular soil attributes. As an example, analysis of Landsat multispectral imagery has been used to identify peatland on the island of Lewis, Scotland (Stove and Hulme 1980).

Another remote sensing technique, which is proving of value in assisting with updating soil survey, is ground-penetrating radar (GPR). Doolittle (1987) explains how the Soil Conservation Service in the United States has been evaluating the potential of GPR to soil survey since the late 1970s. In summary the technique involves the generation of high frequency (10 to 1000 M Hz) short duration pulses of energy which are transmitted into the ground. A proportion of the pulse's energy is transmitted back to a receiving antenna when an interface between layers of different electromagnetic properties is encountered. Stratigraphic or pedologic variations with depth can thus be inferred. In the field, the antenna is towed behind a vehicle which houses the control and recording units. As a result transects can be surveyed so that with appropriate control points, variations in depths of such features as argillic horizon, fragipan, spodic horizon or water-table can be plotted (Doolittle 1987).

GPR has been used in Florida to assist with updating soil survey (Schellentrager et al 1988). Sites for GDR transects were selected to cross the maximum landscape variation within sample areas; an attempt was made to sample each mapping unit at least once. Along these transects, usually one soil boring and description were adequate for identifying diagnostic subsurface horizons. From the GPR transects, the proportion of different soil series could be determined and compared statistically with the original soil survey results. This was achieved by estimating variability within mapping units and thus it was possible to check on correlation decisions. The overall effect of using GPR as a aid to updating soil survey was to reduce the number of map units. Schellentrager et al (1988) compared the costs of conventional soil sampling transects with GPR transects and the results were $59.26 and $17.66 respectively. They conclude that GPR along with statistical analysis provide an effective and efficient alternative to conventional techniques of soil survey update.

3.3   Quality of soil survey data

A soil map, or indeed any type of map, is used as a predictive tool; the aim is to indicate the nature and properties of soils at one or more points or areas. A soil map is designed to answer specific where and what type questions and any user of the results should be aware of the associated errors. An important introductory point to stress is that the use to which the data will be put determines the acceptable level of data quality. It is all too easy to call continually for better and better data, but a broad prediction of soil properties with high associated errors may well be quite acceptable for certain purposes. As Brown (1988: 452) puts it, 'a less-than-perfectly-accurate soil survey that is used by clients wisely, extensively, and in conjunction with other relevant materials is surely of greater value than a meticulously prepared, highly accurate and precise report that, for whatever reasons, never sees the light of day'.

Much of this section will discuss different forms of errors which influence data quality, but it is important to indicate the difference between data *errors* and data *quality*. Errors can be precisely defined and expressed in quantitative form, giving probabilities of values within specified ranges. In contrast, quality is a much more qualitative and subjective characteristic. In popular usage, an item described as being of good quality summarizes an assessment or evaluation. Quality, unlike the estimation of errors, is judged with reference to the use to which the data will be put. The assessment of data quality necessitates the evaluation of errors and is thus conditioned by the defined objectives of the analysis. In the establishment of international standards for analytical techniques, careful consideration is given to the assessment of repeatability and reproducibility. The former measures differences in results as determined from the analysis of identical samples by the same operator in the same laboratory on the same equipment over a short time period. Reproducibility on the other hand measures the differences which emerge from analysing the same material using the same method, but by different operators in different laboratories using different equipment.

Discussion of a hypothetical example provides a useful introduction to the issues associated with data quality. Suppose the need is to produce a map of a 100 ha square showing those areas with a soil depth in excess of 50 cm. Five component stages can be identified in this investigation: definition, measurement technique, sampling errors, data transfer and spatial processing.

Definition

An initial decision is required on the meaning of soil depth, a surprisingly difficult issue. If the results are to be used with reference to cropping, then a definition based on the available rooting zone is necessary. Thus soil depth would need to be taken as the zone within which there is no restriction to root development as posed by an iron pan, a fragipan, a concentration of stones or the presence of bedrock. In the field there may well be differences in opinion as to the concentration of stones which are necessary in order to produce a major impediment to root development.

Measurement technique

The usual method for measuring soil depth is to dig a soil profile or to use a soil auger. The former, although time consuming, gives a direct measure of depth to an identified feature which constrains root development. The use of an auger for estimating soil depth has the merit of speed, but difficulties arise in interpreting the limit which is often due to the occurrence of individual stones. Measures by auger tend to underestimate soil depth available to plants because of the presence of stones. Another method of measuring depth is the use of ground penetrating radar (GPR) as already described. Such a method has the merit of speed but the disadvantage of cost and depends on extrapolating soil horizon patterns from a limited number of

control sites on the basis of reflected signals. Clearly errors can arise from difficulties in interpretation, operator variance and instrumental problems.

Sampling errors

Depth, like any other soil property, varies in space and one task of sampling is to produce measures of variability which are acceptable to the project. The selection of sampling design and intensity thus depends upon the spatial pattern and variability of soil depth. Suppose a decision is made to measure depth by auger using a 50 m grid over the 100 ha square, measurements are also made at grid points immediately outside the square to allow mapping up to the edge of the boundary (Figure 3.2a). In sampling, errors arise not only from variability, but also from inaccurate location of field sampling points.

Data transfer

An obvious potential source of error is in the transcription of field results to a map and their subsequent input to a computer mapping system. Good quality digitizing tables have a resolution of 0.01 or 0.02 mm and thus errors in digitizing are related primarily to the source map. Of particular relevance is the scale of this map; considerable errors can be introduced if the sampling grid is drawn so as to occupy a very small area. The usual practice in soil mapping is for the field survey to be executed at twice the ultimate scale of publication. In the case of sampling the 100 ha square, such an area would measure 10 × 10 cm on a 1:10,000 map. Such a size would be quite useless given that 420 points would have to be located. A minimum working size of 40 × 40 cm for the 100 ha square can be proposed and this would necessitate a 1:2,500 base map. Such a map may have to be produced by the photographic enlargement of a 1:10,000 scale map, and distortion errors would

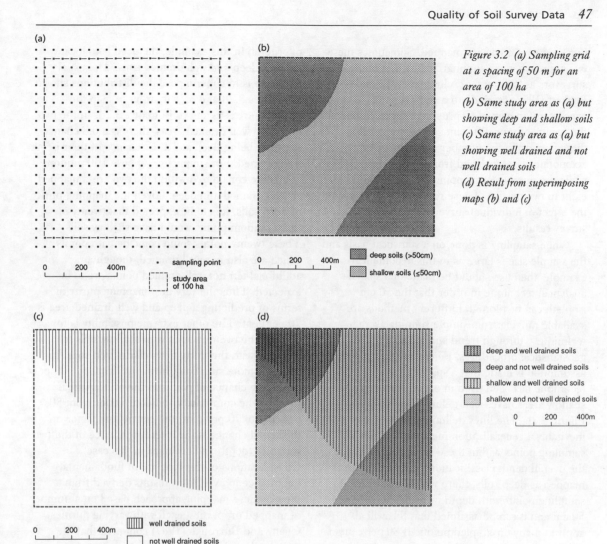

Figure 3.2 (a) Sampling grid at a spacing of 50 m for an area of 100 ha
(b) Same study area as (a) but showing deep and shallow soils
(c) Same study area as (a) but showing well drained and not well drained soils
(d) Result from superimposing maps (b) and (c)

become apparent, especially round the margins of the map.

Spatial processing

Fundamental to all forms of mapping based on field survey is the extrapolation of point observations to areas. This operation is succinctly expressed in the soil depth mapping problem in that the objective is to separate areas of deep soils (defined as over 50 cm) from shallow soils. A variety of spatial interpolation techniques is available, the simplest

being that the field surveyor draws in a boundary between deep and shallow soils based on the measured depth values at the sampling points and on any landscape patterns as evident in the landscape, for example slope changes. Such an approach will inevitably be influenced by the decisions of the surveyor who may adopt one of two extreme approaches. The surveyor may give emphasis to indicating in the greatest possible detail spatial variations through the inclusion of many small areas. The other extreme approach is to group areas as far as possible so that large homogeneous areas are mapped. Sometimes these two approaches are summarized by describing surveyors as 'splitters' or 'clumpers'. Bie and Beckett (1973) carried out a soil mapping experiment in part of Cyprus in order to compare the results of four different soil surveyors. For these surveyors, the number of identified soil taxonomic classes ranged from eight to twenty-five while the number of mapping units also varied from eight to twenty-five. These results clearly highlight the effect of individual surveyors in influencing soil survey results.

When sampling is done on a statistical basis and the sample size is large as in this hypothetical example, then use should be made of a spatial analytical technique in order that the 50 cm isopleth can be plotted. Different methods are available ranging from simple running average techniques, through trend surface analysis to geostatistical procedures. For present purposes, the assumption is made that a spatial analytical technique has been used in order that deep and shallow areas have been delimited as shown in Figure 3.2b. The lines delimiting these areas are inevitably a generalization meaning that not all sampling points within these areas correspond to the overall depth classification. Thus in the areas mapped as deep soils, there will be instances of sampling points with depth measures less than 50 cm and it can be assumed that this will also apply at many unsampled points. If 80 per cent of the sampling points within areas mapped as deep have depth measures over 50 cm, then a probability of 0.8 can be proposed for finding deep soil at any unsampled point within these areas. Such a probability is a statement on the mapping purity of the deep soil class.

This hypothetical example can be further used to introduce some fundamental concepts regarding the combinations of areas. Suppose that during the original field survey, each sampling point was categorized as well drained or not well drained. The same issues of spatial generalization would occur again, with the results being expressed as in Figure 3.2c. Suppose that the mapping purity of the well drained area is 70 per cent. A common request in land evaluation is to locate areas with a given set of criteria; in this example, the need is to locate areas of deep *and* well drained soils. The usual approach is to superimpose the distributions shown in Figures 3.2b and 3.2c in order to map the required areas as shown in Figure 3.2d. In the two deep and well drained areas, there is a 0.8 chance of points being deep and a 0.7 chance of their being well drained. For simplicity, suppose 100 random points are considered within the two areas mapped as well drained and deep. Given the mapping purity of deep soils, it is to be expected that twenty of these random points would have shallow soils. These twenty points could coincide with points which are also not well drained, though an additional ten not well drained points are to be expected. Thus the very best mapping purity in terms of predicting a deep and well drained area is 70 per cent. The other extreme possibility is for none of the twenty points with shallow soils to coincide with the thirty not well drained soils. In such a remote situation, the purity drops to 50 per cent. The chance of points in the overlap areas meeting the combined conditions varies from 50 per cent to 70 per cent; the controlling factor on the actual chance is the interdependence of the two variables (depth and drainage in this case). Considerations of this type are of fundamental importance to evaluation results derived from a filter or sieve mapping approach based on a number of mapped properties, each with varying purities. Chang and Burrough (1987) comment that the 'crisp set' model of soil classes does not accord with reality and processing using logical relationships can give a misleading impression of accuracy to land evaluation results. The problem with defining an area as consisting of well-drained sites is that this is either true or false with respect to individual sites. Chang and Burrough (1987) describe how the application of fuzzy set theory offers considerable advantages given the possibility of defining partial membership of a set. This means that it is possible to give a grade to indicate the extent to which a site belongs to a mapping unit.

In a review of soil survey quality, Brown (1988) states that a user of soil survey would like to have results which had one or more of the following characteristics:

1 perfect accuracy and precision in estimating and mapping particular soil characteristics

2 fully quantified statements of map unit compositions

3 fully quantified representations of delineation boundary characteristics, that is widths, degrees of contrast, estimated error in locations, etc

4 interpolations of soil properties between sampling points, with variances indicated, as can be done using geostatistics (Chapter 8).

(from Brown 1988: 453)

As Brown admits, these ideals may be approached only with high intensity survey such as that described for the 100 ha square in the previous subsection. The more conventional and extensive resource inventory surveys, based on the free survey approach, cannot attain such standards. This is not to question their widespread application and importance, but users need to be aware of factors which influence the magnitude of errors in soil survey.

Despite the availability of detailed and well-tested field handbooks on soil profile description, surveyors investigating the same soil profile will not produce identical descriptions. Surveyors may differ in opinion over component horizons, the description of soil colour, or assessments of such properties as stoniness, abundance of mottles and degree of structural development. Ogunkunle and Izuakor (1988) compared the descriptions of six pedons by two soil surveyors of comparable post-graduate training and experience in dealing with soils in south-west Nigeria. They found good agreement on the number of horizons per pedon, the recognition of the presence and depth of an argillic horizon, iron and manganese concretions, mottling and the description of soil structure. In contrast, they found wide differences concerning the number and depth of A and B horizons, soil colour and texture as determined by feel.

If a soil horizon in a soil profile is sampled twice, and then analysed for particular properties, the differences in the results are explicable in terms of two groups of factors: variation within the horizon

and laboratory errors. Much attention has been given to variability as caused by samples being derived from different points in space. In recent years, increasing attention is being given to variability associated with laboratory analysis. At present the Laboratory Methods and Data Exchange (LABEX) programme is in progress under the auspices of the International Soil Reference and Information Centre (ISRIC) in The Netherlands (Pleijsier 1988). The aims are to assess between and within laboratory differences resultant upon the analysis of identical samples. Early results from the project revealed variation being not less than $+/- 11$ per cent for clay content determination, $+/- 20$ per cent for cation exchange capacity of soil, $+/- 25$ per cent for cation exchange capacity of clay and $+/- 10$ per cent for base saturation. Subsequent efforts have focused on the greater standardization of techniques. As an example, Pleijsier (1988) quotes estimated confidence intervals for the measurement of soil pH in water. A resolution ranging from 4.4 to 5.6 was found using different methods while this improved to 4.7 to 5.3 when the same methods were adopted. The importance of standardization of techniques is underlined. Caution needs to be exercised in the use of laboratory derived data for soil classification as is the case with the US *Soil Taxonomy*; Ogunkunle and Izuakor (1988) propose that more emphasis should be given to field profile measurements to aid classification though as already stated, such field observations are not error free.

As already indicated, any form of spatial interpolation from point observations to the delineation of areal units, involves errors. It is unfortunate that soil maps display soils as occurring as discrete spatial entities while in practice, soils vary in a continuum over the landscape. With the traditional free survey approach to soil mapping, despite attempts at standardization of approach and use of regional correlation, there is still scope for variation in results dependent upon individual approaches by surveyors. Comment was made on the 'clumpers' and 'splitters' with regard to soil classification; exactly the same issue arises with respect to spatial units.

(a)

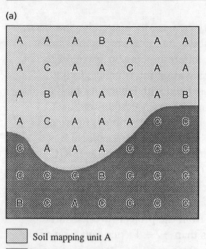

☐ Soil mapping unit A

■ Soil mapping unit C

(b)

☐ Soil mapping unit A

▨ Soil mapping unit B

■ Soil mapping unit C

Figure 3.3 (a) Grid sampling of a hypothetical area with sample points classified according to one of three taxonomic units (A, B or C); the boundary between mapping unit A and C is indicated

(b) Grid sampling at twice the intensity as shown in (a); the more detailed distribution of soil mapping units A, B and C is demonstrated

Differences in approach are revealed when the soils of an area are resurveyed. As an example, Goldin (1988) compares the results of a soil survey of Whatcom County in north-west Washington

completed in 1941 with one conducted between 1980 to 1982. The older survey did not have access to aerial photographs while the more recent survey benefited from these, and from much more specific guidance on soil survey through the use of *Soil Taxonomy* (Soil Survey Staff 1975) for classification, and the National Soils Handbook (Soil Conservation Service 1983) for mapping procedures. A grid sampling frame was placed over the two maps and the results compared. Overall Goldin (1988) found a 70 per cent agreement between the two maps. He explained the differences in terms of the following factors:

1 actual soil changes in the area (mostly destruction of the organic top horizon) – about 10 per cent

2 differences in map unit definition – about 10 per cent

3 differences in field survey techniques (location of boundaries by air photo interpretation versus ground survey) – about 50 per cent

4 noise (short-range soil variation, sampling error, difference in the observation interval) – about 30 per cent.

(Goldin 1988: 108)

As can be seen from these results, the main single factor which explains the difference in the maps is the contrast in survey technique.

These factors account for the differences in the soil maps produced at different times. A closely related issue is the variation in delineation of mapping units according to different scales and intensities. Smaller scale maps require more generalization than large scale maps of the same area. Also, the boundaries of the mapping units on the smaller scale maps will be smoother and there may be a greater grouping of mapping and taxonomic units. This theme is reviewed by Valentine (1981) who also compares examples of different scales of soil maps for the same area. In one of his analyses he compared for the same area soils mapped by the Soil Survey of England and Wales at scales of 1:1,000,000, 1:250,000 and 1:25,000. Through map superimposition he found that boundaries rarely coincided. One major reason for this is the degree of smoothing of boundaries which must take place according to the scale. In essence, sampling intensity decreases as map scale increases to lead to greater simplification of spatial patterns. This can be demonstrated by considering a hypothetical area as described by Valentine (1981). The area has been surveyed on a grid frame at two intensities and sample sites have been allocated to one of three taxonomic units (A, B or C) as shown in Figures 3.3a and 3.3b. The sampling intensity of Figure 3.3a is half that of Figure 3.3b and this would be expressed in the ultimate scale of the published map for the area. In Figure 3.3a two mapping units (soil series A and C) are delimited while with the greater intensity of sampling as shown on Figure 3.3b, three sampling units (soil series A, B and C) can be delineated as well as in a more intricate manner. With more detailed sampling and a larger scale of publication, more inliers and outliers of mapping units can be shown. There are some quite important implications from this example for areas which are to be resurveyed in greater detail. Such an operation will become increasingly common as more detailed information is required for particular localities. In more detailed resurvey, more intricate soil patterns are likely with the additional inclusion of inliers and outliers which perhaps were not identified in the original survey. Also, further subdivision of the original soil mapping legend may not be adequate since further soil taxonomic and thus mapping units may be revealed and these cannot be incorporated into a modified version of the original legend. In other words, a new legend may have to be designed.

3.4 Soil variability

It is an inherent property of soils that they vary in space and measures of such variability are necessary if errors are to be assessed. Campbell (1979) in a

review of spatial variability of soils, comments that although soil variability has been investigated for over sixty years, 'there is surprisingly little formal acknowledgement of its presence in mapping procedures and soil descriptions' (1979: 544). Such a view is not so valid today since some soil surveys are making greater efforts to indicate variability. Furthermore, the use of database systems means that it is much easier to extract data from sampled sites within mapping units thus giving an immediate indication of variability. In this section, the issues associated with variability are introduced: these are variability within individual pedons, variability in taxonomic units within mapping units, and variability in soil properties within mapping units.

Variability within individual pedons

A pedon is the basic three-dimensional unit of soil; similar and contiguous pedons can be grouped together to form polypedons or soil mapping units. To introduce the issue of variability, it is important to consider variations within individual pedons and this can be done by quoting some case studies. An early review of soil variability by Beckett and Webster (1971) revealed that up to 50 per cent of the variability between similar soils occurred within 1 m, a clear indication of the differences which can occur within individual pedons.

Patterson and Wall (1982) collected replicate 1 kg samples from the A, B and C horizons of forty-one pedons in south-west Ontario in order to measure within-pedon variability in particle size, organic matter, calcium carbonate and pH. A total of 492 samples were collected from 126 horizons at points equally spaced around the faces of soil pits. The variability within horizons was expressed in the coefficient of variation which was determined as follows:

$$CV = (s/x)100$$

where CV is the coefficient of variation as a percentage, s is standard deviation and x is the mean. They found mean CV values for sand, silt

Table 3.2 Number of within-pedon samples required to estimate means for selected soil properties at the 95 per cent confidence level

Soil property	Limit of accuracy	Soil horizon		
		A	B	C
% silt	+/− 5.0%	2	3	2
organic matter (%) (A horizon)	+/− 0.5%	3	–	–
calcium carbonate equivalent (%) (C horizon)	+/− 2.0%	–	–	5
pH (CaCl$_2$)	+/− 0.2 units	3	3	2

(source: Patterson and Wall 1982: 638)

and clay to be less than 7 per cent for an A horizon (range of 0–47 per cent); less than 15 per cent for the B horizon (range of 0–88 per cent) and less than 17 per cent for the C horizon (range 0–94 per cent). The low variability values for the A horizon were attributed to the effects of mixing through cultivation. The mean CV values for pH, organic matter (A horizon only) and calcium carbonate (C horizon only) were all less than 10 per cent but with individual highs of 14, 30 and 26 per cent respectively.

Patterson and Wall (1982) calculated the number of samples necessary to estimate a mean value for each analysed property with a specified error range and confidence level. This was determined using the equation

$$n = (t^2 s^2)/L^2$$

where n is the number of samples, t is the value of Student's t distribution with (n−1) degrees of freedom, s^2 is the variance and L is the desired limit of variation. The results are summarized in Table 3.2 which gives the number of within-pedon samples required to obtain reliable estimates of selected soil properties at the 95 per cent confidence level. The results indicate that for the A or B horizons, three replicate samples bulked to a single sample will provide an adequate estimate for the specified soil properties. Greater variability was found in the C horizon, and thus the recommendation is for the bulking of five replicated samples from that horizon. Wilding (1985) comes to a similar conclusion regarding the benefits of bulking samples and he stresses the importance that such samples must come from the same subhorizon. He states that the collection of four samples per horizon followed by mixing prior to analysis, will decrease the probable sampling error by half compared to the analysis of one sample. Such considerations are of particular relevance to soil classification when the soil is being assessed with reference to class boundary values as specified in *Soil Taxonomy* (Soil Survey Staff 1975).

The process of soil survey necessitates the investigation of individual sites (pedons) which, on the basis of field and laboratory data, are allocated to taxonomic units within the classification system. Mapping units at whatever scale will include sites of taxonomic units which do not accord with the mapping unit. This is assessed in terms of mapping purity which, as a percentage, expresses the chance of a random site within a mapping unit coinciding with the taxonomic unit. Targets for purity were set at 85 per cent for the USA, 70 per cent for The Netherlands and 80 per cent for Britain, but as Western (1978) notes, there was little attempt to determine if these levels were being achieved. Before some purity figures are quoted, it is important to stress that purity is influenced by mapping scale and the width of the soil classes as defined within the classification system. Purity will improve if the same classification system is used at increased scale; furthermore, purity will deteriorate if the same soil is mapped at one scale, but with a more and more detailed classification system involving more classes (Western 1978).

In a case study in central Scotland to determine mapping purity, Ragg and Henderson (1980) first reviewed previously published results. They found that no study revealed a mapping purity which reached the target 85 per cent; instead they quote results ranging from 37 per cent to 74 per cent. Bie and Beckett (1971) conclude that many mapping units on published soil maps have less than 50 per cent of the relevant taxonomic unit. Ragg and Henderson (1980) selected a 95 km^2 area which had previously been surveyed and selected four series (Aberdona, Caprington, Macmerry and

Rowanhill). These soils were considered representative of surface water gley soils (stagnogleys) and gley brown forest soils (stagnogleyic brown earths) in central Scotland. A sampling scheme was then designed to be areally representative and a total of 644 sites were identified at which a range of site and soil characteristics was determined. This included the classification of each of these 644 sites and the results are shown in Table 3.3. As can be seen from Table 3.3, the purities ranged from 43 to 66 per cent. Ragg and Henderson (1980) found that the mapping units had better reliability when single soil properties were compared, with values above 84 per cent for topsoil texture, 70 per cent for drainage, and 50 per cent for parent material. The authors do not consider their results as an indictment of the quality of soil mapping since they found that the original delineations of the mapping units were satisfactory. One of the reasons which they suggest for the inclusions was the result of boundary smoothing where small areas were ignored as a result of the mapping scale. Another reason was because of a certain vagueness in the soil classification system. They stressed the need for more tightly defined specifications for the taxonomic units. When they compared soil properties between taxonomic units, they found significant differences, a result which confirms the validity of traditional soil survey approaches. In order to estimate means of soil properties for mapping units which are varied, more sampling points are required than is usually the case in order to produce reasonable estimates. It also needs to be stressed that the fact that a mapping unit falls far short of the target 85 per cent purity level may not be a serious problem. This is because the sub-dominant soils which occur within the mapping unit are likely to be closely related to the named soil series and thus will have properties of similar effect on land use.

Variability within mapping units

If a number of soil samples are collected from one horizon throughout a soil mapping unit in one area, then variation in values is to be expected. This will result from inherent spatial variation within the mapping unit including instances of other soil types as well as from laboratory errors. The level of variation within a taxonomic unit is expected to be less than within a mapping unit since the latter will contain more than one taxonomic unit. Adams and Wilde (1980) tested this hypothesis with reference to the Westmere silt loam, a soil mapping unit in the Wanganui district of New Zealand. This mapping unit is a subdivision of the Westmere soil series and is formed from aeolian andesitic parent materials. Thirty-one profiles were investigated within the mapping unit and eighteen of these were considered to fall within the definition of the Westmere taxonomic unit, giving a mapping purity of 58 per cent. It was thus possible to compare morphological and chemical properties for the mapping and taxonomic units. Overall they found

Table 3.3 Purity of four mapping units in central Scotland in terms of included taxonomic units

Mapping units	Aberdona	Caprington	Macmerry	Rowanhill
Taxonomic units				
Aberdona	52.8	16.1	5.6	14.2
Caprington	13.8	42.9	13.9	6.9
Macmerry	4.1	14.3	51.4	2.5
Rowanhill	12.2	10.7	8.3	65.9
Darvel	4.1	3.6	12.5	0.5
Colluvial soils	4.1	7.1	2.8	3.6
Other units	8.9	5.4	5.6	6.4

(source: Ragg and Henderson 1980: 564)

that variation in morphological properties within the taxonomic unit was always less than that observed within the mapping unit. For one property, structural size, the taxonomic unit had a wider range than the mapping unit. Overall, the results from comparing morphology indicated the general similarity of the mapping and taxonomic unit. For chemical properties, the variability was generally less in the taxonomic unit compared with the mapping unit; only two properties (0.5M sulphuric acid extractable phosphorus and exchangeable calcium) showed a marked contrast. Adams and Wilde (1980) conclude that the decreased variability in the taxonomic unit is generally only slight compared to the mapping unit. Such results again indicate that the inclusions of various sub-dominant taxonomic units within mapping units need not necessarily have much effect on the actual characteristics of mapping units. The adoption of such mapping units can thus be justified for land use purposes.

Although the contrasts in variability between mapping and taxonomic units may not be as marked as expected, any project designed to investigate soil properties within mapping units will find considerable variations. This can be illustrated by taking three case studies from Nigeria where mapping units called land facets were mapped using the free survey approach. The investigations by Areola (1982) and Ameyan (1986a) were designed to test the quality of such facets through determining the variability of soil physical and chemical properties. Areola (1982) investigated two facets which he called the summit and sideslope land facets within the Gwaga Plains in the Federal Capital Territory. His results as summarized in coefficients of variation for these facets and for three horizons are given in Table 3.4. In a similar way Ameyan (1986a) identified three facets in his study within the Keffi plain of northern Nigeria; he terms these facets the interfluve crest, the middle slope and the lower slope. A sampling grid was placed over such facets and three random sites were selected within each 0.5 km square cell. Again the results for coefficient of variation are given in Table 3.4. The other study by Ameyan (1986b) examined the variability within the Ozugbi series as

mapped on alluvium deposited by the river Niger. Two sample areas of 200×200 m were selected and through a stratified sampling design, ninety-eight sample were collected for analysis; the results are given in Table 3.4.

The results from the two land facets in the Gwaga plains (as summarized in columns 1 to 6 in Table 3.4) demonstrate a fairly high degree of variation. Coefficients of variation less than 33 per cent are sometimes taken as indicative of homogeneous areas; on this criterion these facets can be considered as homogeneous in terms of sand content and pH. Care needs to be taken in the interpretation of coefficient of variation values for pH given the arbitrary zero of the pH scale (Webster 1977). In contrast, the coefficients of variation are greatest for exchangeable bases and stone content. In broad terms, Areola (1982) found coefficients of variation of 20–40 per cent for textural properties and 30–60 per cent or more for chemical properties. When he compared the two land facets, almost every property showed no difference between the facets. Ameyan (1986a) found similar results (columns 7 to 12 in Table 3.4); his land facets in the Keffi plain of Nigeria did not differ significantly from each other for most of the studied properties. Exceptions were sand content, exchangeable sodium for topsoils, and pH and exchangeable magnesium for subsoils. The results from the soil derived from river alluvium (columns 13 and 14 in Table 3.4) further demonstrate the wide range of variability values in two small sample areas within one mapping unit. Ameyan (1986b) calculated optimum sample sizes within 5 per cent of the true mean at the 95 per cent confidence level. Two sample numbers were determined for each property since two sample areas were used. Selected results are as follows: sand (450,99), silt (26,917), clay (571,295), pH (8,19), sodium (247,385), potassium (139,1068), cation exchange capacity (1228,1038), base saturation (174,41). Other than for pH, the magnitude of these required sample numbers is huge; the other striking feature is the difference in results from the two sample areas.

It would be very easy to be very disheartened over results such as those given in Table 3.4 since

Table 3.4 Coefficients of variation (%) within soil mapping units for selected soil properties in Nigeria

	(1)	(2)	(3)	(4)	(5)	(6)	(7)	(8)	(9)	(10)	(11)	(12)	(13)	(14)
sand %	12	28	20	8	24	19	7	3	9	30	22	35	54	25
silt %	37	40	29	35	38	45	48	23	89	54	43	55	25	63
clay %	37	50	32	30	47	31	23	20	12	45	49	46	61	44
stones %	285	165	137	203	151	131	—	—	—	—	—	—	—	—
pH	6	8	7	1	1	1	4	6	6	9	6	11	7	11
Ca++ me/100g	39	86	84	55	92	77	56	70	62	66	53	80	—	—
Mg++ me/100g	40	104	91	64	85	84	41	49	42	95	49	101	—	—
K+ me/100g	31	33	49	41	29	49	40	40	43	40	40	35	—	—
Na+ me/100g	32	32	33	22	38	37	41	49	42	200	167	125	37	46
CEC me/100g	38	75	69	45	67	65	39	44	53	51	58	44	92	83
C %	36	22	30	58	35	19	57	63	50	38	47	33	38	51
N %	40	22	20	47	26	25	50	50	30	20	25	10	—	—

(1) Summit land facet, top horizon

(2) Summit land facet, second horizon

(3) Summit land facet, third horizon

(4) Sideslope land facet, top horizon

(5) Sideslope land facet, second horizon

(6) Sideslope land facet, third horizon

(7) Interfluve crest, top horizon

(8) Middle slope, top horizon

(9) Lower slope, top horizon

(10) Interfluve crest, second horizon

(11) Middle slope, second horizon

(12) Lower slope, second horizon

(13) Ozugbi series, sample area 1

(14) Ozugbi series, sample area 2

(sources: (1) to (6) Areola 1982: 11; (7) to (12) Ameyan 1986a: 103–4; (13) and (14) Ameyan 1986b: 1290)

they could be taken to question the basis of soil survey using a land facet approach. Certainly much greater attention needs to be given to assessing soil variability within mapping units. The alternative approach is not to generalize information within mapping units, but to store the survey data for each sampled point and then to use spatial interpolation techniques. Another key point about the results in Table 3.4 is that they are derived from different sampling designs. No attempt was first made to establish the pattern of soil variation. The first stage in any investigation of soil variability ought to focus on determining the scale at which variability occurs. The results in Table 3.4 could be quoted to argue

that these land facets would not be different with respect to agricultural potential and limitations. Ameyan (1986a) compared intraclass variance in relation to interclass variance and concluded that 'in spite of its limitations, subdivision of the landscape into facets appears to be useful in predicting the broad chemical potentials of this environment with a simple level of technology and low density of population' (1986a: 105). It would also be interesting to use such multivariate techniques as cluster analysis or principal components analysis to determine if groupings in the values coincided with land facets. After all, it is the *combination* of soil physical and chemical properties which is of crucial importance to plant growth.

The overall aim of this chapter has been to present a review of the methods of collecting soil data. This chapter along with the preceding one is intended to provide the reader with an overview of land resource survey techniques. The approach has been towards the evaluation of land resources from a biological standpoint and thus geological and geomorphological survey techniques have not been discussed. The importance of soil and climatic data to land resource assessment requires no emphasis since soils are the medium of plant growth and plants need heat and moisture. The remaining chapters of this book are devoted to the ways by which land resource data can be evaluated for particular purposes, especially crop growth.

4

Land Capability

Chapters 2 and 3 examined the methods of land resource survey, with particular emphasis being given to soil surveys. Such methods are designed to produce land resource inventories which provide a key input to any spatial database for assisting with rural land use management and planning. The sequence of chapters in this book reflects the development of land evaluation as an applied science. The foundations of the subject lie in land resource inventories with major geological surveys beginning during the nineteenth century. The development of land capability schemes during the 1930s in the USA marks the beginning of the second major development in the subject, but the widespread adoption of land capability schemes only began after 1960. The assessment of land capability involves an evaluation of the degree of limitation posed by permanent or semi-permanent attributes of land to one or more land uses. It is essentially a negative approach whereby as the degree of constraint increases, so land is allocated to lower classes. Before this is described in greater detail, it is interesting to outline the factors which encouraged the development of land capability schemes.

The American work during the 1930s was a response to the serious soil erosion problems which occurred then, especially in the Mid-West. The prime aim of the classification was to express the risk of erosion and to indicate sustainable land uses. The maps were thus designed to provide an important input to the formulation of soil conservation schemes. Another key factor which encouraged the production of land capability maps was the increasing awareness that conventional soil maps were not being widely used. There are considerable costs associated with the field survey of soils and the associated laboratory analysis, and report and map publication. Land capability maps as interpretations of climatic, relief and soil conditions can be easily used by non-specialists given the categorization of land classes. Land capability maps thus provide an effective way of presenting land resource data in forms readily understood. For Zambia, Woode (1981) considers that soil survey reports are rarely read while land capability maps are used constantly. There, the Federal Department of Conservation and Extension adopted and modified the land capability system of the Soil Conservation Service of the US Department of Agriculture. It is not an interpretation of existing soil maps since these are available only for limited areas. Instead, aerial photo interpretation combined with field sampling are used to determine and map land capability classes. The system has as its main objective the assessment of land capability for rainfed, medium and large-scale farming.

Another factor which has encouraged the use of land capability maps in many countries, especially in the developed world, is the increase in planning control over land use. In Canada for example, there has been the gradual realization that good quality land is of limited spatial extent. Such a result emerges from an appraisal of land resources only as achieved by a land capability assessment. The loss of prime agricultural land round Canadian cities through the spread of urbanization and industrialization has been an issue of considerable concern. The preservation of such prime land for agricultural use is a stated objective in many countries. In Scotland, for example, planning policy is such that there is a presumption against the transfer from agricultural to non-agricultural use if the land capability for agricultural use is in Class 3 Division 1 or better. Land capability maps can be used in the planning process only if they are available on a national basis, a major limitation for many countries. Land capability maps can also play important roles through assisting with land valuation and taxation, and land assessment for subsidy schemes. The aim of this chapter is to describe the approaches to land capability assessment in the USA, Canada, UK, The Netherlands and New Zealand. Particular emphasis is given to how the schemes in these countries have evolved over the years and to the quality of the results.

4.1   Land capability – the American method

An early review of American work on land capability assessment is given by Hockensmith and Steele (1949), but it was not until 1961 that a comprehensive handbook was published (Klingebiel and Montgomery 1961). The technique was evolved by the Soil Conservation Service of the US Department of Agriculture and will be referred to as the USDA method. Integral to the assessment procedure is an evaluation of soil erosion hazards, wetness and soil and climatic limitations. Land capability assessment, as already indicated, is based on a broader range of characteristics than soil properties. Information on slope angle, climate, flood and erosion risk, as well as on soil properties is required. Of course, there is a large degree of interrelation between these types of information and thus to a large extent soil mapping units are grouped together to form capability units.

The prime aim of the method is to assess the degree of limitation to land use or potential imposed by land characteristics on the basis of permanent properties. A scale of land capability grades can thus be envisaged with the degree of limitation and hazard defining the classes. This concept is illustrated in Figure 4.1 with the eight classes of the USDA method. As the degree of

limitation increases, so the range of land use options decreases. Comment needs to be made about the nature of permanent properties. The capability assessment would become quickly redundant if the values of selected properties could be easily changed. For example, a farmer can quickly change the pH value of fields by the application of lime. In contrast, it is far more difficult to modify the slope of the land, the depth of the soil, the effects of past erosion, soil texture, type of clay minerals and water holding capacity. If it is not technically and economically feasible to tackle such problems as water lying on the surface of the soil, lack or excess of water in the soil, stones, presence of soluble salts or exchangeable sodium, then these limitations are considered to be permanent. Under such circumstances these limitations would not be taken into account in capability assessment. Clearly there are difficulties in deciding what is technically and economically feasible and an additional problem is that technical and economic changes mean that any land capability assessment will have to be re-appraised.

The USDA method has three levels in its classification structure.

1   *Capability class*
   This is the broadest category and a total of eight classes are defined and labelled I to VIII inclusive indicating degree of limitation.

2   *Capability subclass*
   These subclasses indicate the type of limitations encountered within the classes. Limitations such as an erosional hazard, rooting zone restriction, and problems of climate, stoniness, low fertility, salinity or wetness are indicated by a letter subscript. For example, class V with major limitations imposed by excess water and climatic characteristics is indicated as Vwc.

3   *Capability unit*
   This is a subdivision of the subclass. Land in one capability unit clearly includes many different soils but has little variation in degree and type of limitation to land use, but in addition is suitable for similar crops under similar farm and soil management schemes. The yield range of crops within capability units in such circumstances should not be greater than 25 per cent.

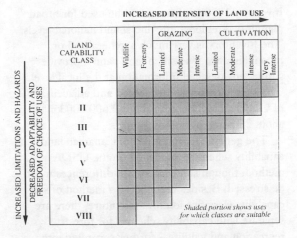

Figure 4.1 Intensity with which each land capability class can be used with safety; note the increasing limitations on the uses to which the land can be safely put as one moves from class I to class VIII (source: Brady 1984: Figure 15.25: 465)

The assignment of any soil mapping unit to a capability class, subclass or unit is possible only if a number of assumptions are made and these are specified fully by Klingebiel and Montgomery (1961). It is important to reiterate the underlying assumption that soils of different type may well be grouped into the same capability class since they share the same degree of limitation. Comments about suitability for specific crops can be made only at the level of the capability unit. A moderately high level of management is assumed on the part of the land users. This level is considered to be 'reasonable' for the area in question. Greater variations in management techniques may well be required within capability classes than between classes. Factors such as distance to market, types of roads, size and shape of the soil areas, location within fields, ability and resources of individual land users, and other characteristics of land ownership are not taken into account.

Klingebiel and Montgomery (1961) provide a full description of the type of land within each of the eight capability classes. The brief summary of these classes as provided by Young (1973: 14–15) is given below. The close association between the abbreviated definitions and Figure 4.1 should be evident. Note that classes I to IV are cultivable

while the remaining classes are not.

Class I   Soils with few limitations that restrict their use.

Class II   Soils with some limitations that reduce the choice of plants or require moderate conservation practices.

Class III Soils with severe limitations that reduce the choice of plants or require special conservation practices, or both.

Class IV   Soils with very severe limitations that restrict the choice of plants, require very careful management, or both.

Class V   Soils with little or no erosion hazard, but with other limitations impractical to remove, that limit their use largely to pasture, range, woodland or wildlife food and cover. (In practice this class is mainly used for level valley-floor lands that are swampy or subject to frequent flooding.)

Class VI   Soils with very severe limitations that make them generally unsuited to cultivation and limit their use to pasture or range, woodland or wildlife.

Class VII Soils with very severe limitations that make them unsuited to cultivation and restrict their use largely to grazing, woodland or wildlife.

Class VIII Soils and landforms with limitations that preclude their use for commercial plant production and restrict it to recreation, wildlife, water supply or aesthetic purposes.

If the USDA method is considered as a fully defined land classification technique, then it can be severely criticized. If the descriptions of the capability classes are examined, a distinct lack of precise quantitative criteria will quickly be very evident. Phrases such as 'gentle slopes', 'moderate susceptibility to wind or water erosion', or 'less than ideal soil depth' clearly lack precision of definition, thus making them liable to diversity of interpretation. However, it can be argued that the strength of the USDA method lies in its flexibility, a viewpoint put forward by Young (1973). Major difficulties arise if any attempt is made to fix rigid limiting values which are relevant to a variety of environments. Consider soil texture: the significance of the textural types (loam, sandy loam, clay loam, etc) will vary according to the climatic regime and to the types of crops and land uses. Thus the lack of precise limiting values gives the USDA method distinct flexibility. The method is better described as a *framework* for land capability assessment since it can be adapted for a wide variety of environmental conditions. Young and Goldsmith (1977) do such an exercise for part of Malawi.

The hopes of Hockensmith and Steele (1949) about the potential uses of land capability maps have been realized to a large extent. They visualized such maps being used by farmers for a wide variety of purposes, by soil conservation officers to determine the conservation needs both at the regional and individual farm levels, and by taxation authorities or lending institutions requiring information about the basic nature of land. Practically all soil survey reports in the USA contain a section on land capability and this information is used widely by advisory and planning agencies. Data on land capability are integral to the categorization of land as prime, though additional considerations such as proximity to markets, availability of transport facilities and land use practices in adjoining areas are also taken into account.

4.2 Land capability – the Canadian method

Land capability assessment in Canada was initiated by the Canada Land Inventory which was established in 1963 as a result of the Agricultural Rehabilitation and Development Act (ARDA) of 1961. This Inventory is a comprehensive survey of land capability and was designed to provide a basis for resource and land use planning (Canada Land Inventory 1970). It is meant to be used for broad planning at regional, provincial and national levels. The Inventory is very much a generalized or reconnaissance assessment and cannot provide sufficiently detailed information at the local level. The survey covers all the settled and adjacent areas of Canada, amounting to about 2,600,000 km^2 or about 25 per cent of the country.

The general approach of the Canadian land capability scheme is modelled on the USDA method, though some important differences must be stressed. Besides there being a method of soil capability classification for agriculture, there are separate land capability schemes for forestry, recreation and wildlife – further separated into ungulates and waterfowl. The species of ungulates (antelope, caribou, deer, mountain goat, moose and mountain sheep) indicate how the capability scheme has been tailored to Canadian conditions. For illustrative purposes, a brief outline is given below of the agriculture and recreation capability schemes; a complete summary of the schemes is provided by Report No. 1 of the Canada Land Inventory (1970).

All the Canadian capability schemes have seven classes in contrast to the eight of the USDA method. The soil capability classes for agriculture can be summarized as follows.

Classes

1 *Soils in this class have no significant limitations in use for crops*
The soils are deep, are well to imperfectly drained, hold moisture well and in the virgin state are well supplied with plant nutrients. They can be managed and cropped without difficulty. Under good management they are moderately high to high in productivity for a wide range of field crops.

2 *Soils in this class have moderate limitations that restrict the range of crops or require moderate conservation practices*
The soils are deep and hold moisture well. The limitations are moderate and the soils can be managed and cropped with little difficulty. Under good management they are moderately high to

high in productivity for a fairly wide range of crops.

3 *Soils in this class have moderately severe limitations that restrict the range of crops or require special conservation practices*
The limitations are more severe than for class 2 soils. They affect one or more of the following practices: timing and ease of tillage; planting and harvesting; choice of crops; and methods of conservation. Under good management they are fair to moderately high in productivity for a fair range of crops.

4 *Soils in this class have severe limitations that restrict the range of crops or require special conservation practices, or both*
The limitations seriously affect one or more of the following practices: timing and ease of tillage; planting and harvesting; choice of crops; and methods of conservation. The soils are low to fair in productivity for a fair range of crops, but may have high productivity for a specially adapted crop.

5 *Soils in this class have very severe limitations that restrict their capability to producing perennial forage crops, and improvement practices are feasible*
The limitations are so severe that the soils are not capable of use for sustained production of annual field crops. The soils are capable of producing native or tame species of perennial forage plants, and may be improved by use of farm machinery. The improvement practices may include clearing of bush, cultivation, seeding, fertilizing or water control.

6 *Soils in this class are capable only of producing perennial forage crops and improvement practices are not feasible*
The soils provide some sustained grazing for farm animals, but the limitations are so severe that improvement by use of farm machinery is impractical. The terrain may be unsuited for use of farm machinery, or the soils may not respond to improvement, or the grazing season may be very short.

7 *Soils in this class have no capability for arable culture or permanent pasture*
This class also includes rockland, other non-soil areas and bodies of water too small to show on the maps.

O *Organic soils (not placed in capability classes)*
(source: Canada Land Inventory 1970: 23–4)

As with the USDA method subclasses are indicated by letters. The Canadian method has a wider range of such limitations than the USDA one. The background assumptions to the Canadian scheme are very similar to those of the USDA method.

In the scheme for classifying land according to recreation capability, the seven classes are differentiated according to the intensity of outdoor recreational use, or the quantity of outdoor recreation which may be generated and sustained per unit of land per annum under perfect market conditions. This last point means that a uniform demand and accessibility is assumed for all areas – in other words location relative to population centres and to existing access are not included in the assessment procedure. Subclasses are defined using a letter notation; some examples are E (land with vegetation possessing recreational value), F (waterfall or rapids), G (significant glacier view or similar experience) and H (historic or prehistoric site). It can be appreciated that the interpretation of *land* varies according to the capability method. With the land capability classification for ungulates, for example, land is categorized according to its habitat suitability for these particular animals.

The Canada Land Inventory (CLI) is one of the most comprehensive and ambitious national inventories of land resources. It was instituted in the early 1960s to aid the targeting of economic development programmes in rural areas. A fundamental objective of the scheme was thus to answer questions on the nature, location and extent of land resources. A crucial aspect in any land evaluation is comparison of alternative land use strategies and the CLI offers such opportunity given the different land capability assessments. Thus through the simple overlaying of different land capability maps for a particular area, it is possible to identify alternative uses such as when land may be graded in the same class for forestry and agriculture. The CLI is thus used as a powerful tool in order to indicate land use options based on physical criteria. The results from such physical assessments can then be used as inputs to economic and social analysis.

Perhaps the most outstanding result from the CLI is the recognition that good quality agricultural land in Canada is limited in extent. For example, only 3.4 per cent of land suitable for agriculture is in the highest capability category with a capacity to grow a wide range of crops including maize, speciality fruits and vegetables. Furthermore, good agricultural land occurs in the immediate vicinity of urban centres. A report by Neimanis (1979) examines the land resource base around Canada's largest cities which are called Census Metropolitan Areas (CMAs). The CMAs, although they occupy only 0.5 per cent of Canada's land area, include 55 per cent of the population. Continued population growth of these CMAs results in considerable demand for land for housing, industry, recreation and transport. Between 1981 and 1986 about 55,200 ha of rural land were lost to urbanization and land with prime capability (Classes 1, 2 or 3) to produce crops accounted for 59 per cent of all converted land. The issue of particular concern is that over 55 per cent of Canada's prime agricultural land lies within a 160 km radius of the CMAs. Furthermore, the nearer the urban centre, the greater is the proportion of good agricultural land. The spatial association of good agricultural land with CMAs is a result of Canada's settlement history, but this is now leading to an increasing conflict between urban and agricultural land needs. In addition, as discussed in Chapter 1, certain areas near CMAs are suited to particular crops, for example, fruit in the Great Lakes peninsula. This industry is under much threat with the expansion of the Toronto-Hamilton-St Catherine's conurbation. A similar issue is evident in British Columbia where there has been considerable loss of fruitland to urbanization in the Okanagan Valley (Krueger and Maguire 1985). Such loss has occurred despite the innovative formation of Agricultural Land Reserves designed to limit the urbanization of prime agricultural land.

The initial objective of the CLI was the publication of land capability maps. Concurrent with research on land capability during the 1960s was the development of computer methods for handling spatial data. In 1971 Canada was the first country to produce a fully operational system, called the Canada Geographic Information System (CGIS). At first the data could be accessed only

through a national mainframe computer. Now priority is being given to the provision of CLI data on inexpensive computer disks to encourage use on readily available microcomputers.

4.3 Land capability – British methods

Before attention focuses on methods currently used in Britain, mention must be made of earlier approaches. The first national assessment of land grade resulted from the Land Utilization Survey in the 1940s (Stamp 1962). Under this method land was graded on the basis primarily of land use characteristics and maps at a scale of 1:625,000 were published. Such information, albeit very generalized and subjective, was all that was available to assist land use planning in the 1950s. By the 1960s there was the growing realization that a more detailed and up-to-date assessment of land was needed. A study group was established in 1962 under the aegis of the Agricultural Land Service of the Ministry of Agriculture, Fisheries and Food, and an *Agricultural Land Classification* was published in 1966. In this scheme land is graded into five classes according to degree of limitation imposed by soil and climatic conditions on agriculture. The degree of limitation is expressed in terms of range of crops which can be grown, the level of yield, the consistency of yield and cost of obtaining the yield (Morgan 1974). Agricultural land classification maps at a scale of 1:63,360 are available for England and Wales. The prime objective of these maps is to assist planning decisions concerning the release of agricultural land for urban purposes. One problem with this scheme is that almost one half of the agricultural land in England and Wales has been classed as grade 3. More detailed assessment of this grade has proved necessary and details are available for defining and identifying three subgrades of grade 3 (Agricultural Development and Advisory Service 1976). A summary and review of this agricultural land classification scheme are provided by Morgan (1974); greater detail is provided below on the more recent version of this scheme (Ministry of Agriculture, Fisheries and Food 1988).

A major limitation of this agricultural land classification scheme is that all upland and hill areas of England and Wales are covered by the two lowest grades (4 and 5). As a result the Agricultural Development and Advisory Service (1980) developed a more refined system for appraising such areas; the approach is also summarized by Cowie and Metcalfe (1982). The main objective is to determine land potential for improvement with a distinction being made between unimproved rough grazings termed hill land and improved land called upland. Hill land is classified according to suitability for improvement and current grazing value while the assessment of upland is dependent upon flexibility of use. The classification of upland or hill land is achieved by assembling information on vegetation, gradient, irregularity and wetness, other available mapped data, aerial photo interpretation, and field survey. A system of overlays is used to allocate land according to the following scheme.

Classification of hill land

H 1A   generally improvable – of high present grazing value

H 1B   generally improvable – of moderate present grazing value

H 1C   generally improvable – of low present grazing value

H 2   mainly improvable but slope or irregularity impose some limitation

H 3   improvements generally severely limited but of moderate or high grazing value

H 4   generally not improvable and of low grazing value.

Classification of upland

U 1   generally suitable for grazing, mowing and occasional arable cropping

U 2   suitable for grazing but mowing and arable cropping are limited by irregularity and/or wetness

U 3W   generally restricted to permanent grassland which is primarily used for grazing due to wetness

U 3S   generally restricted to permanent grassland which is primarily used for grazing due to slope, irregularity, or shallow soils

U 4   mostly rough grazing or with some permanent pasture and not generally improvable because of severe slope, irregularity and/or wetness restrictions.

(source: Cowie and Metcalfe 1982: 54)

The Scottish Office Agriculture and Fisheries Department has not published agricultural land classification maps, though information using a A+, A, B+, B, B−, C and D scale is made available to planning authorities. These lettered grades correspond to very good, good, medium plus, medium, medium minus, poor and non-arable land respectively. The grading is based on a visual survey supported by information on productivity of various farms. This scheme has been replaced by an assessment of land capability for agriculture (LCA) (Bibby et al 1982), and details of this approach are given following an outline of the older land capability system.

In Britain the Soil Surveys developed a Land Use Capability Classification (Bibby and Mackney 1969), modelled on the USDA scheme. The prime aim was to present the results of soil surveys in a form suitable for planners, agricultural advisers, farmers and other land users. As with the American and Canadian schemes, a number of assumptions are specified in the British scheme. For example, the classification is primarily for agricultural purposes. A moderately high level of management is assumed. Land is graded only on the basis of limitations which cannot be removed or reduced at acceptable cost. Distance to markets, and types of roads and farm structure are not taken into account in the assessment procedure. Reference must be made to the scheme for full details of the assumptions. Like the Canadian method, the British one has only seven classes. In particular, class 5 of the USDA method is excluded since it refers specifically to flat wet areas and thus breaks the theme of progressively greater limitations (Mackney 1974). The American subclasses are also used with the addition of a subclass for gradient and soil pattern limitation. A distinctive characteristic of the British method is that classes are more precisely defined with limiting values for particular properties being specified. Climatic characteristics are incorporated in a quantitative manner in order to define three climatic groups as described in Chapter 2. This is done on the basis of the water balance and temperature during the period April to September. The Soil Survey of Scotland has further refined the assessment of climatic conditions by producing one map based on accumulated temperature and potential water deficit (Birse and Dry 1970) and another on exposure and accumulated frost (Birse and Robertson 1970). Similarly the Soil Survey of England and Wales has published national maps showing average maximum potential cumulative soil moisture deficit, accumulated temperature above 5.6°C, median accumulated temperature above 0°C (January to June), mean duration of field capacity in days, and mean potential soil moisture deficit for mid-July adjusted for winter wheat.

The land use capability classes of the Soil Survey scheme can be summarized as follows.

Class 1   Land with very minor or no physical limitation to use.

Class 2   Land with minor limitations that reduce the choice of crops and interefere with cultivation.

Class 3   Land with moderate limitations that restrict the choice of crops and/or demand careful management.

Class 4   Land with moderately severe limitations that restrict the choice of crops and/or require very careful management practices.

Class 5   Land with severe limitations that restrict its use to pasture, forestry and recreation.

Class 6   Land with very severe limitations that restrict use to rough grazing, forestry and recreation.

Class 7   Land with extremely severe limitations that cannot be rectified.
          (source: Bibby and Mackney 1969: 3–4)

An extract from a land capability map is shown in Figure 4.2 with the topography and soils also being shown for the same area which is located to the immediate west of Stirling in the Forth valley of central Scotland. The topographic extract (Figure 4.2a) shows how the terrain ranges from the carselands to the Touch Hills to the south of Gargunnock. The soils include poorly drained gleyed warp soils on the estuarine silts and clays (Stirling Series), well and imperfectly drained brown forest soils on the lower valley slopes (Kippen and Fourmerk Series), and peaty podzols (Baidland Series), skeletal soils and blanket peat on the upper areas. The land use capability map (Figure 4.2c) reflects such soil variation with class 3 land on the carseland, classes 4 and 5 on the lower slopes, class 6 dominant in the peaty podzol and blanket peat areas on the upper and summit slopes and class 7 land restricted to very steep or very thin soil localities. The specific limitations vary from soil wetness and rooting zone limitations on the carselands, to slope and pattern limitations on the lower and middle slopes, to climatic and slope and pattern limitations on the highest land. The close association of topography, soils and land use capability class and subclass should thus be very evident for this area. Despite the inclusion in the Bibby and Mackney (1969) scheme of critical values for defining selected characteristics, problems often are encountered in trying to assign sites to specific land capability classes. To aid this process, Burnham and McRae (1974) produced a useful land-judging form. Rudeforth and Bradley (1972) also developed the approach through writing the classification process in the form of a flow chart. This permitted the automatic allocation of sites to land capability classes in their study in Pembrokeshire (Figure 4.3).

During the late 1970s and early 1980s, the need for revision to the land use capability scheme became increasingly evident. Particular concerns were with improving quantitative guidelines as well as with incorporating better assessments of climatic

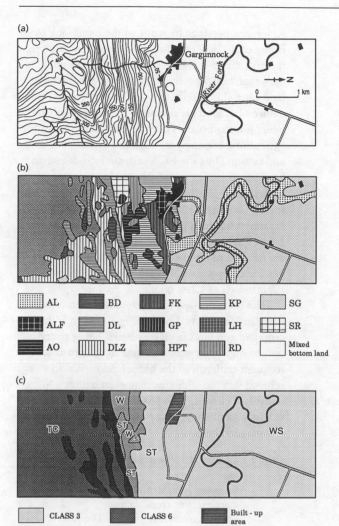

Figure 4.2 Topography, soils and land use capability of an area at Gargunnock in the Forth valley in Scotland
(a) topography (contours in metres)
(b) soils: brown forest soils – FK (Fourmerk), DL (Darleith), KP (Kippen), GP (Glenpark); podzols – RD (Redbrae), BD (Baidland); gley soils – AO (Arnmore), SR (Sorn) and LH (Limpithill); other soils – HPT (hill peat), AL (alluvium), ALF (alluvial fans) and SG (gleyed alluvial soil on silts and clays)
(c) land use capability: specific limitations are indicated by letters – T (topography), C (climate), W (wetness), S (soil)

parameters. In England and Wales the result has been the production of revised guidelines and criteria for grading the quality of agricultural land (Ministry of Agriculture, Fisheries and Food 1988). In Scotland a system for classifying land capability for agriculture (LCA) has been published and an examination of this follows.

The LCA scheme as described by Bibby et al (1982) is based on very similar principles to that of the USDA method (Klingebiel and Montgomery 1961). Similar assumptions are integral to the system; for example, land is classified according to the degree to which its physical characteristics

affect the flexibility of cropping and its ability to produce certain crops consistently. Another is the assumption about the level of farm management; a satisfactory level is assumed though this is taken to mean that it is above the average in the relevant agricultural sector. The obvious key point of difference between the USDA scheme and this new one is the far greater degree of quantitative specification on assessment criteria. The core to the system are the guidelines for assessing the criteria which are used to define the different classes; for current purposes it is instructive to list these limitation types.

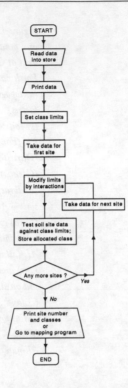

Figure 4.3 Generalized flow chart for soil or land classing by computer (from Rudeforth 1975: 157)

1 CLIMATE
   • maximum potential soil moisture deficit
   • accumulated temperature
   (these are combined as illustrated in Figure 2.4)
   • modification due to exposure (wind speed)

2 GRADIENT

3 SOIL
   • soil structure
   • shallowness
   • stoniness
   • droughtiness

4 WETNESS
   • workability, trafficability and poaching risk

5 EROSION

6 PATTERN

7 VEGETATION
   • rating of plant species and calculation of relative grazing values.

Reference needs to be made to the handbook by Bibby et al (1982) for full details on these limiting factors though it is interesting to give an outline of the vegetation assessment. The earlier scheme of land capability assessment paid little attention to the nature of upland areas, and in a country such as Scotland, the uplands play an important role in the agricultural economy through the grazing of sheep and cattle. Thus the LCA scheme introduced an innovative assessment of the grazing value of upland areas. Ratings are given for individual plant species and then using abundance data, relative grazing values can be calculated for particular areas. Furthermore, bands of relative grazing values are defined to define high, moderate and low grazing categories which are then used in the subdivisions of Class 6 land.

The classification system retains seven classes with land in classes 1 to 4 being suited to arable cropping and land in classes 5 to 7 being suited only to improved grassland and rough grazing. A frequent criticism of the older land capability scheme was the wide diversity even within individual classes. This has been solved by the subdivision of some of the classes into divisions as summarized below.

Class 1 *Land capable of producing a very wide range of crops*
Cropping is highly flexible and includes the more exacting crops such as winter-harvested vegetables. The level of crop yield is consistently high.
(covers less than 1 per cent of Scotland)
(no divisions)

Class 2 *Land capable of producing a wide range of crops*
Cropping is very flexible and a wide range of crops can be grown, but the land may be unsuited to winter-harvested crops. The level of yield is high but less consistently obtained than on Class 1 due to the effects of minor limitations affecting cultivation, crop growth or harvesting.
                (covers 1 per cent of Scotland)
(no divisions)

Class 3 *Land capable of producing a moderate range of crops*
Land in this class is capable of producing

good yields of a narrow range of crops, principally cereals and grass, and/or moderate yields of a wider range including potatoes, some vegetable crops and oilseed rape. The degree of variability between years will be greater than is the case for Class 1 and 2, mainly due to interactions between climate, soil and management factors affecting the timing and type of cultivations, sowing and harvesting.

(covers 15 per cent of Scotland)
Subdivided into two – Division 1 (above average arable land) and Division 2 (average arable land).

Class 4 *Land capable of producing a narrow range of crops*
The land is suitable for enterprises based primarily on grassland with short arable breaks. Yields of arable crops are variable due to soil, wetness or climatic factors. Yields of grass are often high but difficulties of production or utilization may be encountered. The moderately severe levels of limitation restrict the choice of crops and demand careful management.

(covers 11 per cent of Scotland)
Subdivided into Divisions 1 and 2 based on capability for producing forage crops for stock feed.

Class 5 *Land capable of use as improved grassland*
Land in this class is restricted to grass production. Mechanized surface treatments to improve the grassland, ranging from ploughing through rotavation to surface seeding and improvement by non-disruptive techniques are all possible.

(covers 19 per cent of Scotland)
Subdivided into Divisions 1, 2 and 3 based on suitability for improvement.

Class 6 *Land capable of use only as rough grazings*
The land has very severe limitations which generally prevent the use of tractor-operated machinery for improvement. Reclamation of small areas to encourage stock to range is often possible. A range of widely different qualities of grazing is included from very steep land with significant grazing value in the lowland situation to moorland with a low but sustained production in the uplands.

(covers 48 per cent of Scotland)

Subdivided into Divisions 1, 2 and 3 based on the relative grazing values of the vegetation.

Class 7 *Land of very limited agricultural value*
This land has extremely severe limitations that cannot be rectified. Agricultural use is restricted to very poor rough grazing.

(covers 3 per cent of Scotland)

Built-up areas, quarries, etc, account for 2 per cent of Scotland.

For Scotland, land capability maps for agriculture have been published at a scale of 1:250,000 for the whole country; sheets are available at a scale of 1:50,000 for the lowland areas. Such availability is important given that these maps are used to locate areas of prime agricultural land, defined as Class 3 Division 1 or better. Prime land accounts for 5.7 per cent of Scotland's land surface and there is a presumption against the transfer of such land from agriculture.

The equivalent land classification in England and Wales is detailed in a handbook produced by the Ministry of Agriculture, Fisheries and Food (1988). This scheme evolved from the earlier one devised during the early 1960s. The main changes centre on the assessment of climatic, and soil wetness and droughtiness limitations. The subdivisions of Grade 3 land are limited to two subgrades rather than three. The main limiting factors used in this scheme are as follows.

1 CLIMATE
   • average annual rainfall
   • accumulated temperature
   • local climatic factors

2 SITE
   • gradient
   • microrelief
   • flooding

3 SOIL
   • texture and structure
   • depth
   • stoniness
   • chemical status

4 INTERACTIVE LIMITATIONS
   • wetness
   • droughtiness
   • soil erosion.

It may seem surprising to note the inclusion of chemical status assessment since land capability is usually concerned with permanent or semi-permanent limitations. In this scheme the chemical status of soil does not influence land grading where application of fertilizer can correct any deficiencies. Chemical limitations are taken into account only when they have a long-term detrimental effect on the physical condition of the soil, crop yield, range or crops, stocking rates or grazing management. The grades and subgrades are as follows:

Grade 1   Excellent quality agricultural land

Grade 2   Very good quality agricultural land

Grade 3   Good to moderate quality agricultural land (subdivided into Subgrades 3a and 3b)

Grade 4   Poor quality agricultural land

Grade 5   Very poor quality agricultural land

Other non-agricultural land uses constitute land categories, for example urban and woodland areas.

In Britain a key factor which encouraged the development of land capability schemes was the need to preserve good agricultural land. The view was that such land is a fundamental resource and has to be protected in order to maintain and increase agricultural output. During the 1980s there has been a dramatic change in objective given the excessive agricultural production within the European Community. This has led to a variety of schemes designed to encourage farmers to reduce their output such as through set-aside. Afforestation is also seen as offering considerable scope for land use diversification on farms and incentives exist to foster such change. Another dimension is the considerable import bill for timber to Britain. The overall effect is increasing attention being paid to the planting of trees, not just on poor land in the uplands, but also on better lowland land. A system of land capability classification for forestry has been produced to aid decision-making at broad planning levels, to guide land managers and to indicate forestry potential within Britain (Bibby et al 1988). The general approach is

modelled on the land capability scheme for agriculture with assessment based on a number of defined limitations. These are:

CLIMATE
- accumulated temperature
- exposure

WINDTHROW

NUTRIENTS

TOPOGRAPHY

DROUGHTINESS

WETNESS

SOIL
- depth and pattern

The classification process begins with climatic considerations (accumulated temperature and exposure). The resultant land classes are taken as a first approximation for an area prior to further downgrading should this be necessary when other limitations are included. Soil nutrient status is given greater emphasis than in the LCA scheme since trees have to rely more on the natural availability of nutrients than do farm crops. Once all the limitations have been assessed, then land can be allocated to one of seven capability classes for forestry. These are as follows.

Class F1   Land with excellent flexibility for the growth and management of tree crops

Class F2   Land with very good flexibility for the growth and management of tree crops

Class F3   Land with good flexibility for the growth and management of tree crops

Class F4   Land with moderate flexibility for the growth and management of tree crops

Class F5   Land with limited flexibility for the growth and management of tree crops

Class F6   Land with very limited flexibility for the growth and management of tree crops

Class F7   Land unsuitable for producing tree crops
(source: Bibby et al 1988)

These classes are subdivided into subclasses

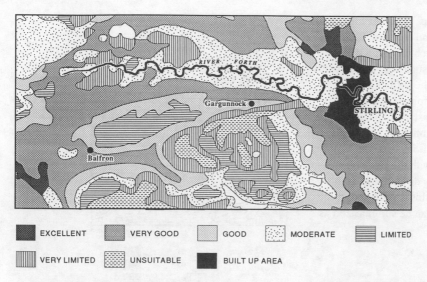

Figure 4.4 Extract from a 1:250,000 land capability for forestry map for part of the Campsie Hills in central Scotland (source: Soil Survey of Scotland 1982)

■ EXCELLENT ▨ VERY GOOD ▦ GOOD ⣿ MODERATE ▤ LIMITED

▥ VERY LIMITED ▩ UNSUITABLE ■ BUILT UP AREA

according to the dominant limitations which are indicated by letters such as c for climate, b for windthrow and n for nutrients. These subclasses can be further subdivided into capability units which can be applied at scales of between 1:25,000 and 1:10,000 when the emphasis is on detailed forest planning. For Scotland, LCF maps showing land capability classes are published for the whole country at a scale of 1:250,000; an extract for part of the Campsie Hills in central Scotland is given in Figure 4.4.

4.4   Land capability – a Dutch method

The Dutch landscape is well known for its intensity of use and land is under ever increasing pressure. Not only is there need to preserve as far as possible the soils most suitable for agriculture which plays an important role in the Dutch economy, but also space must be found for new houses, industrial areas, recreational areas, forestry and roads. There is a long tradition of land evaluation in The Netherlands. The early work during the 1950s on soil survey interpretation is summarized by Edelman (1963) who describes the use of such research primarily for crop production and for land reclamation and improvement. He gives brief consideration to soil surveys in relation to town and

country planning with the main contribution in The Netherlands being the preservation of soils particularly suitable for horticulture. In a review of soil survey applications by Haans and Westerfeld (1970), the marked rise in the use of soil data in the non-agricultural sector is noted and such applications will be discussed in Chapter 5. For present purposes, an outline is given of the older soil survey interpretation for agricultural purposes in The Netherlands.

Soil maps at a scale of 1:200,000 have been the basis for the assessment of soil suitability for arable land and for grassland. Details of the scheme are provided by Vink and van Zuilen (1974) with a summary also in Vink (1975). The first 1:200,000 soil map was completed in 1961, and even before that time the need for a general assessment of the country's soils for agriculture had been identified. The term suitability is used rather than capability and this is defined as 'the degree of success with which a crop or range of crops can be regularly grown on a certain soil, within the existing type of farming, under good management, and under good conditions of parcellation and accessibility' (Vink and van Zuilen 1974: 17). The assessment is made on a qualitative basis with reference to the economic and technological situation of agriculture about 1960. Thus, as with the USDA land capability scheme, various assumptions are necessary before land or soil grading is necessary.

Changes in these assumptions, resultant for example upon the introduction of a new farming layout or new machinery which can cope with difficult soils, mean that the suitability assessments ought to be reappraised. In the British land capability schemes, much emphasis is given to climatic limitations. In contrast, climatic variations within The Netherlands are minimal and hence soil limitations assume paramount importance. Another important point of contrast with the British schemes is that agriculture is divided into arable and grassland activities and this is reflected in the classification system which can be summarized as follows.

MAJOR CLASS BG
Arable land and grassland soils
Soils generally suited to arable land and usually also to grassland.
Subdivided into seven classes (BG1 to BG7).

MAJOR CLASS GB
Grassland and arable soils
Soils generally suited to grassland and in many cases also to arable land.
Subdivided into three classes (GB1 to GB3).

MAJOR CLASS B
Arable land soils
Soils generally suited to arable land, but mostly poorly or not suited to grassland.
Subdivided into three classes (B1 to B3).

MAJOR CLASS G
Grassland soils
Soils generally suited to grassland, but mostly poorly or not suited to arable land.
Subdivided into five classes (G1 to G5).

MAJOR CLASS O
Unsuitable soils
Soils predominantly poorly suited to arable and to grassland.
Subdivided into two classes (O1 and O2) according as to whether the soils are too dry or too wet respectively.

The final category is non-classified soils which include areas of very varying soils or hydrology, sand excavations, foreland soils or urban areas.

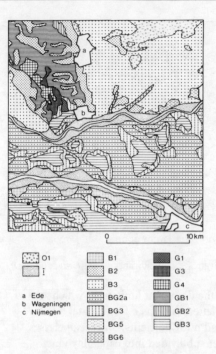

a Ede
b Wageningen
c Nijmegen

O1   B1   G1
I   B2   G3
     B3   G4
     BG2a GB1
     BG3 GB2
     BG5 GB3
     BG6

Figure 4.5 Soil suitability for arable land and grassland in the vicinity of Wageningen, Gelderland, The Netherlands; grades of land suitability are indicated for arable and grassland (BG), grassland and arable (GB), arable (B) and grassland (G); OI and I indicate unsuitable and unclassified soils respectively (source: Vink and van Zuilen 1974: opposite p. 36)

Land suitability for arable land and grassland is illustrated in Figure 4.5 for the Wageningen area. As can be seen, much of the land to the east of a line between Wageningen and Ede is in class B3 – arable land soils of extremely limited suitability. This area coincides with extensive sand deposits on which high podzols have developed; the term 'high' is applied since these soils are not influenced by groundwater. They are thus liable to serious soil moisture deficits as well as nutrient deficiencies. In contrast the clay soils between the rivers Rhine and Waal are classed as BG2a – arable land and grassland soils of wide suitability.

Reference is made to this Dutch system because it differentiates between arable and grassland suitabilities. This reflects the greater priority attached to grassland in The Netherlands compared to the UK. The merit of such an approach is that more specific information is given about land suitability for agriculture. If land is graded in a comprehensive manner for agriculture, then distinctive quality may not be apparent. In Britain, for example, land graded as Class 4 might well be highly suited to animal husbandry. However, the objective of land classification must always be remembered; if an overall assessment is required to aid land use planning, then a multipurpose grading scheme is required. If more detailed comments are needed on land suitability for particular crops or agricultural activities, then more specific classifications are necessary.

4.5   Alternative approaches to land capability assessment

The assessment of land capability in such countries as the USA, Canada, Britain and The Netherlands as already outlined is achieved primarily by interpreting the degree of limitation which land conditions pose to one or more land uses. Prior data exist in the form of climatic, soil and topographic maps. Spatial units are determined by the superimposition of these maps and then graded according to capability. The whole approach is dependent upon the availability of climatic, soil and topographic data. There may well arise situations where adequate data do not exist or are not appropriate to the scale of the analysis. In such circumstances it is necessary to mount special surveys. It is not normally cost effective to collect field and laboratory data for a wide range of land attributes; instead data collection has only to be relevant to the particular land capability classification. There thus arises the need to devise methods for the direct assessment of land capability. The aim of this section is to discuss how such direct assessment can be tackled.

An example of the direct assessment of land capability is given by Woode (1981). He describes how a field sampling programme in Zambia was devised on the basis of an initial aerial photo interpretation. At the sampling sites, the following twelve characteristics were recorded:

- effective depth of the soil
- texture of layer 0–20 cm
- texture of layer 20–40 cm
- texture of layer 40–60 cm
- texture of layer 60–90 cm
- hindrances to cultivation
- limiting material
- slope of site
- observed erosion severity
- wetness (drainage) factor
- colour of subsoil
- parent material (if known).

Reference is then made to a classification system in order to determine the capability class for each site. In the first instance a decision is made concerning which of the four primary divisions is applicable, that is arable land (suited to long-term intensive use), marginal arable land (suited to a limited range of crops or requiring extensive improvements for arable production), grazing land only, and unsuitable land for arable cropping or grazing. Further subdivision into subclasses is also described by Woode (1981). Mapping of land capability is done by spatial extrapolation using aerial photographs.

The attraction of this type of approach is that only data relevant to the capability classification are collected. If the data are stored in their original form as in a database system or geographic information system, then changes in the classification as well as data updates or corrections are easy. Use can also be made of a land judging form as given by McRae (1988) to permit the allocation of individual sites to land capability classes. Such a form provides an easy way to apply the Scottish system of land capability assessment for agriculture (Bibby et al 1982). Each property is considered in turn and an assessment is made for the best possible class. The approach is based on the principle of limiting factors whereby the first estimate of the overall assessment is determined by

the worst component score. Thus if all properties
are rated at Class 2 with the exception of one at
Class 4 division 1, then the overall assessment
should be Class 4 division 1. McRae (1988)
recommends that results should be confirmed only
after a check is made with the description of classes
as given in the full handbook to ensure correct final
decisions.

At all times it must be remembered that the
prime aim of land capability assessment is to aid the
planning or management of land use. Dumanski et
al (1979) give an appropriate example of capability
analysis to aid planning of the urban fringe to
Ottawa in Canada. They provide a map of soil
capability for agriculture as well as a set of maps
indicating various land factor restrictions (wetness,
drainage variability, flood hazard, bedrock
occurrence, stoniness, natural fertility, soil structure
and droughtiness). As a result they are able to
identify areas deemed suitable for urban expansion
– areas which avoid the best agricultural land as
well as localities which pose particular problems to
construction. This Canadian study emphasizes the
importance of developing capability schemes with
close reference to the needs of the users of the
results. A similar point is made by Osunade (1987)
with reference to the needs of small farmers in the
humid tropics. Criticism is made of the extensive
mapping of soil series or associations in Nigeria
since the resultant mapping units convey little to
small farmers. Instead, emphasis is given to land
facets since these not only corresponded with
integrated landscape units but also are recognized
by small farmers as expressed in local terms for
river-side, plain, lowland, footslope, freeslope, hill
crest. In other words priority has to be given to
providing land capability information for landscape
units which are perceived as different and distinct
by local farmers. Land capability interpretation of
these slope units is likely to be better accepted and
understood by farmers.

4.6   The influence of land capability on yield and land value

As discussed at the beginning of this chapter, many

schemes of land capability assessment can be traced
back to the American system of Klingebiel and
Montgomery (1961). The essential aim is to
evaluate the combined effects of climate, relief and
permanent soil conditions on land use limitation
and productive capacity. Although a capability
classification does not provide a productivity rating
for specific crops, some relationship is to be
expected between land capability and crop yield.
Guidance on anticipated yields from land capability
classes is not usually given since factors other than
permanent or semi-permanent physical constraints
influence yield. An exception is the Canadian
system for assessing land capability for forestry
(Canada Land Inventory 1970). For each class a
yield range is given on the assumption that forest
growth is solely dependent upon the natural state of
land without improvements such as fertilization,
drainage or amelioration practices (Table 4.1).
Such an approach is particularly appropriate for
Canadian conditions given the extensive nature of
the forest land resource. In the equivalent British
land capability system for forestry, no guidance is
given on anticipated yields. However, Bibby (1990)
presents average yield class figures for the
capability classes (Table 4.2); he stresses that such
figures mask considerable variation and should be
used only in calculations of national production
potential.

To examine further the relationship between
land capability and yield, reference is made to three
case studies – two in Canada and one in England.
Comment has already been made on the urban
pressures on the fruit growing area in southern
Ontario resultant upon the expansion of the
Toronto conurbation. Van Liet et al (1979)
investigated the effects of soil, climatic and
management variables as well as capability class on
the yields of apple trees in this area. For the latter
analysis, use was made of a specialized land
capability classification for tree fruits. Classes 1 to 3
were capable of sustained production of fruit crops,
class 4 was marginal and class 5 not capable of tree
fruit production. Analysis of variance indicated an
overall significant yield difference with average
apple yields of 0.85, 0.71, 0.60 and 0.47 kg/cm^2
respectively from land capability classes 1 to 4. On

Table 4.1 Expected gross merchantable timber for different land capability classes for forestry according to the Canada Land Inventory (1970)

Capability class	Yield (cubic metres per hectare per year)
1	>7.7
2	6.4–7.7
3	5.0–6.3
4	3.6–4.9
5	2.2–3.5

Table 4.2 Relationship between land capability class for forestry and yield class of sitka spruce; yield class is the maximum mean annual increment, measured in cubic metres per hectare, which a stand of trees is capable of attaining during its lifetime

Forestry class	Average yield class	95% confidence interval
F1	—	—
F2	22.0	16–28
F3	22.1	17–25
F4	20.0	17–24
F5	17.4	14–21
F6	13.9	11–17
F7	9.9	7–13

(source: Bibby 1990: 19)

the basis of such results, van Liet et al (1979) propose that land capability data should be used to aid local and regional planning of agricultural lands. They found a poor relationship between apple yield and soils as mapped at the series level. In the second Canadian study Peters (1977) investigated the correlation between the yields of cereal crops (wheat, oats and barley) and agro-climates and soil capability in Alberta. It needs to be recalled that the Canadian system of assessing soil capability for agriculture does not include a climatic assessment. Some statistically significant differences were obtained within agro-climatic regions according to soil capability, but the main conclusion was that variations in yield could best be correlated with agro-climatic conditions. Peters (1977) concludes that yield predictions based on agro-climatic, soil series and soil capability data can be the basis to land use planning in the province.

The third selected study is provided by Burnham et al (1987) who examined the relationship between crop yields and soil type and agricultural land class in south-east England. Data were obtained using a farm business survey for nearly 200 farms in the region. For 115 of these farms it was possible to determine the predominant soil type, soil parent material and agricultural land grade. Yield data for twelve harvest years (1974–85) were obtained for six principal crops (winter wheat, winter barley, spring barley, winter oats, oilseed rape and maincrop potatoes). It was found that brown soils did not give higher yields than stagnogleys; similarly brown calcareous earths did not outperform rendzinas except for potatoes. The overall impression is of little relationship between yield and soil type. As an example of positive results, soils formed on brickearth (a loamy drift) gave consistently higher yields. The results from comparing yields with agricultural land class indicate weak relationships (Table 4.3). The extreme right-hand column of Table 4.3 indicates differences in yields between agricultural land classes which were shown to be statistically significant. Of note is the result that winter barley on class 1 land outyields class 2. In contrast yields from oilseed rape show no relationship to land class. The study by Burnham et al (1987) also investigated patterns of yield variability from year to year and they found a general tendency for yields to become more variable between good and bad years on poorer grades of land; this was especially noted on grade 4 land even though in good years the yield from such land may equal or exceed the returns from grade 3 land.

In any discussion of the relationships between land capability class or agricultural land grade and yield, it needs to be recalled as already stated that such classifications are not designed to predict land performance. The two Canadian studies and the English one demonstrate that some relationships exist, but there are many other factors not integral to capability assessment which can affect yields.

Crop	Agricultural land class				Significant differences at 5% or better
	1	2	3	4	
winter wheat	115	110	94	93	1>3
winter barley	124	110	97	80	1>2>3,4
spring barley	115	109	98	77	1,2>4
winter oats	107	118	94	90	1,2>3,4
oilseed rape	105	107	109		—
maincrop potatoes	102	104	101	71	1,2,3>4

Table 4.3 Yield of principal crops in south-east England (1974–85) by agricultural land classes as a percentage of the average yield

(source: Burnham et al 1987: 97)

Land capability classifications for forestry tend to be more satisfactory as a basis for yield predictions because of lower levels of input and management compared to agriculture. If the specific objective is to assess land in terms of yield potential, then a fertility evaluation is required. As an example, Sanchez et al (1982) describe a fertility capability soil classification (FCC). It is a technical soil classification system which groups soils according to their fertility constraints. Letter codes are assigned for three categorical levels – type (topsoil texture), substrate type (subsoil texture) and modifiers. Examples are as follows.

TYPE
S: sandy topsoils (loamy sands and sands)
L: clayey topsoils (<35 per cent clay but not loamy sand or sand)
C: clayey topsoils (>35 per cent clay)
O: organic soils (>30 per cent organic matter to a depth of 50 cm or more)

SUBSTRATE TYPE
S: sandy subsoil (texture as in type)
L: loamy subsoil (texture as in type)
C: clayey subsoil (texture as in type)
R: rock or other hard root-restricting layer

MODIFIERS
g: gley (soil or mottles =<2 chroma within 60 cm of the soil surface and below all A horizons, or soil saturated with water for >60 days in most years)
d: dry (ustic, aridic or xeric soil moisture regimes; subsoil dry >90 cumulative days per year within 20–60 cm depth)
e: low cation exchange capacity (applies only to plough layer or surface 20 cm, whichever is shallower; CEC<4 meq/100 g soil by sum of bases plus KCl extractable Al (effective CEC), or CEC<7 meq/100 g soil by sum of cations at pH7, or CEC<10 meq/100 g soil by sum of cations plus Al plus H at pH 8.2).

(source: Sanchez et al 1982: 284–5)

Following the assignment of such codes to soil mapping units, it is then necessary in this system to interpret these codes in terms of attributes of direct relevance to plant growth. Examples of interpretation for types and substrata types are S (high rate of infiltration, low water-holding capacity), L (medium infiltration rate, good water-holding capacity); examples of modifiers are g (denitrification frequently occurs in anaerobic subsoil; tillage operations and certain crops may be adversely affected by excess rain unless drainage is improved by tiling or other drainage procedures; good soil moisture regime for rice production), h (low to medium soil acidity; requires liming for Al-sensitive crops such as cotton and alfalfa). As a result mapping units can be characterized by a string of codes using these letters.

This FCC system has been tested with data on soil profiles and fertilizer response from Brazil, Peru, Colombia and the United States. Sanchez et al (1982) conclude that the system is a meaningful tool for relating fertility limitation to crop yield response for a wide variety of soils and crops. They find that yields cannot be predicted from their FCC classification given the influence of factors not related to fertility. Nevertheless, the FCC is a useful system for providing interpretations of soil maps.

If some relationship exists between land capability and agricultural or forestry yield, then in a free market economy capability class should also be reflected in land value. In practice, many factors influence the price of rural land and the proximity to urban centres is an obvious one as well as the quality of any associated house. Nevertheless, it is possible to isolate the effect of land capability and this can be demonstrated with reference to a case study in Scotland (Davidson 1989).

Renfrewshire with its old county town of Paisley is situated to the immediate south-west of Glasgow and along the southern side of the Firth of Clyde. Marked variation in accessibility within the old county can be excluded since the whole area is small and lies within Glasgow's commuter belt to mean that the effect of accessibility on rural land sale values could be ignored. Data on fifty-one rural land sales over 10 hectares for the period 1981 to 1986 were obtained from the Land Register. The boundaries of land capability classes and divisions for agriculture (LCA) were digitized for each of the properties which were sold. It was thus possible to measure the areas of these classes and divisions on each property and then to calculate an overall score for LCA. This was achieved by converting the LCA classes and divisions to a scale with a range of 10 points covering each class. The mid-point of class 1 was allocated a score of 5, the mid-point of class 2 a score of 15, the mid-point of class 3 a score of 25, etc. The details are given in Table 4.4. It should be stressed that the basis to the scoring system as given in Table 4.4 can be questioned since the LCA scheme was not designed to be so rigidly quantified. Nevertheless, some type of scoring method had to be devised if a measure of average LCA was to be derived for each land sale. This was achieved by multiplying the LCA index by the fractional extents of each LCA class and summing these. For example, if an area

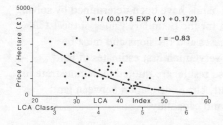

Figure 4.6 Curvilinear regression analysis between price per hectare and LCA index for rural land sales in Renfrewshire between 1981 and 1986
(source: Davidson 1989: 41)

consisted of 60 per cent class 3 division 2, 30 per cent class 4 division 1 and 10 per cent class 5 division 2, then the overall index can be calculated as follows:

$$(0.60 \times 27.5) + (0.30 \times 32.5) + (0.10 \times 45.0) = 30.75$$

The LCA index derived by this method reflects the spatial extent of different classes and divisions for each land sale.

The best fit function between land price and LCA index is of the form $Y = 1/\{A\exp(X) + B\}$ as shown in Figure 4.6. A correlation coefficient of r equal to -0.83 expresses a strong negative relationship between price per hectare and LCA indices. A similar result ($r = -0.87$) is obtained when the analysis is limited to sales without buildings. An interesting observation from the plot of price per hectare against LCA index is that the scatter of points appears more marked in the LCA range 25.0 to 40.0 (classes 3 and 4) than for index values of more than 40 (classes 5 and 6). The inference is that the variation in price per hectare is less in the LCA classes which are considered not suitable for arable cultivation. Using the best fit curvilinear model, the following ranges can be predicted for LCA classes and divisions based on sales from 1981 to early 1986.

Class 3	Division 1	£3770–£2860
Class 3	Division 2	£2860–£2040
Class 4	Division 1	£2040–£1390
Class 4	Division 2	£1390–£910
Class 5		£910–£360
Class 6		£360–£140

These price bands have been determined by solving the equation for the boundary values of the LCA index for classes and divisions and must be regarded as very much first estimates of land values. These results are quoted to demonstrate in this case study clear correlation between land values and land capability.

4.7 Land capability: an overview

As discussed at the beginning of this chapter, the early American system of land use capability assessment was developed in order to identify sustainable forms of land use. Soil erosion assessment was the key factor. The development, refinement and application of land use capability schemes in many countries is a clear indication of their value in aiding land use planning and management. The main application of land capability assessments has been as a means of identifying good or prime agricultural areas – land for which there ought to be a presumption against non-agricultural use. The limited extent of such good land was discussed in relation to Canada where the loss of such land, for example in the Niagara peninsula, has been a pressing issue for

many years. The implementation of any policy to protect prime agricultural land obviously requires the availability of a definition of such land as well as maps to portray spatial distributions. In Scotland, for example, land capability maps for agriculture are available at a scale of 1:50,000 for the whole of the lowlands; there is a presumption against the loss from agriculture of prime land which is classified as Classes 1, 2 or 3 division 1. The basis to such a policy is increasingly under challenge for two reasons. First, there is the issue of agricultural overproduction in western Europe and North America, thus the non-release of prime agricultural land will tend to perpetuate overproduction. Second, land which has high capability for agriculture will very likely also be highly suited to other uses. Such pressures become particularly acute in urban fringe areas on prime land where there are major pressures resulting from housing, industrial and transport demands.

The need for a more integrated approach to land use can be illustrated with reference to the development of forestry indicative strategies in Britain. The British government is seeking to encourage the expansion of forestry in an environmentally acceptable way. An annual planting target of 33,000 ha has been set in addition to planting within the farm woodlands scheme and the vast bulk of new planting is expected to be in

Class/division	Capability of land	LCA index
Class 1	Very wide range of crops	5.0
Class 2	Wide range of crops	15.0
Class 3 Division 1	Moderate range of crops	22.5
Division 2		27.5
Class 4 Division 1	Narrow range of crops	32.5
Division 2		37.5
Class 5 Division 1		42.5
Division 2	Improved grassland only	45.0
Division 3		47.5
Class 6 Division 1		52.5
Division 2	Rough grazing only	55.0
Division 3		57.5
Class 7	Very limited agricultural value	65.0

Table 4.4 LCA indexes in relation to capability classes and divisions (source: Davidson 1989)

Scotland. Regional planning authorities there are encouraged to devise forestry indicative strategies which should be integral to structure plans. Although forestry is not subject to planning control, forestry indicative strategies are seen to be helpful in two ways. First, they provide a framework to aid responses in relation to forestry grant applications, and second, they signal to landowners and other forestry investors the opportunities and sensitivities of forestry development. The identification of areas suited to forestry needs to take into account the occurrence of the following: good agricultural land; land suitability for forestry; ecological, landscape, water and heritage resources; tourism and recreational opportunities. In essence such forestry indicative strategies are designed to attract forestry investment into areas which are ecologically suited to tree growth and are not constrained by major conservation issues. The other objective is to protect from afforestation areas which are less suited to tree growth and contain sensitive land resources of conservation value. Strathclyde Regional Council has produced a forestry indicative strategy and an extract for the area bordering the Firth of Clyde is shown in Figure 4.7. As already stated, information on land capability for agriculture and forestry is an important input to the sieve mapping process, but many other issues concerned with nature conservation, landscape quality, archaeology and maintenance of existing agriculture are integral to the analysis. The end result is the identification of *preferred areas* (land which is likely to be attractive to forestry investment and where there are no major constraining interests), *potential areas* (land which is suited for forestry development, but where there is at least one sensitive issue), *sensitive areas* (land on which the number, intensity or complexity of issues is such as to make it extremely sensitive to forestry development), and *unsuitable areas* (land which is physically unsuited for producing tree crops and existing built up areas).

The development of forestry indicative strategies demonstrates that data from land capability surveys need to be incorporated in an integrated approach to land use planning. The results from land capability assessment should not be taken in

themselves as recommendations for land use, a point stressed by Flaherty and Smit (1982) who instead recommend the evaluation of land resources which incorporates demands, requirements or goals of societies including those of the future. Consideration of land ownership patterns is another crucial component in any attempt to predict or control land use. Flaherty and Smit (1982) argue that neither land classification schemes nor overlay techniques can provide a means of analysing competing land uses. Instead they suggest that mathematical programming procedures can deal with the issues associated with allocating limited resources between competing activities assuming specified conditions and goals are stated. One great advantage of using such techniques is that assumptions and goals can readily be varied by changing the constraints. The evaluation of alternative options is an essential ingredient of current land evaluation methodology and the adoption of a modelling approach achieves such an objective.

The inflexible nature of a land capability classification poses other limitations in terms of application to changing issues. The alternative approach is to store all the base land resource data

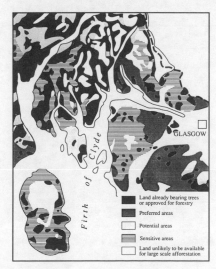

Figure 4.7 A forestry indicative strategy for part of Strathclyde Region in Scotland
(source: Strathclyde Regional Council)

in a geographical information system (GIS) and to carry out processing according to specific requirements. The advantages of flexibility, ease of data update, modification of classification or scoring methods according to specific objectives and the ability to integrate with modelling all become evident. Such computer processing requires that assumptions in the land evaluation procedure have to be explicit. As one example, Hammond and Walker (1984) describe a simple computerized method for capability analysis based on grid data. Scores are awarded for each land characteristic in every cell and then an overall capability can be determined based on the weighted means of the component scores.

Despite these clear merits of a GIS and

modelling approach to land evaluation, there is still a need for the publication of land capability maps. Such maps have the advantages of ready access to many people and furthermore can be readily understood by non-specialists. It was never intended that they should be the basis for land use prescription, but rather that they indicate on ecological criteria the degree of constraint to one or more land uses. As already demonstrated, land capability can also provide in certain situations first estimates of expected yields as well as land values. Land use planning at the strategic level is all about drawing lines on maps; land classification is thus essential and land capability maps must constitute one important dataset.

5

Methodology of Land Evaluation

In a review of the use of soil survey data for quantitative land evaluation, Bouma (1989) states that soil surveys in many countries have reached a crucial stage. He believes that increasing emphasis will be given to the interpretation and application of soil survey data. In the western world this can be explained by the availability now of many soil maps and associated data. The rise in public concern with planning issues in rural areas along with policy objectives of land use diversification mean that sophisticated techniques of land evaluation will be increasingly used in order to identify alternative land uses. In the developing world as discussed in Chapter 1, the evaluation of land resources will increasingly become a key process to agricultural planning. Basic questions such as the type of soil or agricultural land grade may still be asked, but the clear trend is towards the posing of more difficult questions which require more complex analysis. Current concerns in land evaluation are with applications of GIS technology, and modelling and spatial analysis. However, such developments are dependent upon an underlying land evaluation methodology. In the late 1960s the world Food and Agricultural Organization (FAO) realized the need for some kind of methodological framework to aid agricultural planning. Another problem was that many countries had or were in the process of developing their own land evaluation methods and the FAO feared that major problems of information exchange would result. In 1970 a working group was established to develop a Framework for Land Evaluation and the result was a publication with this title. For simplification this document will be referred to as the FAO *Framework*. Readers are encouraged to examine the full document (FAO 1976) as well as some of the preliminary publications (Brinkman and Smyth 1973; FAO 1975). The aims of this chapter are to outline the nature of the FAO *Framework*, give some examples of its application, review developments in the methodology since the original publication in 1976 and to discuss the parametric approach to land evaluation using indices of land quality.

Before attention turns to the FAO *Framework*, it is useful to note the contrasts between the *Framework* and schemes of land capability as discussed in Chapter 4. The *Framework* is a set of methodological guidelines rather than a classification system and the intention is for it to be applied to any land evaluation project in any environmental situation and at any scale. It is an ecological analysis whereby land mapping units are evaluated with reference to defined land utilization types which also incorporate social, economic and technological descriptions. In contrast land capability schemes have as their main focus the grading of land according to degree of limitation posed to one or more land uses; assumptions are made about such aspects as level of management, farming structure and location. Kanyanda (1988) provides an interesting report on the experience in Zimbabwe when he compares the well established land capability system there with the FAO *Framework*. The capability system was evolved from the USDA one and has as its main objectives the identification of the most intensive land uses which do not result in erosion as well as to indicate land use limitations. The Zimbabwe capability scheme grades land from Classes I to VIII and is thus a simple practical system, easy both to use and apply.

Zimbabwe land capability	FAO guidelines
Refers to a range of uses (broad agricultural base)	Refers to tightly defined use or practice
Limited — adopted for commercial areas especially for conservation purposes	Flexible
Applicable for farm planning (scales larger than 1:15,000)	Applicable at all levels of scale from national to farm planning
Employs the use of land characteristics which remain more or less constant over time	Employs the use of land qualities with their dynamic nature
Can be executed by a single worker eg agricultural officers	Calls for a multi-disciplinary approach (pedologist, agronomist, economist, etc)
More concern for conservation of land resources and less concern for people	Takes into account land and socio-economic settings
A physical classification with no proper economic considerations	Allows for an economic and social analysis
Not a productivity rating for specific crops	Rating for specific crops and farming systems

Table 5.1 Comparison of the Zimbabwe Land Capability system with the FAO Framework

(source: Kanyanda 1988: 38)

The main disadvantages of the system are its limited nature, lack of flexibility, overemphasis on limitations rather than on potentials, and its design for commercial farming systems. Thus according to Kanyanda (1988), difficulties arise in trying to apply the system to peasant areas. He contrasts the objectives and assumptions of the Zimbabwe Land Capability scheme with those of the FAO *Framework* (Table 5.1).

5.1 The FAO *Framework for Land Evaluation*

In the early discussions about this *Framework*, much thought was given to the definition of land. The conclusion was to view land as *areas* composed of physical characteristics which are or may be of importance to human use. The objective of land evaluation is to judge the value of an area for defined purposes. The evaluation need not be limited to assessment of environmental characteristics, but the exercise can be extended to the point where the economic viability, the social consequences and the environmental impact of the proposals are also analysed. In addition to referring to what is meant by land, any introductory outline of the *Framework* needs to list the six principles upon which the approach is based. These are as follows.

1 *Land suitability is assessed and classified in relation to particular land uses*
This principle recognizes that land uses vary in their requirements so that a field highly suitable for one crop may be unsuitable for another.

2 *Evaluation requires a comparison of the inputs and outputs needed on different types of land*
This could be done by comparing the costs of production with the economic returns of different types of land.

3 *A multidisciplinary approach is required*
Contributions from such specialists as crop ecologists, agronomists, pedologists, climatologists, economists and sociologists are necessary in order to make a comprehensive and sound assessment of land suitability for a specified use.

4 *The evaluation is made with careful reference to the physical, economic and social context of the area under investigation*
It is fairly obvious that any land use proposals have to be realistic for an area. It is important to take into account such factors as cost of available labour and skills of the labour force.

5 *Suitability refers to use on a sustained basis*
The proposed use of land must not result in its degradation through processes such as wind erosion, water erosion or salinization.

6 *Different kinds of land use are compared on a simple economic basis*
This means that the suitability for each use is assessed by comparing the value of the goods produced to the cost of production.

It should be evident that there is a certain degree of overlap between these principles. Fundamental to the approach is the identification of relevant land uses in the first instance in order that the evaluation procedure is executed with specific reference to these land uses. This means that the land use requirements of the various land uses have to be established and then the actual characteristics of land mapping units have to be assessed in terms of how well they can provide optimum conditions. This comparison of land mapping units with land use requirements is known as matching.

The *Framework* (FAO 1976: 1–2) proposes that a land evaluation project should be able to answer questions of the following type.

How is the land currently managed, and what will happen if present practices remain unchanged?
What improvements in management practices, within the present use, are possible?
What other uses of land are physically possible and economically and socially relevant?
Which of these uses offer possibilities of sustained production or other benefits?

What adverse effects, physical, economic or social, are associated with each use?
What recurrent inputs are necessary to bring about the desired production and minimize the adverse effects?
What are the benefits of each form of land use?

Various steps are necessary in order for the evaluation exercise to answer these types of questions. In the first instance there must be the clear statement on the objective of the study. Selection of relevant land characteristics (attributes of land which can be measured or estimated) is possible only within the context of a particular study. Two strategies are possible according to the FAO *Framework* once the objectives of a study are stated (Figure 5.1). In the two-stage approach, an economic and social analysis may follow on from a qualitative land classification, while in the parallel approach the analysis of the land and land use relationships proceeds concurrently with economic and social analysis. Land use capability assessment is an example of the first stage of the two-stage approach, and as demonstrated in Chapter 4, the results can be directly incorporated into planning decisions. Alternatively, the results of a capability

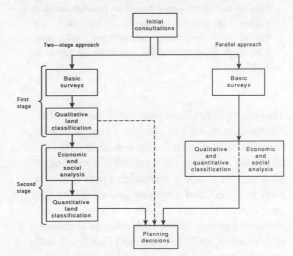

Figure 5.1 Two-stage and parallel approaches to land evaluation
(source: FAO 1976: 6)

assessment can be subjected to an economic and social analysis to provide a quantitative land classification which can be applied to planning, In essence the evaluation of land suitability means the assessment of land mapping units with respect to defined land uses which are physically, economically and socially appropriate to the area. An ecological basis to the evaluation methodology is thus clear and in order to discuss such a methodology, consideration needs to be given to the use of various terms.

A distinction is made between a *major kind of land use* and a *land utilization type*; the former is a major subdivision of rural land use, for example pasture land, forestry or recreation, whilst the latter is a type of land use described in greater detail (FAO 1976). It must be stressed that land utilization types are described not only in terms of actual land uses or crops, but also with reference to such factors as type of market orientation (subsistence or commercial production), capital intensity, labour intensity, technology employed, infrastructure requirements, size and configuration of land holdings, land tenure and income levels. An example of a land utilization type as given in the FAO *Framework* (1976: 10) is

> rainfed annual cropping based on groundnuts with subsistence maize, by small holders with low capital resources, using cattle-drawn implements, with high labour intensity, on freehold farms of 5–10 ha.

This example neatly demonstrates the type of information needed to describe a land utilization type. It is also possible to have *multiple land utilization types* (two different uses co-existing together, for example recreational uses within forestry areas), and *compound land utilization types* (areas treated as one utilization type though various forms of use may follow each other in sequence – a crop rotation, or different areas of land within the same functional unit – a mixed farm with both arable and pasture).

The task of detailed land evaluation is to assess land mapping units in terms of land utilization types. This makes it necessary to recognize *land qualities* which are 'a component regime of the physical land conditions with a specific influence on land use performance' (Beek 1977: 147). Four types of land qualities can be described for exemplification (Beek and Bennema 1972; FAO 1976; Beek 1978):
land qualities related to

1 *Plant growth* (for example, availability of water, nutrients, oxygen for root growth, etc).

2 *Animal growth* (for example, hardships due to climate, endemic pests and diseases, nutritive value of grazing land, etc).

3 *Forest growth* – natural or plantations (annual increments of timber species – influenced by many qualities listed under (1), pests and diseases, types and quantities of indigenous timber species, etc).

4 *Management and inputs* (terrain factors affecting mechanization, construction and maintenance of roads, size of potential management units, etc).

Land qualities are dynamic attributes and are assessed from land characteristics which are land attributes that can be measured or estimated. A distinction is made between *single land qualities* such as moisture content, depth to water-table, and *compound land qualities*, which cannot be directly measured (Bouma et al 1986). There is increasing attention being given to the quantitative determination of compound land qualities by using transfer functions which mathematically relate several land characteristics to the qualities.

The distinction between land qualities and land characteristics can be demonstrated by considering erosional hazard. This problem is best assessed by analysis of the interaction of such factors as slope length, slope angle, rainfall intensity, and soil permeability etc, rather than by the individual assessment of these component characteristics. Thus the FAO *Framework* recommends that land units should be evaluated for land uses in terms of land qualities. To achieve such evaluation, *diagnostic criteria* are recognized; these may be land qualities or characteristics, but they are known to have a clear effect on land use output or potential. Critical values are associated with diagnostic criteria so that suitability classes can be defined. The FAO *Framework* considers the land quality 'oxygen available in the root zone' to demonstrate the nature of diagnostic criteria. In this case, soil mottling, soil drainage class or natural vegetation could be used as diagnostic criteria for assessing oxygen availability.

Details of twenty-five land qualities relevant to rainfed agriculture are described in *Guidelines: Land Evaluation for Rainfed Agriculture* (FAO 1984a). It is instructive to select from this report one land quality, moisture availability, as an illustration of the assessment procedure. Crops obviously require moisture for growth and there is also the potential hazard of drought to cause severe stress and ultimate death. Soil moisture stress progressively increases from field capacity towards the permanent wilting point, but crops vary in their response to such stress. Thus there are different critical soil moisture thresholds at which crops begin to suffer. Also the severity of soil moisture stress depends on the development stage of the crop, for example maize is particularly sensitive during the flowering stage. In a similar way crops vary in their response to drought; some crops can withstand substantial periods of drought, for example sisal and pineapple, while others, for example maize, are sensitive to short spells of drought. Also, the timing of drought incidence is critical; the occurrence of drought during crop emergence and establishment poses the greatest danger. These considerations have led to three subdivisions of the land quality *moisture availability* being defined, total moisture, critical periods and drought hazard.

Total moisture

A wide variety of methods is available for estimating moisture availability and some of these can be summarized as follows:

1   mean annual rainfall, or rainfall during the growing season

2   specified confidence limits for either of the above, eg 75 or 90 per cent probability of exceeding specified rainfall amounts

3   moisture surplus, estimated indirectly and approximately from values of monthly temperature and rainfall, related by a formula

4   moisture surplus calculated as excess of rainfall over potential evapotranspiration, for the whole year, the growing season, or confidence limits for either of these

5   the duration of the agro-climatic growing period

6   modelling rain-soil-crop moisture balance over the growing period.

(source: FAO 1984a: 82–3)

FAO recommend another method based on the calculation of the *relative evapotranspiration deficit*, $(1 - ETa/ETm)$, where ETa is the actual evapotranspiration (the amount of water actually transpired by the crop plus that evaporated from the soil surface), and ETm is the maximum evapotranspiration (the amount of water that would be transpired by the crop, plus that evaporated from the soil surface, if available water was not limiting). The relative evaporation deficit gives an index of soil moisture availability ranging from 0.0 (no deficiency) to 1.0 (total crop failure). In order to calculate this index, data are required on rainfall, potential evapotranspiration, temperature, and coefficients for individual crops (Doorenbos and Kassam 1979).

Critical periods

If it is known that the crop under evaluation is particularly sensitive to soil moisture stress during a particular period, then the relative evapotranspiration deficit can be calculated for that period.

Drought

A measure of drought incidence is the percentage

of years when crops fail due to lack of moisture. Thus annual variations in soil moisture budget need to be assessed in relation to the demands and tolerances of individual crops. The recommended method by FAO is to calculate the probability that soil moisture will fall to wilting point over the whole of the rooting zone during the growing season or, in the case of perennials, during the whole year. The sequence of steps is as follows:

1 For each crop under consideration, estimate (a) the rooting depth, (b) the number of days that it can survive without available moisture.

2 For each soil type present, estimate the soil moisture storage, calculated as available moisture multiplied by thickness of horizons, within the rooting zone.

3 Estimate the rate of potential evapotranspiration, which is the rate of soil moisture depletion in the absence of rainfall.

4 By combining steps (2) and (3), followed by step (1), obtain the number of days without rainfall that would cause drought damage to the crop.

5 From daily, weekly or ten-day rainfall data, construct frequency duration curves, giving the probability of occurrence of dry spells of given duration, (a dry spell is taken as a period which has cumulatively less than some assumed amount of rain, eg 10 mm).

6 By combining steps (4) and (5), estimate the probability of occurrence of drought damage.
(source: FAO 1984a: 84)

In the actual assessment of moisture availability, many difficulties are posed as a result of data availability and quality. In practice the selected method of assessment is strongly influenced by data considerations. As an example it is interesting to summarize part of a land evaluation procedure in Kenya. The Kenya Soil Survey have devised methods for rating land qualities relevant to conditions in that country; Kiome and Weeda (1988) explain the rating for availability of water. The objective is to rate this land quality according to water availability during crop growing seasons. This requires calculation of a water balance on a monthly basis. Data inputs are P (average monthly

rainfall total) and C (surface runoff coefficient). If runoff data are unavailable, reference has to be made to tables in order to obtain estimate values of C based on vegetation or land use, slope angle and soil textural class. Effective rainfall (EP) is calculated as follows:

$$EP = (1 - C) P$$

Climatological statistics are used to determine potential evaporation (Eo) and thus potential evapotranspiration (Et) is calculated by the simple equation:

$$Et = 0.66 Eo$$

For simplification, differences in Et according to crop are ignored. Easily available water (in the pF range 2.3 to 3.7) can be determined from soil moisture retention curves, but normally estimates are necessarily based on textural class, for example a silt loam has 8 cm/m of easily available water compared with 5 cm/m for a sand. In order to calculate the total easily available water, note needs to be taken of effective rooting depth of crops (the depth to which the crop develops 80 per cent of its roots) as well as the actual depth of the soil. Thus a crop with an effective rooting depth of 50 cm in a silt loam has a total easily available soil moisture storage capacity (S) of 40 mm. Kiome and Weeda (1988: 106) define the criteria for good plant growth as follows:

(EP + dS)/Et	>1	one full growing month
(EP + dS)/Et	0.5–1	sufficient water for germination and ripening of annual crops. For perennial crops, reduced growth and counted as 0.5 of a growing month.
(EP + dS)/Et	<0.5	insufficient for growth

EP: effective rainfall (rainfall − runoff)
dS: surplus soil water balance from previous month, up to the maximum soil moisture storage capacity for the relevant soil depth class
Et: potential evapotranspiration

As a result, monthly water balances can be

calculated and then the number of months with sufficient water for crop growth. Soil moisture surplus from one month is clearly carried over to the next month. In this Kenya method, it is this number of months with adequate water which is used to rate the land quality availability of water.

As already indicated, quantitative land evaluation depends upon the quantitative assessment of land qualities. Use is being made, especially in The Netherlands, of two types of transfer functions: continuous transfer functions (based on mathematical equations) and class transfer functions (based on class data, for example soil mapping units). Determinations of soil moisture retention curves and thus available water are very time consuming; thus there is much merit in being able to predict available water from standard soil analytical results, for example percentages of different particle size classes as well as organic content. Bouma et al (1986) give an example of a continuous transfer function for moisture retention:

$$\theta(h = -100 \text{ cm}) = b_0 + b_1.H + b_2.L + b_3.S_v$$

where $\theta(h = -100 \text{ cm})$ is the water content at a pressure head of -100 cm, b_0 through b_3 are coefficients determined by regression analysis, H is per cent organic matter, L is per cent clay and S_v is 1/dry bulk density. Other examples of continuous transfer functions are given by Breeuwsma et al (1986) in their study dealing with evaluating soils in terms of application of fertilizers, liquid manures and sludges. The three critical land qualities are travel time of water from the soil surface to the water-table, cation exchange capacity (CEC) and phosphate sorption capacity (PSC). CEC is of importance to cation movement, especially heavy metal cations, and PSC is of particular importance to high rates of application of liquid manure. As an example, equations are given for predicting CEC from measures of organic matter and clay contents while PSC is determined from measures of oxalate extractable iron and aluminium. The study of Breeuwsma et al (1986) is of particular interest because following the calculation of the land qualities, results were processed and plotted in a geographical information system (GIS).

An important issue associated with land qualities

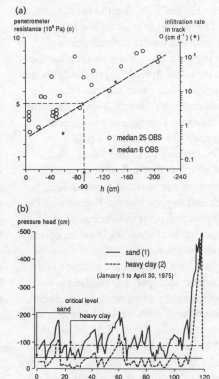

Figure 5.2 (a) The relationship between penetrometer resistance of surface soil and pressure head (h)
(b) A plot of calculated pressure heads for a depth of 5 cm below the surface in a heavy clay and a sand; these values are used to determine the number of days with adequate trafficability in any given period, using threshold levels of the pressure head as independently determined for both soils
(source: Bouma and van Lanen 1987: 109)

is the identification of threshold values. By this is meant the recognition of land quality values of significance to particular types of land use or management. As an example, Bouma and van Lanen (1987) consider the relationship between soil moisture tension and penetrometer resistance. Penetrometer resistance increases linearly with increasing soil moisture suction (Figure 5.2a). They propose for a heavy clay soil a threshold penetrometer resistance value of $5 \times 10^5 Pa$ which corresponds to a threshold pressure head of -90 cm. This value is used to identify periods of trafficability, times at which land can be cultivated, as illustrated in Figure 5.2b. A different threshold pressure head (−40 cm) is selected for a sand and the results in terms of longer trafficability are illustrated on Figure 5.2b. As can be seen for the period 1 January to 30 April 1975, trafficability was possible throughout these four months except for a few days, a pattern very different from trafficability on the heavy clay soil. Bouma and van Lanen (1987) emphasize the importance of field observations in deriving threshold values, the implication of which is that soil surveyors will increasingly have to use portable tensiometers, penetrometers and oxygen meters. Bouma and van Lanen (1987) conclude that the derivation of threshold values for land qualities is an important function for future soil surveys.

Once relevant land qualities are selected and assessed, the next critical stage in the land evaluation process is to compare the requirements of land utilization types with the land qualities of individual mapping units. Figure 5.1 outlines the steps involved in land evaluation, but gives no indication of the ecological foundation. To illustrate how land use considerations are incorporated into land evaluation methodology, the procedure as described in the *Framework* is summarized (Figure 5.3). The first step labelled 'initial consultations' describes the preparatory work – a clear statement on the objectives of a study, the intensity and scale of the survey and the type of suitability classification to be used. At an early stage of the project the 'kinds of land use' must be specified, though some modification of these may be necessary as the evaluation project proceeds. From a list of land uses considered relevant to the area, the required environmental conditions for each land use are determined. This may sound a straightforward task, but many difficulties are quickly encountered since detailed information on requirements of many land uses is inadequate. Practically all land evaluation projects require some type of physical resource survey – commonly a soil or soil-landform survey, and the results are presented in the form of 'land mapping units' backed with appropriate analytical data. From this basic land inventory, 'land qualities' can be postulated by a knowledge of the appropriate land use requirements and limitations. This

'comparison of land use with land' is the key process in land evaluation since this is the crucial stage where the land and land use data, as well as economic and social information, are brought together and analysed.

The results of this lead to the suitability classification. As already mentioned, the term *matching* is used to describe the process by which the requirements of land uses are compared with land conditions in order to estimate or predict land use performance. Beek (1975) draws a distinction between qualitative and quantitative matching; with the former, a conversion table allows each utilization type to be graded in terms of degree of limitation posed by particular land characteristics. An example is given in Table 5.2 in which degrees of depth limitations are defined for four different land utilization types. With quantitative matching, the assessment of land qualities is based on measured cause and effect relationships between the qualities and the land utilization types. As indicated on Figure 5.3, the comparison of land use with land may not only consist of matching, but also include economic and social analysis and perhaps a study of environmental impact. On the basis of such comparison, a land suitability classification scheme can be defined which allows the presentation of results.

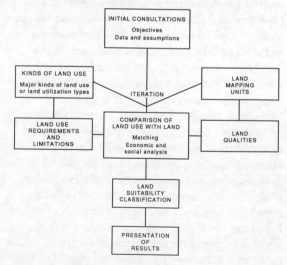

Figure 5.3 Processes involved in land evaluation (from FAO 1976: 28)

Land utilization type	Degree of depth limitations					
	0	1	2	3	4
Cereals and pasture (rainfed)	>90	40–90	20–40	10–20	0–10
Annual root crops (rainfed)	>90	60–90	40–60	0–40	0–40
Deep-rooting perennials	>150	90–150	50–90	20–50	0–20
Irrigated farming	>150	100–150	50–90	20–50	0–20

Table 5.2 Guidelines for the interpretation of soil depth limitations for selected land utilization types (depth values in cm)

(from FAO 1975: 113)

Figure 5.3 is a concise summary of the evaluation procedure, but in practice many difficulties are encountered. The methodology assumes that specific requirements of land uses or crops are known, but detailed information on the optimum requirements of land uses or crops is often inadequate. Information of the type illustrated in Table 5.2 is needed on individual crops for a wide range of properties and an example is given in Table 5.3. Such information is often difficult to acquire, but Dent and Young (1981) provide a useful summary of climatic, soil and water requirements for a range of crops and in addition list land qualities relevant to rainfed agriculture and how these can be estimated from land characteristics. Land qualities are of crucial importance since they provide the link between land resource inventories and land evaluation results. Only relevant land qualities should be assessed so that they can be used to grade land into the output or suitability classes appropriate to the land utilization type. This is best achieved by a land quality/output analysis whereby the outputs in the form of yields, or erosional losses, for example, are correlated with land qualities. In order to carry out such statistical analysis, data from many field experiments are necessary and in practice, such information is not usually available.

The FAO *Framework* describes a scheme for land suitability classification. The term *suitability* is used rather than *capability* to avoid any potential confusion with the American and other capability schemes. According to the FAO *Framework*, 'land

suitability is the fitness of a given tract of land for a defined use' (1976: 17). Four levels of decreasing generalization are defined:

1 *Land suitability orders*   reflecting kinds of suitability
2 *Land suitability classes*   reflecting degrees of suitability within orders
3 *Land suitability subclasses*   reflecting kinds of limitation, or main kinds of improvement measures required, within classes
4 *Land suitability units*   reflecting minor differences in required management within subclasses.
(FAO 1976: 17)

At the order level, an assessment is made as to whether the land is suitable or not for sustained use of the kind under consideration and yielding benefits which justify the inputs. Classes indicate the degree of suitability – up to a maximum of five, though three is common. Examples of classes are highly suitable (S1), moderately suitable (S2) and marginally suitable (S3). Subclasses indicate the type of limitation and are represented by lower-case letters, for example S2m for suitable land of class 2 with the specific limitation of moisture availability. The most detailed level in the classification structure is the unit. Units obviously are of the same class and subclass, but they vary in their production characteristics or in minor aspects of their management requirements. This level in the structure is designed to be applicable to individual farms. Units are indicated by arabic numbers, eg

Crop requirement			Factor rating			
Land quality	Diagnostic factor	Unit	Highly suitable S1	Moderately suitable S2	Marginally suitable S3	Not suitable NS
Oxygen availability	Soil drainage class	Class	Well drained Excessive	Moderately well drained	Imperfectly drained	Poorly Very poorly drained
Rooting conditions	Effective soil depth	cm	>120	50–120	30–50	<30
Nutrient availability	Soil reaction	pH	5.5–7.5	4.8–5.5 and 7.5–8.0	4.5–4.8 and 8.0–8.5	<4.5 and >8.5

Table 5.3 An example of the FAO method for identification and presentation of crop (sorghum) requirements

(source: FAO 1984a: 62)

S2m−1, S2m−2, etc. Reference must be made to the *Framework* for full details; Dent and Young (1981) give much practical guidance on the implementation of the *Framework* while FAO (1984a) has published guidelines for field workers.

According to the two-stage approach (Figure 5.1), the results from the first stage are then subjected to detailed economic analysis in the second stage. Some simple quantitative economic analysis should normally be integral to the first stage evaluation in order to ensure that the proposed kinds of land use or land utilization types are both ecologically and economically viable. For the second stage detailed economic analysis constitutes the major part of the land evaluation process. It is beyond the scope of this book to describe such analytical procedures, but it is important to repeat one of the underlying principles behind land evaluation following the FAO *Framework*. Evaluation requires a comparison of the inputs and outputs needed on different types of land; in economic terms this means a comparison between input costs and output returns. Inputs result from such costs as fertilizers, seed, chemical sprays, tractor fuel, capital borrowing, machinery depreciation, labour; outputs refer to the value of produce. Financial data on such inputs and outputs

are the basis of gross margin analysis which indicates the profitability of individual farming systems. In essence this is obtained by subtracting a farmer's gross annual income from the production costs and overheads. The resultant gross margin can then be calculated per hectare and used for defining land suitability classes. Such an analytical procedure is satisfactory if substantial capital investment is not involved.

Where substantial investment is necessary during the initial period of a project, account needs to be taken of increased production over a number of years. This is especially the case in irrigation schemes or where extensive drainage is necessary. A form of economic analysis called cash-flow accounting is used in order to set initial investment costs against future benefits. If an initial investment of £P gains compound interest at an annual rate of r (expressed as a decimal, eg 0.05 for 5 per cent), then the investment will be worth $£P(1 + r)^n$ after n years. Expenditure and benefits could thus be calculated for different years by adding compound interest and converting the results to a common date for financial comparison. Dent and Young (1981) explain the advantages of carrying out this type of calculation in reverse since investment costs are incurred near the beginning of a project; this process is described as discounting. For example, expenditure of £100 in year 2 would require an initial investment of £90.90 if the discount rate (r) is 0.1 (10 per cent). In general terms a cost incurred or benefit of £P in n years' time has a present value V equal to $£P/(1 + r)^n$. The value $1/(1 + r)^n$ is called the discount factor and is used to multiply any actual cost or benefit to give present or initial value. This method is described and exemplified by Dent and Young (1981) and their approach is also followed by FAO (1984a). Dent and Young (1981) explain how after an initial period in a land development project, annual costs tend to level out. Suppose this situation arises after the fifth year of a project, then tables of cumulative discount factors can be used for the following six to twenty years. Discounted cash-flow analysis is only applicable to production units such as farms; as already stated it is a method for setting initial investment against future benefits over periods usually ranging from twenty to thirty years.

The FAO (1984a) *Guidelines* conclude their description of economic land evaluation by stressing three critical aspects. First, the results are time dependent since they vary according to prices and costs. Thus fluctuations in results are inevitable. Second, an economic analysis does not provide a single quantitative measure of land suitability since results vary according to mode of expression, for example per hectare or per capita, as well as according to different land uses. The results are also dependent upon choice of discount rate and assumed length of project. Third, the nature of assumptions incorporated into economic analysis has a significant effect on the results. This is particularly relevant to social cost-benefit analysis of capital investment in developing countries where family labour is common and there is a lack of a free market. The FAO (1984a) *Guidelines* propose that economic analysis should not be the sole criterion of land suitability. As an example, subsistence crop production may not be viable in financial terms, but may well be justified in terms of meeting the food needs of local people. Where substantial investment is proposed, then there is a stronger case for justifying economic land evaluation.

In summary, a land suitability report based on the FAO *Framework* should include details of the following:

1   the context, in a physical, social and economic sense; background data and assumptions in the approach

2   description of land utilization types or major kinds of land use

3   maps, tables and textual matter showing degrees of suitability of land mapping units

4   management and improvement specifications for each land utilization type with respect to each kind of land use considered, together with the diagnostic criteria

5   economic and social analysis of the consequences of the various kinds of land use considered

6   the basic data and maps from which the evaluation was obtained

7   information on the reliability of the suitability estimates.

Manual procedures both for construction of matching tables or transfer functions and for calculation of suitability are time-consuming and liable to error; thus there are merits for automating the FAO procedures. Rossiter (1990) stresses the value in having a microcomputer program which would act as a framework or shell, but would allow investigators to customize their own land evaluation projects. As a result an Automated Land Evaluation System (ALES) has been devised in Cornell University (Rossiter and van Wambeke 1989). ALES can perform both physical and economic suitability analyses. For the former, land qualities are determined directly or indirectly and then the investigator builds decision rules regarding land use constraints in order to assign mapping units to land suitability classes. For the economic evaluation, gross margins are predicted for each land unit for each land use. A frequent criticism of economic land evaluation is that the results are quickly outdated; the outstanding merit of using ALES is that any new or revised economic parameters can be input and the evaluation repeated with results almost instantly available.

Van Lanen and Wopereis (1991) demonstrate how an expert system was developed within ALES in order to evaluate land in The Netherlands for receiving animal manure in the form of injected slurry. Slurry on arable land is required by Dutch law to be ploughed into the soil by the day following surface application. For grassland, ploughing is not possible and thus there is the need to evaluate such land for receiving slurry by injection. The analytical approach was to define a land utilization type comprising intensively grazed and managed dairy farms on which slurry was applied by injection. This is achieved by the use of specialized farm equipment which injects slurry at a depth of 15 to 20 cm and 50 cm apart. Central to the use of ALES was the design of decision trees to evaluate suitability for three land qualities, accessibility and physical quality of topsoil and subsoil. Modifications to the decision trees were necessary as a result of information collected from interviews. One merit of using ALES is the ability to change decision rules easily. The overall results revealed that in several of the major grassland regions in The Netherlands, less than 40 per cent of the land is suited to slurry injection. Thus the Dutch government has not incorporated slurry application by injection into environmental legislation.

5.2 Applications of the FAO *Framework for Land Evaluation*

An introductory example of using the FAO *Framework for Land Evaluation* is provided by Chinene and Shitumbanuma (1988) who evaluate the suitability of a proposed state farm of 600 ha in northern Zambia for commonly grown crops. A semi-detailed soil survey was carried out at 1:30,000 resulting in six mapping units though the marshland unit was, for obvious reasons, excluded from the land evaluation. As already described, land evaluation requires the specification of land qualities which have to be assessed on the basis of

defined characteristics. In this study land qualities are assessed on the basis of soil survey data; climatic data are excluded because a rainfed growing period of about 160 days usually occurs and this is adequate for most arable crops. For the study area in Zambia there was an absence of data on the performance of the land use types in relation to the qualities; thus the authors rate on a subjective basis each quality from 1 (the best) to 5 (the worst). These qualities can be summarized as follows.

1 *Soil moisture availability*
assessed from determination of bulk density and moisture content at -10 kPa and -1500 kPa (these are moisture contents corresponding to field capacity and permanent wilting point, thus the difference gives available moisture)

2 *Oxygen supply to the root zone*
assessed from the soil drainage classes

3 *Availability of plant nutrients*
assessed from measures of cation exchange capacity, pH, base saturation, and phosphate fixation; component scores were awarded for these four analytical properties and then summed to provide an overall rating for this land quality

4 *Erodibility*
assessed during field survey.

Following the definition of ratings for individual land qualities, minimum rating scores for land qualities had to be specified according to the different land uses (Table 5.4). The final step involved the matching of land qualities as they occurred within individual mapping units in order to grade land suitability.

An example of the results is given in Table 5.5. Tables such as this one are usually based on the principle of limiting factors – the suitability class is determined by the rating of the most severe limitation. However, this rule should not be applied in every case; as an example, Chinene and Shitumbanuma (1988) consider that severe problems of nutrient availability can be overcome if a high level of farm management with high inputs can be assumed. This Zambian example of applying the FAO *Framework* neatly summarizes the

Land use	Moisture availability	Oxygen availability	Nutrient availability	Erodibility
Maize	1	2	2	2
Sorghum	2	2	3	2
Cassava	3	2	4	2
Coffee	2	2	2	2

Table 5.4 Minimum requirements of land uses in terms of ratings for optimum productivity; a rating of 1 indicates the best and 5 the worst

(source: Chinene and Shitumbanuma 1988: 180)

approach though the authors highlight the qualitative and subjective aspects of their methodology. In particular they stress the importance of incorporating crop yields. Such an approach is discussed for Zambia by Kalima and Veldkamp (1987). They define two groups of land qualities – climatic land qualities (CLQ) and edaphic land qualities (EDQ). The first group are based on climatic characteristics of importance to agriculture while the second depend upon one or more soil characteristics. They rate these qualities separately depending upon the requirements of the land utilization types. This is achieved by determining yield reduction as a percentage from what the land utilization type could produce under reference or ideal conditions. For example, a yield reduction figure of 70 per cent means that in a particular locality a crop achieves only 30 per cent of the yield obtained in an area with optimal growth conditions. As a result the rating of land qualities can be done on a quantitative basis and an example is shown in Table 5.6. Following the rating of individual land qualities for different land utilization types, matching is possible to permit the assessment of mapping units in terms of their suitability. Again the principle of limiting factors is the basis to overall assessment. Chinene (1991) reports the full development of the Zambian Land Evaluation System (ZLES) for rainfed agriculture which evolved from the earlier study by Kalima and Veldkamp (1987). A total of twenty-one land qualities and seventy-four subqualities are defined with subqualities described as intermediate between land qualities and land characteristics. In this system the land quality which results in the lowest

suitability class determines the overall result. Predicted yields per suitability class for different crops were compared with data as obtained from four locations. With the exception of one area, significant correlations were found between expected and actual yields, though the range of actual yields was greater than anticipated, reflecting variation in management within defined input levels.

One of the early studies to use the FAO *Framework* is by Young and Goldsmith (1977) who carried out a survey of the Dedza area in central Malawi, a region of 1935 km^2. A conventional soil survey, supported by extensive use of aerial photographs, permitted the identification of seven soil landscapes. These landscapes were evaluated in terms of six major kinds of land use: arable farming for annual crops, the cultivation of perennial (tree and shrub) crops, livestock production, extraction from natural woodlands, forestry plantations and a combination of tourism with production. The description of these major kinds of land use included economic data on net income per hectare and per capita. Young and Goldsmith next decided upon relevant land qualities for each of the major kinds of land use. The process of matching was then possible by comparing the requirements of the land use with the land qualities of the mapping units. The availability of the economic data meant that a quantitative suitability evaluation could be made with results expressed in terms of net income per hectare and per capita according to land utilization type and soil management unit. The results indicated that the greatest margins per hectare could come from mixed farming, annual

	Land uses			
Mapping unit	Maize	Sorghum	Cassava	Coffee
1	S3f	S2f	S1	S3f
2	S3f	S2f	S1	S3f
3	S3f	S2f	S1	S3f
4	No,f	S3o,f	S2o,f	No,f
5	No,f	No,f	No,f	No,f

Table 5.5 Suitability classification of the mapping units on Musaba state farm, Zambia

S1   Highly suitable
S2   Moderately suitable
S3   Marginally suitable
N   Currently not suitable
f   Fertility limitation
o   Oxygen availability limitation

(source: Chinene and Shitumbanuma 1988: 181)

ELQ Al-sat (%) (30–50 cm depth)	0–10	10–20	20–40	40–60	60–80	80–100
ELQ rating	0	1	2	3	4	5
Crop						
Sunflower	0	0–50	100	100	100	100
LUT rating	1	2	4	4	4	4
Maize, tobacco and millet	0	0	0–50	75–87.5	100	100
LUT rating	1	1	2	3	4	4
Cassava, groundnut and sorghum	0	0	0	0–50	75–87.5	100
LUT rating	0	1	1	2	3	4
Rice	0	0	0	0	0–50	50–75
LUT rating	0	0	1	1	2	3

Table 5.6 Yield reduction from reference yields as caused by aluminium toxicity in Zambia; the reduction is expressed as a percentage and is used to rate the land utilization type according to degree of yield limitation

(source: Kalima and Veldkamp 1987: 51)

crops with livestock, followed by forest plantations and arable farming without livestock. A loss was estimated from the cultivation of coffee, but such a result is highly dependent upon the price of coffee which was very variable during the 1970s. The results of the quantitative economic analysis are added to the results of the qualitative evaluation so that land use alternatives can be suggested for each soil management unit. These alternatives are physically practicable, economically viable and environmentally sound. The study by Young and Goldsmith is particularly interesting because it carries out both a qualitative, mainly physical, and a quantitative, chiefly economic, analysis. Their reaction to economic analysis within land evaluation is one of caution since they recognize the short-term validity of such research. As discussed near the end of section 5.1, prices and costs can quickly change thus invalidating results, and Young and Goldsmith also encountered difficulties in making assumptions about discount rates.

5.3 Parametric indices of land quality

It can be readily appreciated that there is considerable merit in being able to produce a number, ranging say from 1 to 100, which expresses land suitability for one or more specific crops. Points or scores are awarded to individual land resource factors and then an overall score is determined by the use of particular models, for example additive or multiplicative ones whereby component points are added or multiplied respectively. As an example of an additive system, Fenton et al (1971) describes how soil mapping units in Iowa were rated. Yield information is a critical input whereby soils and weather conditions are first assessed in terms of suitability for growing corn. Areas with the most favoured conditions are given a corn suitability rating of 100. The guidelines specify a range of slope and precipitation factors each with component ratings; deviations from ideal land conditions are assessed by subtracting the component ratings from the ideal score of 100. Fenton (1975) describes how each soil mapping unit in Iowa was assigned a ratings and the results are shown to produce an equitable assessment of land for taxation purposes. The best known multiplicative index as developed by Storie in California also had taxation as its main application. The ratings can be calculated as follows:

$$SIR = (A_1 \times A_2 \times A_3 \ldots A_n)/100^{(n-1)}$$

where A_1, A_2, A_3, ... A_n are values of land individual properties on the scale 0 to 100.

The original Storie index rating as developed in the 1930s was obtained by multiplying ratings for soil profile, texture of surface soil, and modifying factors such as drainage, slope or alkalinity. The system has been gradually revised over the years with slope being introduced as a separate factor, with more classes of soil profile development and with slight changes in scores for component variables (Storie 1976). The system has been widely modified and applied; for example, Leamy (1974) describes how it has been used in New Zealand to aid farm valuation assessment and Lal (1989) applies a modified Storie index to rate the productivity of sixty-four benchmark soils in India. In this Indian study, the rating is on the basis of four factors, characteristics of the physical profile, surface texture, slope and a group of other factors such as drainage, nutrient status and erosion. Correlation coefficients are computed between the Storie index and the yield of wheat under current ($r = 0.67$) and improved ($r = 0.57$) management levels.

One problem with a multiplicative approach is that if component scores are very low or high, they have a considerable impact on the overall index. This problem is minimized by taking a cube root as demonstrated by Koreleski (1988) who describes adaptations of the Storie index rating to Poland. A habitat fertility (HF) index is defined as

$$HF = (S \times W \times C)^{0.33}$$

where S is soil quality, W water conditions and C climatic conditions. Soil quality is assessed according to thickness, organic content, pH and amount of skeletal material. The water term indicates yield risk according to soil moisture deficiency whilst the climate term is based on duration of growing period. Koreleski (1988) points out that the form of the equation makes the habitat fertility index largely dependent upon the value of the poorest factor, an appropriate emphasis given the principle of limiting factors. Results from applying the index are shown to correlate highly with land productivity ($r = 0.89$); furthermore the index can be combined with measures of cultivation difficulty and erosion hazard to provide measures of overall agricultural habitat value.

In a review of the development of soil ratings in the USA, Huddleston (1984) distinguishes between inductive and deductive ratings. The former are based on inferences about the effects of individual soil and weather characteristics on crop growth and yield. The approach is based on knowledge of the crop growing requirements and factors influencing yield; as already explained, formulae based on addition, multiplication or some other function are used to combine the scores into one overall index. As an example of the inductive approach, reference is made to the model for evaluating productivity as described by Larson (1987). The basis to this model is that soil is a major determinant in crop yield; the model does not incorporate variations in climate, management and crop varieties and is applicable to deep-rooted crops in north central USA. The productivity index (PI) is calculated as follows:

$$PI = \sum_{i=1}^{r}(A_i \times C_i \times D_i \times WF_i)$$

where A_i is sufficiency of available water capacity, C_i is sufficiency of bulk density, D_i is sufficiency of pH, WF_i is a weighting factor and r is the number of horizons in the rooting zone. As can be seen from the model, nutrient status is not directly considered limiting to crop growth though soil pH provides some indication. Bulk density is used as an estimate of resistance to root development. Each of the three key variables, available water, bulk density and pH, is scored in the range 0.0 (most limiting) to 1.0 (no limitation). Larson (1987) provides tables, graphs and equations for the determination of these component scores which are then multiplied and summed for the horizons in the rooting zone, 1 m of soil depth. The success of the model in predicting yield is indicated by regression of corn yield on the productivity index accounting for 71 per cent of the variability in yield. Integral to the study was an investigation of the effect of soil erosion on the productivity index and thus on longer term yield. If there are subsoil conditions less favourable to crop growth than above, then the effect of erosion is to bring such limitations nearer the surface. This is achieved by the use of a weighting factor which varies according to the amount of eroded soil. As a result productivity indices can be predicted according to severity of

soil loss. Such figures could be input into a geographical information system in order to display future productivity patterns under different land conservation strategies.

With the deductive approach, the analysis begins with yield data. The simplest approach would be to correlate soil types with yield of particular crops in an area and then to rate such soils on that basis. Anderson and Robert (1987) describe how this type of approach has been refined in Minnesota through the use of a geographical information system. The calculation of a crop equivalent rating goes beyond the simple correlation of yield with soils. In Minnesota the aim was to provide weighted average productivity ratings for land management units. Special software had to be developed in order to retrieve soil survey data on a land ownership basis. Each ownership parcel is masked in the GIS so that component soils are identified and measured. Crop equivalent ratings can then be computed for each management unit with local adjustments for such characteristics as climate, drainage and land under pasture and forest. The results are used to assist with decisions on which areas of land should be retained for agriculture; guidance on land sale or rental value is also possible.

The deductive approach is well represented in soil potential ratings which form part of a system of agricultural land evaluation and site assessment (LESA), devised by the US Department of Agriculture (Wright 1984; McCormack and Stocking 1986; McCormack 1987). In the land capability approach to land evaluation discussed in Chapter 4, emphasis is given to assessing the degree of limitation or hazard to land use. In contrast, soil potential ratings give emphasis to the positive attributes of soil and on the performance of soils. As McCormack and Stocking (1986: 38) state, 'soil potential (ratings) adopt the positive stance of emphasising solutions and not problems, the best use of land and not avoidance, and optimal performance not failure'. The overall objectives of LESA are to assist with agricultural land protection programmes. There are two parts in the LESA process, first an assessment of soils in terms of their quality, and second, evaluation of individual sites with reference to their economic and social viability as farmland. The assessment of the soil potential index (SPI) is integral to the first process. The index is a measure of the soil's relative quality and is defined as follows:

SPI = P − (CM + CL)

The performance standard (P) or yield in an area is based on the most productive soils which are managed at minimum cost while preventing soil degradation and off-site damage. The aim of setting the performance standard is to be able to identify areas of suboptimal performance with reference to yield or which would incur considerable cost in tackling soil limitations. Corrective measures (CM) are an index of additional costs above the defined standard as given for P. Continuing limitations (CL) may well exist after corrective measures, for example costs associated with the maintenance of terraces or land drainage. McCormack and Stocking (1986: 39) provide a useful summary of the steps necessary to establish soil performance ratings:

1   definition of performance standard (P)

2   determination of the relevant soil and site conditions

3   specification of degree of limitation posed by each soil and site condition; this is to help farmers and local experts to understand the management needs of soil

4   effects of use are specified

5   corrective measures (CM) are then identified for each of the soil and site conditions for which they are needed; local experts must judge which corrective measures are selected based on the costs of alternatives

6   the costs of the selected corrective measures are agreed and an index system places corrective measures and continuing limitations on the same basis as performance standard

7   continuing limitations are similarly determined and indexed

8   calculation of soil performance indices for land areas.

This procedure is aided by the use of worksheets as demonstrated in a test of the method in Zimbabwe (Stocking and McCormack 1986). Particular advantages of the method are the incorporation of data from farmers and local experts, and the approach is based on an economic analysis of performance.

A key problem in devising an index of land quality or performance is the identification and appropriate weighting of controlling factors. Following the deductive approach, yield data for one or more crops in an area can be assembled alongside data on a range of climatic and soil properties. Then it is possible to determine using statistical analysis which factors most explain variation in yield. Such factors can then be incorporated into an index which provides a very good indicator of yield. As an example of an investigation using this approach, Gbadegesin (1987) describes how soils in a study area in south west Nigeria were rated for maize production. The project was based on a sample of fifty farms, all 1 ha in size, and on each, the same variety of maize was grown under very similar fertilizer and management strategies. Maize yield was determined over a two-year period using sample quadrats; in addition, four vegetative parameters of maize were measured as surrogate yield variables; for one example, number of leaves per plant. Soil samples from the top 20 cm were analysed for twenty different physical and chemical properties. As a result, Gbadegesin (1987) was able to investigate the correlation between the five yield parameters and the twenty soil properties. The use of a stepwise regression technique allowed the identification of the independent variables which contributed most to the variation in yield. The outstanding result was that organic matter contributed 58.4 per cent overall to maize yield followed by 13.1 per cent for available moisture; figures for the remaining factors were below 2.4 per cent. Thus a soil rating for predicting maize yield was proposed on the basis of the organic matter content and available moisture with these factors being weighted 4.5 to 1.0. Such weightings are demonstrated in a scoring system for these two soil properties. The scores as given in Table 5.7 are

Organic matter		Available moisture	
Range of values (%)	Score	Range of values (%)	Score
<0.50	4.5	<5	1
0.51–1.00	9.0	6–10	2
1.01–1.50	13.5	11–15	3
1.51–2.00	18.0	16–20	4
2.01–2.50	22.5	21–25	5
>2.51	27.0	>26	6

Table 5.7 Scales for scoring organic matter content and available moisture; scores are multiplied to provide an overall index for indicating maize productivity in south-western Nigeria

(source: Gbadegesin 1987: 36)

multiplied to provide an index of soil productivity for maize in this region. The results can be provided in the form of indices, as predictions of actual yield figures or in a simple productivity classification. The merit of this type of approach is that there can be confidence in the index values given that the method is based on soil-yield correlations. A disadvantage of the approach is that the results will not necessarily be applicable to other crops and other areas. Further calibration of indices would be necessary.

McRae and Burnham (1981) list fifteen advantages and disadvantages of parametric systems. Among the advantages are

1 Once a rating is defined as a function of specific attributes, its determination becomes straightforward, quantitative and consistent.

2 Ratings are measured on an interval or continuous scale which makes the calculation of average figures for farms or fields an easy operation;

furthermore, such a scale is preferred to an ordinal one if the rating is to be used for taxation purposes.

3 The approach is flexible; if sensible results are not obtained, then changes can be made to the included variables and their mathematical association.

Some disadvantages that can be highlighted include

1 There is a danger that a parametric system can be taken to give an objective measure; in fact, there is a high degree of subjectivity involved in the selection of variables and how the function is expressed.

2 A crucial problem is interaction of factors and how combinations affect land use or crop yield.

3 Ratings developed and tested in one area for a specific crop may have to be redefined for application in other localities.

6

Soil Survey Interpretation

For many years in countries with soil survey institutes, a common attitude was that soil survey was a basic and fundamental activity. The prime objective was to produce soil maps with associated reports and the application of such data was primarily left to other users. The assumption was that data from general purpose soil surveys were applicable to a wide variety of land use planning and management issues. During the 1960s and 1970s there was a growing realization, especially in such countries as the USA, Canada and The Netherlands, that soil survey had to be justified on its usefulness rather than just on its resource inventory value. As Beckett (1981: 289) states,

> when soil surveys are justified publicly it is on their practical value, so they should be assessed on their practical value too, that is on how the existence of a soil map and its supporting documentation has enabled the members of a community to conduct their activities more economically, or to do more things for the same investment, than they could have done without it.

This led him to discuss the costs and benefits of soil surveys. Survey costs are closely related to required precision and specificity; for any one area, beyond a certain level of survey precision, costs markedly increase in relation to the additional information produced. The assessment of soil survey benefits is difficult, one problem being that for any area, there always exists some knowledge on soil properties in advance of a survey. The relationship between survey costs and increase in profit resultant from such information is shown in Figure 6.1; in practice there are many difficulties associated with determining the precise form of these curves. Also, it should be noted that subdivision of landscapes beyond a certain size threshold is irrelevant, for example to farmers, who require minimum sizes of fields for efficient management.

6.1 Multi-purpose soil survey interpretation

The interpretation of larger scale soil maps for land use planning purposes can be illustrated by an extract from a Dutch 1:25,000 map. Dekkers et al (1972) demonstrate how the 1:25,000 soil map for the area of Brouwhuis to the immediate south-east of Helmond can assist with the structure-plan for Helmond. As can be seen from Figure 6.2a, the soils are derived from non-calcareous sands. The soils are classified using the system specified by de

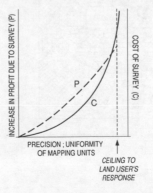

Figure 6.1 Graphs showing the increase in cost (C) of soil survey according to level of required precision and the increase in profit (P) through better land management as a result of the soil data (source: Beckett 1981: 310)

(a) SOILS

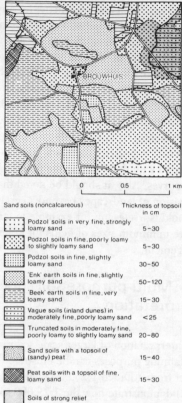

```
0        0.5        1 km
```

Sand soils (noncalcareous)	Thickness of topsoil in cm
Podzol soils in very fine, strongly loamy sand	5–30
Podzol soils in fine, poorly loamy to slightly loamy sand	5–30
Podzol soils in fine, slightly loamy sand	30–50
'Enk' earth soils in fine, slightly loamy sand	50–120
'Beek' earth soils in fine, very loamy sand	15–30
Vague soils (inland dunes) in moderately fine, poorly loamy sand	<25
Truncated soils in moderately fine, poorly loamy to slightly loamy sand	20–80
Sand soils with a topsoil of (sandy) peat	15–40
Peat soils with a topsoil of fine, loamy sand	15–30
Soils of strong relief	

(b) WATER–TABLE CLASSES

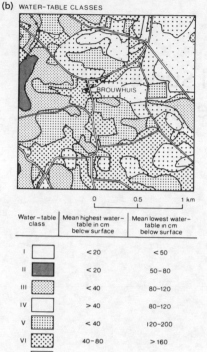

```
0        0.5        1 km
```

Water–table class	Mean highest water–table in cm below surface	Mean lowest water–table in cm below surface
I	< 20	< 50
II	< 20	50–80
III	< 40	80–120
IV	> 40	80–120
V	< 40	120–200
VI	40–80	>160
VII	80–120	>200
VIII	>120	>200

Water–table classes I & IV do not occur in this area

(c) SUITABILITY FOR ARABLE

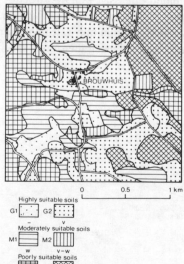

```
0        0.5        1 km
```

Highly suitable soils
G1 [ ]   G2 [ ]
              v
Moderately suitable soils
M1 [ ]   M2 [ ]
   w   v–w
Poorly suitable soils
W1 [ ]   W2 [ ]
   ww   vv

G1 ⟶ G2 decreasing suitability in class G

Limitations

None/slight	Moderate	Severe	Description
–	v	vv	moisture deficiency
–	w	ww	excess of water

(d) SUITABILITY FOR PASTURE

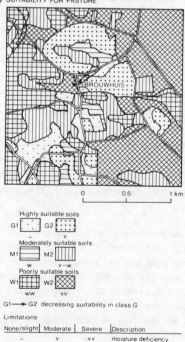

```
0        0.5        1 km
```

Highly suitable soils
G1 [ ]   G2 [ ]
              v
Moderately suitable soils
M1 [ ]   M2 [ ]
   w   v–w
Poorly suitable soils
W1 [ ]   W2 [ ]
   ww   vv

G1 ⟶ G2 decreasing suitability in class G

Limitations

None/slight	Moderate	Severe	Description
–	v	vv	moisture deficiency
–	w	ww	excess of water

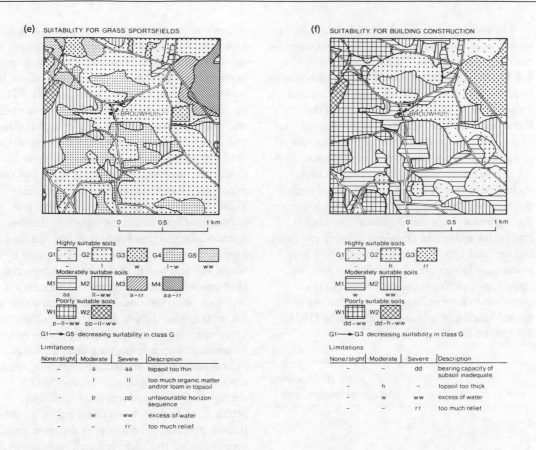

Figure 6.2 Soil and suitability maps for the vicinity of Brouwhuis: (a) soil map; (b) groundwater table map; (c) suitability for arable land; (d) suitability for pasture; (e) suitability for grass sportsfields; (f) suitability for building construction (from Dekkers et al 1972)

Bakker and Schelling (1966), but for present purposes mention need be made only of the soil mapping units on Figure 6.2a. Three types of podzols are present and these vary in texture and thickness of topsoil. 'Beek' earth soils display hydromorphic characteristics – for example a non-aerated subsoil within a depth of 80 cm. The fact that 'vague' soils are associated with inland dunes should make their nature clear. Dutch soil maps at the scale of 1:50,000 and 1:25,000 also show water-table classes, but this information has been excluded from Figure 6.2a since it is given in

Figure 6.2b. The depth and fluctuation of the water-table are of marked importance and the water-table classes are defined in the key to Figure 6.2b. Figures 6.2c–f illustrate the interpretation of basic soil data for different land uses. As can be seen, the soils are assessed in the first instance as high, moderately or poorly suitable for the particular land uses. These three categories are further subdivided according to degree of suitability, with information also being given on the type of certain limitations as well as an indication as to whether such limitations are moderate or severe.

The preceding description of Figures 6.2c–f in no way considered how the soils were evaluated for the different land uses. Fairly clearly, the soil conditions had to be evaluated with reference to the requirements of the particular uses. Haans and van Lynden (1978) and Haans (1978) stress the importance of assessment factors in the execution of this task. These are particular combinations of soil properties relevant to specific land uses. Table 6.1 lists seven assessment factors and indicates their varying relevance to five land uses. Fertility status rather surprisingly is relevant only to forestry, the argument being that differences in natural fertility for arable and grassland farming can easily be corrected by application of fertilizers. These assessment factors are usually divided into five classes; an example is the subdivision of the assessment factor drainage status according to mean highest groundwater depth. Haans (1978) defines the classes as follows:

Class	Mean highest groundwater depth below surface (cm)
1	>80
2	40–80
3	25–40
4	15–25
5	<15

The next step is a comparison of specific land use requirements with the classes of the assessment factors. For example, the significance of these various drainage status classes could be assessed with reference to arable farming or to specific crops. This is usually achieved by informal procedures based on experience and empirical research. Some combination of classes would usually be possible and then groupings of classes from several assessment factors would define overall suitability classes (highly, moderately and poorly suited as in Figures 6.2c–f).

This Dutch example exemplifies how a series of interpretative maps can be derived from the original soil survey. Clearly such interpretation requires evaluative skills as well as an appreciation of the nature and properties of the soil mapping units. One common criticism of soil maps is that highly detailed legends and associated terminology provide barriers to comprehension by non-specialists. In a survey of soil maps users, Msanya et al (1987) recommend that soil reports should provide better and easier guidance on their use as well as clearer and simpler legends. Many soil survey reports in the USA and Australia have achieved these objectives, illustrated for example in the soil survey report for Orange County in New York state (USDA 1981). On the inside cover is a clear summary of how to use the report. In the first instance, the soil unit symbols for the required area have to be identified; such location is eased by the use of soil unit boundaries printed on an aerial photograph mosaic. Summaries of the relevant soil series can then be consulted, but of particular value for encouraging the use of the report is the comprehensive set of tables giving a wide range of information for each mapping unit. Tables give information on soil productivity, yields of different crops and pasture, guidance on woodland management and productivity (for example, problems of erosion, seedling mortality, windthrow hazard, potential productivity of common trees, recommended trees for planting), recreational development (in particular degree of limitations for camp areas, picnic areas, playgrounds, paths, trails and golf fairways), wildlife habitat potentials, building site development (problems likely to be encountered with shallow excavations, dwellings without basements, dwellings with basements, small commercial buildings, local roads and lawns), sanitary facilities (problems of septic tanks and sanitary landfill), sources of construction material (roadfill, sand, gravel and topsoil), water management (issues associated for example with ponds, reservoirs, embankments, waterways and terraces), engineering properties (engineering classification, particle size fractions and Atterberg limits), and physical and chemical properties (permeability, available water capacity, soil reaction, shrink-swell potential and soil erodibility). In summary a tremendous amount of soil interpretation is presented in the survey report and readers are guided to their particular requirements.

Assessment factor	Land use					*Table 6.1 Assessment factors and their use for various land uses in The Netherlands*
	Arable farming	Grassland	Forestry	Recreation development	Low rise	
Drainage	+	+	+	+	+	
Moisture supply	+	+	+	+		
Bearing capacity topsoil		+		+		
Workability	+					
Structural stability	+					
Bearing capacity subsoil					+	
Fertility status			+			

(from Haans 1978)

6.2   Soil survey interpretation for housing development

When one or more houses are to be constructed, then the interpretation of soil maps can prove to be of benefit. Soil information can be used to predict a range of problems which can be encountered in the construction of new houses and provision of associated services. Unfavourable soil conditions can cause problems in terms of structural stability of buildings, corrosion of concrete pipes, failure of septic tanks, pollution from rubbish being buried in unsuitable soils, or cracking and pot-holing of roads laid on poorly suited soils. The results of soil surveys in proposed new urban areas can be of great assistance in identifying special design precautions which will be necessary to deal with specific problems. The cost-benefit of such surveys in the USA has been estimated by Klingebiel (1966) as 1 to 100. A similar cost-benefit ratio has been obtained for Massachusetts where Zayach (1973) has calculated that there is more than a $110 benefit for each dollar invested in a soil survey. Given the very clear cost advantages, it is perhaps surprising that soil surveys geared to urban needs have not become very common, though there are a few clear exceptions. In Britain, the tradition is for urban areas to be excluded from routine soil survey.

Credit must be given to the North Americans for first encouraging the application of soil data to urban needs. Pettry and Coleman (1973) describe how Fairfax County in Virginia was the first to employ a soil scientist for multipurpose soil interpretation on a county basis and had an urban soil programme in operation by 1955. Support for such a programme resulted from mistakes being made in selecting sites for schools and other buildings where extra costs were incurred through ignorance of soil conditions. Widespread publicity of these avoidable costly ventures clearly indicated the need for an urban soil programme. Failure of septic tank systems also caused much alarm; some of these tanks had been installed in soils with seasonally high water-tables. The urban soil survey was to locate areas with seasonally high water-tables and soils which were too shallow, as well as areas subject to periodic flooding. Pettry and Coleman (1973) also describe the problems of structural stability to illustrate the value of urban soil survey in Fairfax County. Unusually deep snow occurred during the winter of 1961, and landslides followed the ultimate thaw. It was discovered that these slides occurred on soils of similar type, namely where marine clays were overlain by sandy soils. Such soils were mapped and building permits are issued only if a method of minimizing slide susceptibility has been designed. Soils which expand in volume according to moisture content

Soil characteristics and properties	Engineering properties	
Undisturbed soil		
Texture, pH drainage	Metal conduit corrosion potential	
Drainage, texture, kind of clay, organic matter content	Suitability for road subgrades	
Drainage, texture, kind of clay, organic matter content	Suitability for building foundations	
Drainage, texture	Susceptibility to frost action	
Texture, kind of clay, organic matter content	Shrink–swell potential	
Texture and structure of B and C horizons	Percolation rate	
Surface texture, permeability, drainage	Trafficability (non-vehicular)	
Disturbed soil		
Texture, kind of clay, organic matter content	Suitability as fill material	
Texture, organic matter content	Suitability as lining for water storage units	
Texture, organic matter content	Suitability as topsoil	

Table 6.2 List of engineering properties of soils which can be deduced from soil properties and characteristics

(from Bartelli 1962: 101)

(certain clays, for example montmorillonite), also pose problems for the construction and maintenance of roads.

Bartelli (1962) argues that contractors, farmers, area planners, engineers and home owners ought to have the basic results of a soil survey and in a form appropriate to their needs. He demonstrates how detailed soil maps can be used to predict certain constructional difficulties. Table 6.2 shows which engineering properties can be deduced from soil characteristics. The table also indicates how soil surveys can aid with locating fill material for foundations of buildings or roads. Of course, such interpretation from soil maps does not mean that more detailed site investigations and laboratory analyses will not be necessary; however, as Bartelli (1962) stresses, the interpretation of soil maps allows the recognition of troublesome soils at an earlier stage.

The application of soil information is best illustrated by discussion of an example and a study by Murtha and Reid (1976) of the Townsville area in Queensland, Australia. Townsville is situated at the mouth of the Ross river (Figure 6.3). To the north and west of this river a featureless plain, broken only by a few inselbergs, gradually rises to piedmont slopes which fringe the base of a coastal scarp. The land to the south of the Ross river is dominated by various mountain ranges with limited areas of alluvium along the major streams. A littoral zone composed of mangroves, mudflats, salt pan and beach ridges is extensive.

The soil maps accompanying the report are at a scale of 1:100,000 and an extract at a reduced scale is given in Figure 6.3. Eight broad soil groups are present; groups 1 to 5, subdivided into more detailed units, and groups 6, 7 and 8. The soils of the eight broad classes can be summarized as follows.

1   Cracking clays

These soils expand and contract according to moisture content. The grey clays (1a) occur chiefly

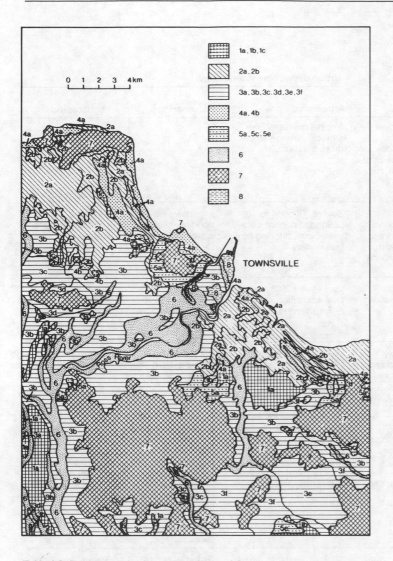

Scale: 0 1 2 3 4km

Legend:
- 1a, 1b, 1c
- 2a, 2b
- 3a, 3b, 3c, 3d, 3e, 3f
- 4a, 4b
- 5a, 5c, 5e
- 6
- 7
- 8

TOWNSVILLE

Figure 6.3 Soils in the Townsville area, Australia; the legend is provided in Table Figure 6.3 (from Murtha and Reid 1976)

Table 6.3 Description of soils present in Figure 6.3

Dominant soil		Major characteristics of dominant soil	Urban development limitations		
Map unit	GSG*		Agronomic	Engineering	Landscaping
1a	Grey clay.	Gilgaied cracking clays with dark grey, strong medium blocky-structured heavy clay A horizons over grey or grey-brown, coarse blocky heavy clay subsoils. May be mottled at depth.	Severe. Low fertility, slow internal drainage, poor surface drainage (water ponded in depressions).	Expansive clays cause problems in all engineering applications. Surface drainage very slow.	Severe limitations, difficult plant establishment, few adapted species, limited access due to water ponding.
1b·	Black.	Very dark grey to black, strong fine blocky-structured	Moderately severe. Low to moderate fertility, slow	As above.	As above.

Table 6.3 Continued

Dominant soil		Major characteristics of dominant soil	Urban development limitations		
Map unit	GSG*		Agronomic	Engineering	Landscaping
		heavy clay A horizons over dark grey or black coarse blocky heavy clay subsoils. Moderate to high amounts of carbonate below 30 cm. may become grey or brown at depth.	internal drainage. Poor surface drainage where there are gilgai.		
1c	Grey clay.	Dark grey heavy clay A horizons with prominent gley mottles. Subsoils are dark grey heavy clays with prominent olive-grey, orange and red mottles.	Severe. Flooded for prolonged periods each year. Some flooding by tidal waters.	Expansive clays, flooding, shallow water table.	As above, some flooding by saline waters.
2a	Solonchak.	Dark brown saline muds under mangroves and saline clays on salt pan.	Very severe. Subject to tidal inundation, very high salt levels.	Subject to tidal inundation and storm surge. Low bearing strength for foundations.	Limited to salt-tolerant species.
2b	Solodic.	Thin (10–15 cm) strongly bleached silty loam or clay loam A horizons over dark grey or dark grey-brown heavy clays, strongly mottled yellow and red at depth.	Very severe. High salt levels due to occasional tidal inundation, low fertility.	Subject to tidal flooding. Permanent water table at about 60 cm.	As above.
3a	Solodized solonetz.	Very thin (15 cm) strongly bleached silty or sandy loam A horizons with abrupt change to brownish or greyish heavy clay B horizons. Alkaline reaction in subsoils.	Very severe. Moderate to high salt and very high exchangeable sodium in the clay B horizon. Very poor physical properties, low fertility, impeded drainage.	B horizon clays have very poor drainage and low bearing capacity when wet. They are highly dispersive with adverse chemical properties causing corrosion of underground services.	Very severe limitations, few adapted species, soil amelioration difficult and costly.
3b	Solodic, solodized solonetz.	Very thin (2–5 cm), light grey-brown sandy or silty loam A_1 over very strongly bleached sandy loam A_2. Total A horizon depth ranges from 15 to 25 cm. Abrupt change to whole coloured or mottled grey or yellowish heavy clay B horizons with alkaline reaction.	Severe. Similar to 3a, but as depth of A horizon increases severity of limitation lessens.	As for 3a but as depth of A horizon increases, engineering properties improve. May be some expansive clays in the B horizon and many are highly dispersive.	Severe limitations, impeded drainage, limited species adapatability. Need to import loam for lawn establishment.
3c	Solodic.	As above but total A horizon depth exceeds 25 cm, may be as deep s 80 cm.	Moderate, as for 3b.	As for 3b.	As above but limitations are less severe.
3d	Solodic.	Thin (3–5 cm), light grey-brown sandy or silty loam A_1 horizon over very strongly bleached sandy loam A_2 horizon. Abrupt change to motled light grey or	Moderate, as for 3b, but internal drainage is better.	As for 3b, but limitations less severe.	As for 3c.

Table 6.3 Continued

Dominant soil		Major characteristics of dominant soil	Urban development limitations		
Map unit	GSG*		Agronomic	Engineering	Landscaping
		yellow-grey heavy clay B horizons with mildly to strongly acid reaction.			
3e	Red podzolic.	Dark brown or dark grey-bbrown loam A₁ and slightly paler loam A₂ horizon. Abrupt change at 10–15 cm to dark red, strong blocky-structured medium clay B horizon grading to weathered parent material from 60 cm.	No major limitations, reasonable nutrient levels and fair internal drainage.	Nil.	Few limitations. Many adapted species available.
3f	Yellow and brown podzolic.	Dark grey-brown sandy loam to loam A₁ over weakly developed A₂ horizon. Abrupt change at 15–25 cm to yellow or brown, medium to heavy clay, blocky-structured B horizons.	No major limitations. Moderate fertility levels, internal drainage may be slow but not excessively impeded.	May encounter some of the problems associated with units 3a and 3b, but much less severe.	As above.
4a	Siliceous sand.	Uniform coarse sands. Profile development dependent on age of beach ridge.	Severe. Extremely low fertility, very low water-holding capacity.	Subject to erosion and storm surge on beach fronts, may require compaction and stabilisation for foundations.	Limited by low water availability. No restriction with supplementary irrigation and fertilization.
4b	Siliceous sand.	Uniform sands with deep, very strongly bleached A₂ horizon and mottled pale yellow, colour B horizon.	Severe. Very low fertility, low water-holding capcity.	May require compaction and stabilisation for foundations.	As above.
5a	Red earth.	Grey-brown loamy sand to sandy loam A horizons overlying red or yellowish red sandy clay loam to sandy clay B horizons.	Moderate fertility levels, no major limitations.	No restrictions.	Very few restrictions, large range of adapted species.
5c	Yellow earth.	Grey-brown loamy sand or sandy loam A horizons overlying yellow or reddish yellow sandy clay loam B horizons which grade to coarse gravels below 1–1.5 cm.	Moderate to low fertility, no other restrictions.	No restrictions.	Few restrictions, large range of adapted species, fertilisation advisable.
5e	Yellow earth.	Dark grey-brown loak A₁ horizons overlying mottled yellow-brown and red clay loam to light clay D horizons at about 60–80 cm.	Moderate to low fertility, impeded drainage at 60–80 cm.	Sink hole and gilgai microrelief, expansive clay D horizons cause problems with road and building foundations.	As for unit 3c.
6	Alluvial soil, red earth.	Wide range of soils on younger alluvium.	No restrictions other than likelihood of flooding.	Subject to flooding, otherwise no restrictions.	No restriction of species, use may be restricted due to flooding.
7		Very wide range of soils on hilly and mountainous terrain. All soils have gravel on surface and	Similar soils would be expected to behave as in the groups already	Instability of steep slopes a major problem. Difficult to	

Table 6.3 Continued

Dominant soil	Major characteristics of dominant soil	Urban development limitations		
Map unit GSG*		Agronomic	Engineering	Landscaping
	throughout the profile. Rock outcrop is common.	described.	provide access and services in many areas.	
8	Reclaimed land including dumping of domestic and industrial wastes and sand pumping.		Subsidence of fill material and in many areas the low bearing strength of underlying mangrove mud is a major restriction.	Little restriction although adequate top dressing needed for lawn establishment.
*GSG Great Soil Group			Degree of severity followed by major limiting factors. In soil with marked texture contrast unified classification of both surface soil and subsoil is given.	

(from Murtha and Reid 1976)

on the main plains and on the backswamp deposits of the larger alluvial plains; they are furthermore distinguished by the presence of gilgai microrelief. The black earths (1b) occur on alluvium of more local origin, on floodplains of smaller streams and on gentle piedmont slopes of areas of basic parent materials. Gilgai microrelief is only weakly developed. Mapping unit 1c is also a grey clay, but areas mapped in this category are subject to prolonged flooding.

2 Saline soils

The salinity of these soils is due to flooding by tidal waters. Soil of the solonchak mapping unit (2a) corresponds to areas of mangroves and saline clays on salt pans. Map unit 2b has a sodic soil as the dominant type; this soil is subject to occasional tidal inundation and is further distinguished by a strongly bleached A horizon overlying dark mottled clays.

3 Duplex soils

This group encompasses a range of soils, but their common characteristic is the contrast in texture between the upper and lower horizons. Map units 3a, 3b, 3c and 3d are dominated by solodic and solodized solonetz soils. These soils are distinguished by a thin, light grey-brown sandy loam A_1 horizon overlying a very strongly bleached A_2 horizon of the same texture. In marked contrast the B horizon has a clay texture. Solodic and solonetz soils both have saline C horizons and the former has a distinctive blocky structure in the B horizon compared with a strong columnar one for the latter. A solodized solonetz soil has a strongly bleached A_2 horizon which is not present in a solonetz. The detailed differences between map units 3a, 3b, 3c and 3d can be appreciated by study of Table 6.3 which accompanies Figure 6.3. The other duplex soils are the red podzolics for map unit 3e and then yellow and brown podzolics for map unit 3f. These soils are all acidic and have a contrast in texture from loams or sandy loams in the upper horizons to clays in the B horizons. They all have weakly developed bleached A_2 horizons and are subdivided according to the colour of the B horizons.

4   Uniform sands

These soils occur on the beach ridges fringing the coastline and on older stranded beach ridges. Soils in map unit 4a are formed on coarse siliceous sand and the degree of profile development depends upon the age of the beach ridges. With soils in map unit 4b, also formed on siliceous sand, a bleached A_2 horizon is very evident as well as a mottled B horizon. These soils occur on the older beach ridges.

5   Gradational soils

The duplex soils exhibit a sharp contrast in texture within their profiles while gradational soils vary more gradually in texture. In the map extract only map units 5a (red earth) and 5c and 5e (yellow earths) are represented. A red earth with an unbleached A_2 horizon present, has an acid reaction throughout the profile. The texture grades from loamy sand or sandy loam in the A_1 horizon, to sandy clay loam or light sandy clay in the B horizon. Red earths occur on piedmont slopes. The yellow earth soils are more variable than the red earths, though they have similar general profiles. Fairly obviously the B horizons of the red earths are dominantly red compared with yellow for the yellow earths.

6   Soils on young alluvium

This soil group is included in one map unit (6) and embraces a wide range of soils developed on young alluvial floodplains, terraces and levees. The most extensive areas of soils mapped in this unit flank the lower course of the Ross river.

7   Soils on hilly and mountainous terrain

This map unit includes a very wide range of soils, though they all have gravel on their surfaces and throughout their profiles. Extensive areas of map unit 7 occur to the immediate south of Townsville (Mount Stuart Range) and to the south-east (Muntalunga Range).

8   Reclaimed land

Soils in this unit are man-made through the dumping of domestic and industrial wastes and sand pumping. They occur within and adjacent to the urban area of Townsville.

The major characteristics of the dominant soil in each map unit are summarized in Table 6.3 which accompanies Figure 6.3. The table also gives a summary of agronomic, engineering and landscaping limitations posed by soil conditions, information which Murtha and Reid (1976) consider useful for the planning of urban development. These three groups of limitations merit consideration in turn.

In an assessment of soils for urban planning, information on soil suitability for agriculture is usually included so that new urban areas are not zoned on the better land. This is not the case for the Townsville area since the surrounding region is low-density beef cattle grazing land. Thus Murtha and Reid (1976) recommend that the urban development should take place on soils with lesser agronomic limitations since these soils generally have fewer engineering limitations. In detail they suggest that the better types of soil should be reserved for public facilities or open space with urban development planned around these more favoured soils, though some soils pose so many difficulties that they should not be used for any purpose.

Table 6.3 also illustrates how information relevant to engineering can be presented according to soil map units. Structural failures and foundation failures of roads occur in Townsville because of a lack of understanding of soil physical and chemical properties (Murtha and Reid 1976). Particular problems are posed by the expansive clays (map unit 1) which also occur in the duplex soils (map unit 3). Soils with moderate to high levels of exchangeable sodium in their subsoils are highly susceptible to gully erosion. This implies that great care must be taken with the design of drains. Road failures can often be linked with the use of highly dispersive clays as foundation materials. Galvanized steel pipes corrode very rapidly if laid in the B horizons of the duplex soils which are highly alkaline, have moderate to high exchangeable sodium, and moderate salt levels. Some subsoils of the cracking clays and duplex groups also have significant sulphate contents which would indicate a concrete corrosion problem. Again, remedial measures are necessary.

The final column in Table 6.3 shows how soil information can be interpreted to aid the landscaping of the Townsville area where the tasks are to stabilize the foreshore, plant trees along streets, improve school yards and playgrounds, plant parks and develop urban gardens. The foreshore problem is essentially one of trying to stabilize the movement of sand by establishing sand-binding plants. Along the highways and streets, the need is to select trees, shrubs or plants appropriate to soil conditions. For example, the duplex soils pose severe limitations to tree growth. Soils which are poorly drained and which puddle under heavy pedestrian usage when wet, are unsuitable for school yards and playgrounds unless expensive treatment is undertaken. Murtha and Reid (1976) also argue that the home gardener can save money and effort if he knows the potential or limitations of his soil type with reference to plants or shrubs.

For a Canadian example of a soil survey geared specifically to urban planning, reference is made to the study by Lindsay et al (1973). In this case, a soil survey programme was integral to the planning process for Mill Woods, a suburb of Edmonton in Alberta. Soils were examined on a grid pattern with the distance between grid intersections being 76.2 m. Soil samples were collected at every second intersection and analysed for water-soluble salts,

electrical conductivity, soil reaction (pH), particle size distribution, Atterberg limits and total nitrogen and total carbon contents. Soils were then evaluated in terms of landscaping potential. Some, for example, had fairly serious limitations with regard to establishing lawns. The solonetzic soils which were mapped posed problems with respect to compaction and trafficability. A major engineering hazard which emerged from the survey was the potential corrosion of concrete structures and underground conduits because of subsoil salinity in certain soils.

These studies in Australia and Canada are essentially negative in approach in that the degrees of limitation posed to urban planning were assessed. McCormack and Johnson (1982) argue that a method using soil potential ratings is a more positive approach to relating land to its use; they demonstrate such a approach with reference to assessing soil potential for onsite sewage disposal in a county in Florida. The need was to develop a method for assessing soils in terms of the operation of septic tanks for individual homes, ensuring that effluent did not appear at the soil surface at any time. The soil mapping units were scored for such a land use by the determination of a soil potential index (SPI) as determined from the equation $SPI = P - (CM + CL)$ where P is an index of performance or yield, CM is the index of costs of corrective measures, and CL is the index of costs resulting from continuing limitations. Reference needs to be made to the original publication for details of costs (McCormack and Johnson 1982), but the end result is the determination of soil performance indices for the different soils; a five-fold classification of soils could then be produced in order to categorize soils ranging from those of very high potential to very low potential for onsite sewage disposal.

6.3 Land evaluation for irrigation

About one-third of the world's land surface suffers from a moisture deficiency which presents a major constraint to agricultural development (Zonn 1977); currently about 16 per cent of the world's arable area is irrigated. Any significant increase in agricultural output from arid and semi-arid regions is dependent upon new irrigation schemes. Such projects are highly expensive and necessitate very careful planning to ensure ultimate environmental, economic and social success. Bergmann and Boussard (1976) provide a *Guide to the Economic Evaluation of Irrigation Projects*. They identify four stages in the planning process prior to actual construction and these are listed below.

1 *Outline survey*
This is the initial survey to provide a rough outline of the project by discussing it with hydrologists, soil surveyors and agricultural officers, all familiar with the study area.

2 *Preliminary project*
Reconnaissance field surveys of pedological, hydrological, topographical and geological conditions are carried out to assess the environmental feasibility of the proposed scheme.

3 *Feasibility report*
The results from the previous stage permit an analysis of the proposed project including an economic evaluation. The first estimates of returns on overall investment should become available. Also, estimates are made of the economic viability of farms which will be established on completion of the irrigation scheme.

4 *Definitive project*
The detailed survey work and resultant planning are undertaken only if the results from stage 3 are favourable. In stage 4, topographical, pedological, geological, climatological and hydrological conditions are investigated in detail. Such data combined with information on costs of construction of the scheme including new roads, farms, etc, as well as estimates of crop returns, allow a thorough economic appraisal of the project. If the project is to proceed, then the data collected during the definitive project stage are also used for the detailed planning of the project.

These stages are described to illustrate how the planning of irrigation projects requires an integrated approach; soil survey work is only one type of input to the planning process. If adequate soil maps are available, then these may be interpreted to assist with the outline survey for an irrigation proposal. If the project continues to the definitive stage, then special purpose soil surveys will be essential. Thus soil information is required at varying levels of detail ranging from introductory qualitative assessments at stage 1 to intensive field sampling combined with the laboratory determination of many soil properties at stage 4. A definitive text on irrigation is provided by Hagan et al (1967) while FAO (1985) has produced detailed guidance on land evaluation procedures.

Soil survey work is necessary not only at various stages of an investigation for an irrigation project, but also for different purposes. New crops are usually grown in an area following the installation of an irrigation scheme, and thus soils must be assessed in terms of their suitability for these crops. Soil types also influence the methods of irrigation. For example, soils with a high storage capacity can be irrigated with large quantities of water infrequently (for example, flood irrigation), while soils with a high rate of infiltration have to be irrigated frequently, but with smaller quantities (for example, by sprinkler methods). Soil surveyors, besides describing soil types before irrigation, have to predict the effect of irrigation on soil characteristics since many physical, chemical and biological changes may be induced. Maletic and Hutchings (1967) postulate possible changes in soil structure through modification of salinity level, an increase in exchangeable sodium, a change in organic matter content and an alteration of clay minerals. The marked increase in the downward movement of water may result in the translocation of clay, ultimately producing an argillic horizon which will impede the movement of water. Changes in cation exchange capacity as well as in the amounts of such salts as calcium sulphate and calcium carbonate may also occur. Information on the quality of the applied water is also essential since such water, if it contains a high suspended or chemical load, will influence the soil. For example, if the suspended sediment load is over 100 ppm, then the clogging hazard with trickle systems of irrigation is considered to be severe (FAO 1985);

Potential irrigation problem	Units	Restriction on use		
		none	slight to moderate	severe
Salinity (affects crop water availability)[a]				
EC_W	ds/m	<0.7	0.7–3.0	>3.0
(or)				
TDS	mg/l	<450	450–2000	>2000
Infiltration (affects infiltration rate of water into the soil: evaluate using EC_W and SAR together)[b]				
SAR = 0– 3 and EC_W =		>0.7	0.7–0.2	<0.2
= 3– 6 =		>1.2	1.2–0.3	<0.3
= 6–12 =		>1.9	1.9–0.5	<0.5
= 12–20 =		>2.9	2.9–1.3	<1.3
= 20–40 =		>5.0	5.0–2.9	<2.9
Specific ion toxicity (affects sensitive crops)				
Sodium (Na)[c]				
surface irrigation	SAR	<3	3–9	>9
sprinkler irrigation	me/l	<3	>3	
Chloride (Cl)[c]				
surface irrigation	me/l	<4	4–10	>10
sprinkler irrigation	me/l	<3	>3	
Boron (B)	mg/l	<0.7	0.7–3.0	>3.0
Miscellaneous effects (affects susceptible crops)				
Nitrogen (NO_3–N)[d]	mg/l	<5	5–30	>30
Bicarbonate (HCO_3) (overhead sprinkling only)	me/l	<1.5	1.5–8.5	>8.5
pH		(Normal range 6.5–8.4)		

Table 6.4 Guidelines for the interpretation of water quality for irrigation

[a] EC_W means electrical conductivity, a measure of the water salinity, reported in deciSemens per metre at 25°C (dS/m) or as previously reported in millimhos per centimetre at 25°C (mmho/cm); they are numerically equivalent. TDS means total dissolved solids, reported in milligrams per litre (mg/l).

[b] SAR means sodium absorption rate. SAR is sometimes reported by the symbol ^RNa. At a given SAR, infiltration rate increases as water salinity increases. Evaluate the potential infiltration problem by SAR as modified by EC_W.

[c] Values for sodium and chloride applicable to sensitive tree and woody plants with surface irrigation; many annual crops are less sensitive to these specifications. With overhead irrigation and low humidity (<30 per cent), sodium and chloride absorbed through the leaves of sensitive crops can cause damage.

[d] NO_3–N means nitrate nitrogen reported in terms of elemental nitrogen (NH_4–N and Organic–N should be included when wastewater is being tested).

(source: FAO 1985: 140)

the problem is considered moderate with suspended solids in the concentration range 50 to 100 ppm while values below 50 ppm pose only a slight clogging hazard. Guidelines for interpreting chemical attributes of water quality for irrigation are given in Table 6.4 which summarizes the following problems resulting from the use of poor quality water.

1 *Salinity*

Excessive accumulation of salts in the root zone of crops induces salt-induced drought; crops vary in their sensitivity to this problem.

2   *Infiltration*
The rate of infiltration is influenced not only by soil properties, but also by water quality. Water with a low salt content (low electrical conductivity) poses problems given the resultant poor infiltration. This is due to the capacity of pure water to incorporate soluble components (eg calcium). Also relevant is the relative ratio of sodium to calcium and magnesium (SAR); at a given SAR, infiltration rates increase as water salinity increases (Table 6.4). Carbonates and bicarbonates also influence infiltration.

3   *Toxicity*
This results when the applied water adds certain elements to the soil in concentrations which impair crop yields. In arid and semi-arid regions, the critical elements are usually boron, chloride and sodium.

4   *Miscellaneous*
Table 6.4 indicates restrictions on use which can result from abnormal pHs and excessive levels of nitrate nitrogen and bicarbonate.

The evaluation of land for irrigation requires data on the project area (eg location, population, nature and types of farms, water rights, land tenure systems, standard of living), topography, climate, soils, water resources, drainage, present land use, environmental health and social and economic conditions. FAO (1985) lists the following data as relevant to an inventory of climate.

1   climatic type

2   radiation (eg photosynthetically active radiation, net longwave and net shortwave radiation, sunshine hours)

3   temperature (eg monthly means of daily maximum, minimum and mean temperatures, actual monthly maximum and minimum temperatures)

4   relative humidity (eg monthly means of morning and afternoon vapour pressures)

5   evapotranspiration (eg measures on different time-intervals, reference crop evapotranspiration)

6   precipitation (eg totals, means and standard deviations for different time-intervals, rainfall intensity and erosivity)

7   wind speed (eg weekly means of wind speed)

8   storm incidence (eg frequency and intensity).

In terms of soils, it is possible to list the following field observations, field tests and laboratory analyses particularly relevant to irrigibility:

1   *Field observations*
Texture; depth to bedrock, hardpan, sand, gravel, caliche or other root zone limitation; structure; consistence; colour; mottling; kind and sequence of horizons; drainage conditions; depth to water-table.

2   *Field tests*
Infiltration rate; hydraulic conductivity or permeability; soil strength.

3   *Laboratory analyses*
Particle size distribution; bulk density; porosity; clay mineralogy; surface area; availability of nutrients including sodium; cation exchange capacity; soluble salts; base saturation; electrical conductivity of saturation extract; soil reaction (pH); organic matter content; carbon and nitrogen; exchangeable cations; available phosphorus; total contents of P, K, Mg, Na, Cu, Mn, Zn, B, Fe, Al, As, Ni, Cr; calcium and magnesium carbonates; gypsum; available water capacity (field capacity and permanent wilting point); plastic and liquid limits; structural stability; effect of leaching on salt content.
(based on Maletic and Hutchings 1967: 133–4;
FAO 1985: 46–7)

It can be readily appreciated that it is rare for all these observations and measurements on soil properties to be executed; the level of detail required in an investigation depends upon the stage of the analysis and the amount of money available to fund laboratory testing. In land evaluation for irrigation, despite the potential relevance of a very wide range of soil attributes, the crucial issue is that the need for irrigation is controlled by the balance between rainfall, the ability of soil to store moisture during periods of drought and crop moisture requirements. In unsaturated soil, water in pore space is held under suction or negative pressure. Field capacity (FC) is defined as the moisture content of soil in the field after rapid drainage has ceased. In the literature, different soil water potentials are taken to correspond to field capacity, for example -5 kPa, -8 kPa, -10 kPa and -33 kPa. Dent and Cook (1987) argue that it is vital to determine the appropriate soil water potential corresponding to field capacity for particular soils. Total available water is determined by subtracting the moisture content corresponding to the permanent wilting point (soil water potential of -1500 kPA) from the moisture content at field capacity; as Dent and Cook (1987) demonstrate, considerable variations result in estimates of total available water from using slightly different soil water potentials corresponding to field capacity. The soil moisture deficit (SMD) refers to the amount of water required to raise moisture status to that of field capacity. Potential soil moisture deficit is obtained by subtracting rainfall from potential evaporation. In a study of the long-term frequency of irrigation need in Norfolk, Dent and Scammell (1981) adopted the following steps:

1   Estimation of potential soil moisture deficit for each crop.

2   For each soil series, the amount of water before the onset of stress was calculated from soil water retention characteristics and adjusted for the rooting depth of the crop, according to the stage of growth.

3   Prediction of required irrigation when the potential water use by the crop exceeds the amount of water stored within the rooting zone between the upper limit of available water and the maximum soil water tension for optimizing yield.

The results are shown in Table 6.5 and they illustrate the effect of soil type on irrigation requirements. Dent and Scammell (1981) stress the importance of soil water retention characteristics for irrigated agriculture and suggest the relevance of such physical properties in soil survey.

The task of soil assessment is to evaluate the results of field observations and tests and laboratory analysis in terms of suitability for irrigation. The significance of particular soil attributes will vary according to such issues as the natural climatic regime, the method and rate of irrigation, the proposed crops, the quality of the irrigation water, and the availability of finance to overcome any particular soil problem. For guidance, Maletic and Hutchings (1967: 135) give advice on soils suitable for sustained irrigation in the western USA. These soils are permeable and have field-measured hydraulic conductivities ranging from 1.27 to 127 mm/hr, textures ranging from loamy sand to friable clay, cation exchange capacities more than 3 meq/100 g, depths to root limiting influences varying from 30.5 cm to 152.4 cm or more, water-holding capacities varying from 6.25 to

Soil series	texture	spring barley	sugar beet	potatoes
Adventurers, deep phase	peat	4	8	17
Adventurers, shallow phase	40 cm peat on compact till	9	13	17
Sheringham	fine sandy loam	12	16	18
Hall	40 cm fine sandy loam on sand	14	18	19
Beccles	fine loamy on clay	16	17	19
Freckenham	sand	19	19	20

Table 6.5 Years out of twenty in which irrigation is required for maximum yield of selected crops on particular soil series in Norfolk

(source: Dent and Scammell 1981: 56)

25.00 cm/m, salinity levels at equilibrium with the irrigation water at 8 mmhos/cm or less, and exchangeable sodium not more than 15 per cent. In addition, the level of the water-table must be maintained naturally or artificially at such a depth to prevent oxygen deficits and the accumulation of soluble salts or exchangeable sodium within the rooting zone of plants. The soil requirements are reproduced in order to demonstrate properties and values considered significant for assessing the irrigability of soils in the western USA. As already stated, these requirements must be varied according to area and proposed crops; for example soils with cation exchange capacities less than 3 meq/100 g may produce good yields under irrigation in the tropics and crops also vary in their tolerances to saline conditions.

Description and the intensive sampling of soils followed by many laboratory analyses are normal for stage 4 (the definitive project) in the planning process of irrigation schemes. The need at stage 2 (the preliminary project) is to carry out a rapid assessment of soils in terms of their irrigability. If the area has been mapped by standard soil survey, then careful examination of the mapping units may suggest those particularly suitable or unsuitable for irrigation. The essential problems are that routine soil survey does not produce all the data for assessing the irrigability of soils, and in addition the boundaries of soil mapping units may not coincide with boundaries corresponding to differences in soil suitability for irrigation. However, a soil survey carried out by standard techniques, but geared towards the needs of an irrigation project, can produce useful results.

An illustration of this is provided by the investigation of an area of c. 1020 ha proposed for irrigation to the immediate east of Lusaka in Zambia (Yager et al 1967). The soils of the area were surveyed by routine methods resulting in a map showing the distribution of soil series and soil phases. Then each of these soils was assessed with reference to an irrigability classification which was designed to represent a simple land evaluation of soil and slope factors related to the ability to produce crops under irrigation. The prime factors were slope, soil depth, texture, permeability, drainage, water-holding capacity and infiltration rate. Six classes were then defined though no occurrence of grades 1 and 5 were found. Class 2 was described as moderately good, class 3 as fairly good, class 4 as not irrigable except under special conditions while class 6 was land unsuitable for irrigation due to shallow depth. The classes were further divided according to specific limitations with the letter t indicating a slope difficulty, d a wetness limitation and s a difficulty resultant upon the sandy nature of upper soil horizons. The results of the investigation are shown on Figure 6.4; the solid lines indicate the boundaries between the original soil series and phases which have been interpreted using the irrigability classification. The original report by Yager et al (1967) gives information on the mapping units to justify their assignments to the irrigability classes. The size of the proposed dam combined with the evaporation rate allowed the estimation that about 280 ha could be irrigated; Yager et al (1967) state that the class 2 soils are the most suitable to receive such water though they stress that more detailed investigations will be necessary to aid the design of the actual irrigation scheme.

A number of studies could have been selected to illustrate this approach whereby soil mapping units are interpreted in terms of their suitability for irrigation. For example, a detailed investigation has been carried out by Maker et al (1972) for Sierra County in New Mexico. In this study, the eighteen soil associations are evaluated not only with respect to irrigation, but also with regard to suitability for engineering purposes. It should also be noted that projects concerned with assessing soils for irrigation are not limited to those parts of the world with a distinct dry season. For example, the soils in the Mustair valley in Switzerland have been investigated with the specific objective of identifying areas particularly suitable for irrigation (Peyer et al 1976).

As with land use capability or suitability schemes, there is much advantage if one particular framework proves applicable to a wide range of studies concerned with land and irrigation. The system developed by the United States Bureau of Reclamation (USBR) for their irrigation development schemes in the USA has been applied in many other countries, often after certain modifications. Details of this scheme are provided by the USBR (1951) and Maletic and Hutchings (1967); Vink (1975) and FAO (1985) provide summaries. It needs to be stressed that the USBR scheme incorporates economic analysis from the outset. The scheme defines land classes according to the relative degree of payment capacity which is the amount of money left to farmers after they have paid all costs (excluding water charges) and an allowance is made for family living. Predictions about variations in payment capacity are extremely useful from the planning stance; for example larger farm units might be allocated to land with a lower payment capacity. To achieve such an assessment, there has to be collected not only information about physical attributes, but also data necessary to predict crop yields. The scheme is a specialized form of a land classification survey and a standardized method for recording and presenting information through the use of symbols is integral to the method. The scheme does not specify critical factors in order to define the land classes since projects vary in area, development goals and economic circumstances. However, all projects using the scheme categorize land into the following six classes albeit on different bases.

Class 1   ARABLE land that is highly suitable for irrigated farming on a sustainable and high yield basis; high payment capacity.

Class 2   ARABLE land of moderate suitability for irrigated agriculture; suited to a narrower range of crops, more expensive to develop or less productive than class 1 land.

Class 3   ARABLE land of marginal suitability to irrigated farming; such land usually has a serious single deficiency or a combination of moderate deficiencies; under appropriate management, such land can provide adequate payment capacity.

Class 4   SPECIAL USE LAND land suited only to special uses, eg fruit or rice.

Class 5   NON-ARABLE land assessed as unsuited to arable farming on the basis of particular problems, eg excessive salinity, occurrence of flooding; further investigations are required to reclassify the land.

Class 6   NON-ARABLE unsuitable land for irrigation development as a result of, for example, steep slopes, rough topography, inadequate drainage.

Subclasses are indicated by letters to indicate the particular limitations, for example s (soil), t (topography) and d (drainage).

Closely related to the USBR system is the FAO (1985) one entitled *Guidelines: Land Evaluation for Irrigation*. Part one of the FAO report gives detailed procedures of land evaluation and land suitability classification for irrigated agriculture and is based on the FAO (1976) *Framework for Land Evaluation*. The second part gives technical information on individual factors commonly of importance in specifying critical limits in land suitability classification. The prime aim of land evaluation for irrigated agriculture is to predict future conditions after development has taken place. Benefits to farmers as well as to regional or national economies need to be predicted; furthermore any

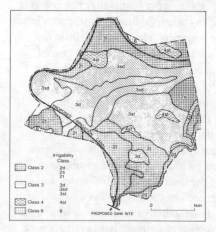

Figure 6.4 The Chalimbana area of Zambia according to suitability for irrigation (classes are described in the text) (from Yager et al 1967)

environmental impact has to be evaluated. As with the FAO *Framework for Land Evaluation*, assessment for irrigated agriculture must be done with reference to alternative kinds of land use or land utilization types. Of particular importance to irrigation schemes is the comparison of predicted outputs with inputs required to produce these outputs. Thus economic assessment is of crucial importance; 'it is most important to achieve a land classification that reflects differences in the long-term productivity and profitability of the land under irrigation rather than one that focuses only on physical differences without regard to their economic implications' (FAO 1985: 5). Of course any recommended land use types must be sustainable on a permanent basis within the irrigation system. In other words land degradation should not result, or at least some financial allowance needs to be made for any remedial action, for example to control soil erosion.

The land suitability orders, classes and subclasses of the FAO *Framework for Land Evaluation* are discussed in Chapter 5. A distinction is made between present suitability of land and potential suitability after a major improvement has been made; an irrigation project is an obvious example of this situation. The *Guidelines: Land Evaluation for Irrigated Agriculture* (FAO 1985) subdivide potential suitability into two categories.

1 *Provisionally irrigable land*   this assessment is done on the assumption that water can be supplied, but without detailed knowledge of the supply or the project and land development costs. Net farm income is recommended as a convenient measure of land suitability class and this is determined by subtracting both the variable and fixed costs from the gross value of production. As stated, project costs are generally not known at this stage and are not taken into account in estimating net farm income.

2 *Irrigable land*   land in this category was first designated as provisionally irrigable, but further investigation has shown it to be suitable for defined land utilization types, taking into account water supply, incremental area-specific development costs, common project costs, and benefits. The recommended standard procedure

for measuring the suitability of irrigable land is *net incremental irrigation benefit* (NIIB) which is a measure of the potential increase in productivity of a unit area of land. It is calculated by estimating the difference in net benefit to a unit area of land with and without the project, taking into account farm investment and operating costs, returns from agricultural land use, project investment, and operating and maintenance costs.

(FAO 1985: 13)

Land suitability classes (ie S1, S2, S3, N1, N2) for land utilization types which incorporate irrigation can be defined on the basis of economic or physical measures. Net farm income and net incremental irrigation benefit are economic measures as already explained while a land productivity index is used to assess physical suitability. In the *Guidelines: Land Evaluation for Irrigated Agriculture* (FAO 1985), a land productivity index is defined as the physical productivity of land for a specific use, relative to that of the best land. Thus the top yield for Class S1 for a particular land utilization type might be 100 per cent with the top of S2 set at 80 per cent, S3 at 60 per cent, etc, as appropriate. Such assessment can be done for present as well as for potential suitability when the irrigation project is in operation. Determination of land productivity indices is likely to take place at the reconnaissance stage and in advance of economic evaluation.

The main steps to be followed according to the *Guidelines: Land Evaluation for Irrigated Agriculture* (FAO 1985) can be summarized as follows:

1 *Select the land utilization types (LUTs) which are to be evaluated*
Provide a full description of each LUT.

2 *Develop the land suitability class specification*
On the basis of requirements and limitations, identify class-determining factors for each LUT; quantify critical limits for the different classes (eg S1, S2, S3, N1, N2).

3 *Field survey and mapping of provisionally irrigable classes and subclasses*
Survey, delineation and description of land units; determine for each land unit which land qualities and land characteristics are class determining for the selected LUTs; match the critical limits of

each land use requirement or limitation with the nature of the land units; combine individual class-determining factor ratings to obtain a tentative land suitability classification for each LUT on each land unit.

4 *Presentation of the results of the provisionally irrigable classification*
Provide maps, legends, descriptions of each LUT; recommendations on input and management.

5 *Determination and mapping of irrigable land*
Revisions of results from stage 4 on the basis of information on water supply and economic data; additional field survey; revision of classification to determine which areas can be irrigated under an economically and financially viable project plan; predict economic results of each selected LUT; prepare reports for investment and management.

Examples of completed projects designed to investigate the irrigation potential of particular areas can be selected from studies by the Overseas Development Natural Resources Institute (ODNRI). Work has been done in Ethiopia (Makin et al 1976) in Botswana (Mitchell 1976) and Cyprus (Water Development Department, Cyprus 1982). A paragraph in this book can do little justice to these large projects. The Ethiopian survey around Lake Zwai is comprehensive, covering such topics as the evaluation of the water resources and agricultural potential which leads to proposals for irrigation development and economic evaluation. The land classification scheme is based on the USBR scheme and the results indicate that the overall area suitable for irrigation is restricted more by soil and topography than by availability of water. The study in eastern Botswana by Mitchell (1976) is more limited in objective since his prime concern was to assess the irrigation potential of soils. The survey is a reconnaissance one with maps at a scale of 1:500,000 showing irrigation potential. Land facets are the basic mapping units which are evaluated in terms of irrigation potential using the method of Thomas and Thompson (1959), but modified to meet local needs and which also conform broadly with the land classes of the USBR scheme. Land facets were delimited by the analysis of patterns on aerial photographs. Such patterns

resulted from variations in landform (relief, degree of dissection, steepness and shape of slope) and lithological differences. Thus the identified land facets were areas of land with similar drainage density and slope characteristics, with similar lithology and consequently similar soils. In essence the land systems approach was adopted. Field surveys were then necessary to describe and sample soil types in the various facets and such information allowed the estimation of irrigation potential. The project in Cyprus is also of a reconnaissance nature (Water Development Department, Cyprus 1982). Figure 6.5 is an extract from original maps at a scale of 1:250,000 from this Southern Conveyor Project (SCP) in Cyprus. In advance of information on water supply and development costs, areas can be classified as having irrigation potential (provisionally irrigable) as shown in Figure 6.5. When such information has been incorporated into the analysis, then project irrigation areas (irrigable land) are mapped.

The case studies summarized in this chapter so far have been concerned with soil or land classification schemes designed to define irrigability classes for agricultural development. Parametric methods can also be used with the production of some index to express suitability. Bowser and Moss (1950) trace the development of soil rating methods relevant to irrigation; they describe how the Saskatchewan Soil Survey in 1936 began to carry out such research although similar work had been initiated in Alberta by 1930. Bowser and Moss propose that the rating of soils for irrigation should follow the same basic approach as the rating of soils for unirrigated agriculture though, of course, different emphasis has to be given to soil characteristics. For example, in a semi-arid area, a top rating might be given to a heavy textured soil for unirrigated agriculture while for irrigation purposes, prime significance would be given to soils of medium texture. Bowser and Moss propose that the following seven factors ought to be considered in classifying and rating soils for irrigation: salinity, soil profile type, nature of soil parent material, soil texture, degree of stoniness, erosion hazard and topography. These seven factors are subdivided into component types. The resultant seven ratings

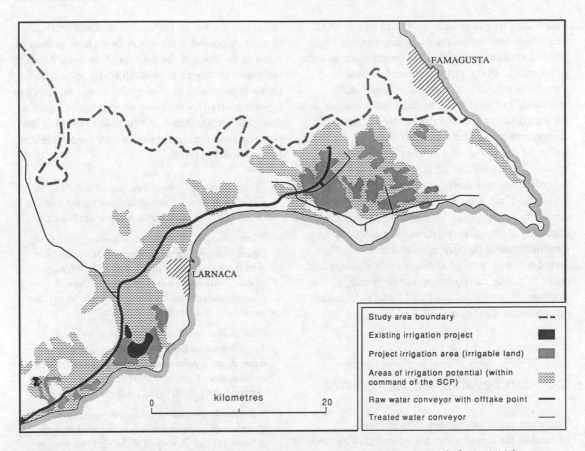

Figure 6.5 Land as proposed in the Southern Conveyor Project in Cyprus to have irrigation potential after an initial survey; further analysis of water supply and development costs resulted in the mapping of project irrigation areas (source: Water Development Department, Cyprus 1982)

are multiplied together to give an overall score which allows the classification of a site according to its suitability for irrigation. Bowser and Moss thus produced a well-defined parametric method for rating soils though they stressed that it was to be used only as a guide since personal judgement was still required to check the results. They also appreciated that irrigation may well change key soil properties and thus account must be taken of this in the evaluation procedure.

The study by Bowser and Moss was rather advanced for its day since it is only in more recent years that parametric methods of soil assessment have become common. It is interesting to mention the parametric method proposed by Sys and Verheye (1974) since there are clear similarities

with the Bowser and Moss (1950) approach. Sys and Verheye (1974) state that the suitability of soils for irrigation in arid and semi-arid areas is mainly influenced by seven factors: texture, soil depth, calcium carbonate, gypsum status, salinity and alkalinity content, soil drainage and slope. The value of an overall index is obtained by multiplying ratings which are listed by Sys and Verheye. It is then possible to assign sites to one of five classes ranging from very suitable to completely unsuitable. The Sys and Verheye method gives greater emphasis to soil chemical properties than is the case with the Bowser and Moss (1950) rating index.

The experience in Alberta of developing a land classification for irrigation is interesting because the Province in 1968 passed an Act which required that land within irrigation districts has to be classified irrigable before irrigation water licences can be granted (Pohjakas 1987). The consequence was the development of the rating approach to land irrigability assessment and this approach has continued to be refined into the 1980s. A Basic Soil Rating (BSR) is first determined by multiplying component ratings for a soil profile factor, the nature of the underlying geology and the soil texture. Values for the BSR are then modified according to soil salinity, sodicity levels and drainage. Thus soils are rated according to their capability for irrigation. Assignment to final land capability classes for irrigation takes place after consideration of topographic features which includes not only relief attributes, but also size and shape of fields, earth moving requirements, stoniness, brush/tree cover and surface drainage requirements (Pohjakas 1987).

6.4   Land evaluation for forestry

There are many similarities between land evaluation for forestry and for irrigation. The scale of analysis can vary from the national or regional down to the local. At the reconnaissance level, evaluation may be limited to the interpretation of existing general purpose soil maps and other environmental data, but as the scale of analysis increases, special purpose surveys will be necessary. Integral to evaluation for forestry and irrigation is assessment of the different forms of impact. If an area is afforested, prior to such action, evaluation should have assessed, for example, the impact on water yield and quality, landscape quality, local economy, and recreational activities.

With land evaluation for forestry, it is important to realize the diversity of applications. When dealing with national or regional assessments of land suitability for afforestation, then land capability schemes for forestry are most appropriate. The systems of land capability assessment for forestry in Canada and in Britain have already been described in Chapter 4. The main use is to aid decision-making at the broad regional or national levels. As already discussed, such assessments have proved of value as an input to the process of devising forestry indicative strategies at regional scales in Scotland. Other applications of land evaluation to forestry can be summarized by outlining experience in Japan as described by Mashimo and Arimitsu (1986). They perceive land evaluation for forestry being relevant to the following issues.

1   *Timber production*   the rating of land according to forest productivity which is assessed on the basis of soil type and elevation (a temperature index).

2   *Water resources*   of particular importance is the capacity of catchments to minimize fluctuations in river discharge; this is dependent upon attributes of soils, surface geology, slope and altitude. A point-scoring method is used to provide an overall measure of water retaining capacity.

3   *Flood control*   attributes of catchments have a direct impact on the flood hazard in downstream areas. Again a point-scoring system is used, based on measures of altitude, slope and ravine density, to provide an overall rating on flood hazard.

4   *Soil conservation*   of particular relevance is the incidence of landslides which occur after periods of heavy rainfall. A rating for the likely incidence of such slope failures is determined on the basis of attributes of surface geology, slope and ravine density.

5   *Forest recreation*   people are attracted to forests because of their scenic and wildlife qualities, possibilities for walking, camping and sports activities, and for features of heritage or cultural value. Forests are classified according to an overall assessment of these attributes.

Mashimo and Arimitsu (1986) describe a site classification system for evaluating large areas of forest in Japan. Each grid cell is scored for the five forest functions as summarized above. In a case study of the River Tone basin, they superimposed the ratings for the five forest functions in order to propose areas with different management objectives.

Land evaluation for forestry using the land capability approach or a rating scheme as illustrated in this Japanese example, is based on the interpretation of existing soil, geological, climatic and topographic maps. As the scale of land evaluation becomes more detailed, it is increasingly likely that special purpose surveys will be necessary. The techniques of land resource survey as discussed in Chapter 2 are applicable to forestry in a way similar to any other form of crop production. The key issue is that the survey technique generates data on appropriate land characteristics from which land qualities relevant to forestry can be evaluated. This subject of resource surveys for forestry is examined in detail by Valentine (1986) who discusses description and classification systems, the stages in soil survey and issues of scale and intensity, the planning and execution of such soil surveys, and the evaluation of the results.

In any land evaluation analysis for forestry, a yield prediction is necessary in order to determine economic viability. Data on species, stocking densities, ages, heights, diameters at breast height and volumes can be collected from sample plots during a forest inventory. From age and volume measurements, growth rates can be determined, for example mean annual increment which is the average volume added per year. In practice it is difficult to estimate volume. Instead yield class (or site index as in North America) for a particular forest block and species can be determined from data on top height and age as shown in Figure 6.6 for sitka spruce. Top height is defined as the mean height of the 100 trees of largest diameter at breast height (dbh) per hectare; these may not necessarily be the tallest trees (Hamilton and Christie 1971). A yield class of 12 means a maximum mean annual increment in the range 11–13 cubic metres per hectare. Thus from areas of well-established forest, yield classes can be determined for different compartments or sample plots which can then be correlated with soil, climatic and topographic conditions. Such a system for predicting the productivity of sitka spruce in upland areas of Britain is explained by Worrell (1987). Data on location, elevation, topex value (a measure of exposure), aspect and soil type require to be obtained; then through the use of tables and diagrams the potential yield class of sitka spruce can be estimated.

Land evaluation for forestry can have a variety of objectives. The selection of tree species which gives the greatest yield of timber may be the most obvious, but other concerns might be landscape aesthetic quality, nature conservation, water catchment, soil conservation, recreation, or assistance with planting and management strategies. Following the FAO (1976) *Framework for Land Evaluation* which is equally applicable to forestry, contrasting objectives need to be fully defined so that data on relevant land characteristics for the land utilization types can be collected. The application of the *Framework for Land Evaluation* to forestry is detailed by FAO (1984b). Four major kinds of land use are distinguished – commercial forestry, community forestry, environmental forestry and recreational forestry. The main objective of commercial forestry is the production of timber for sale while community forestry is dedicated to providing particular needs of local people, for example fuelwood and building materials. Environmental or conservation forestry has objectives of nature or soil conservation. These

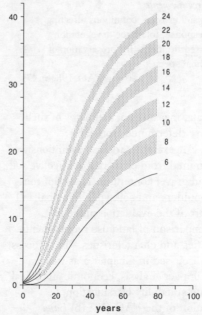

Figure 6.6 General yield class curves for sitka spruce; yield class is determined from age (years) and top height (metres) (source: Hamilton and Christie 1971: 13)

four major kinds of land use can be subdivided into a wide range of land utilization types through the provision of much more detailed descriptions. Following such descriptions, land use requirements and limitations need to be specified as illustrated by the following list for production forestry.

1   *Growth requirements*
    Radiation, temperature, moisture, aeration, nutrients, rooting conditions, salinity/sodicity, toxicities, climatic hazards (fire, frost, wind), physiographic hazards (flood, landslides), pests and diseases.

2   *Requirements based on estimates of forest volume, growth and yield*
    Present forest stands, estimated growth rates, estimated survival rates, estimated yield of non-timber products.

3   *Management requirements*
    Mechanized operations, harvest operations, road construction and maintenance, internal access, nursery sites, vegetation clearance, size of potential management units, location (existing and potential accessibility).

4   *Conservation requirements*
    Tolerance to soil erosion, conditions affecting streamflow response, tolerance to vegetation degradation, requirements for preservation of plant and animal species.

                              (from FAO 1984b: 47)

From survey data, measures or estimates of such land qualities are determined from land characteristics. For example, rooting conditions could be determined from estimates of effective soil depth, stone and gravel content, incidence of rock outcrops and boulders and soil type. The final and most crucial part of the evaluation procedure involves the comparison of land use requirements with land qualities and characteristics – the process of *matching* as discussed in Chapter 5 as well as environmental impact analysis, economic and social analysis and land suitability classification.

The application of the FAO (1984b) *Land Evaluation for Forestry* can best be illustrated by an example. Booth and Saunders (1985) report a study in a largely unlogged area of about 49,000 ha,

comprised mainly of eucalypt forest, in New South Wales, Australia, where the aim was to test the methodology. The aim was to produce a multiple use plan for the allocation of land uses within the Wandella-Dampier area in the extreme south-east of New South Wales. Use was made of a previous land resource survey which described and mapped 249 land units using the land systems approach as outlined in Chapter 3. Eight land utilizations types were defined, in summary.

LUT 1   Multiple use natural forest – general

LUT 2   Multiple use natural forest – special emphasis on recreation

LUT 3   Multiple use natural forest – special emphasis on visual resource protection

LUT 4   Multiple use natural forest – special emphasis on flora and fauna protection

LUT 5   Multiple use natural forest – special emphasis on catchment protection

LUT 6   Undeveloped natural forest

LUT 7   Preserved natural forest

LUT 8   Not available for land use zoning

The aim was to assess the suitability of each mapping unit for the different land utilization types. Suitability class S1 corresponds to highly suitable, S2 moderately suitable, S3 marginally suitable, N1 currently not suitable and N2 permanently not suitable. Required land characteristics were specified in order to allocate land units to these suitability classes for each land utilization type. For example, suitability for LUT 2 (multiple use natural forest – special emphasis on recreation) was assessed according to the present or absence of the following three features at one or several points within a land unit:

1   a perennial stream

2   a potential scenic vantage point with a view to a 'feature landscape' within 5 km

3   greater than 25 per cent of the area included rainforest type vegetation.

Suitability was rated as S1 for land units possessing all three factors, S2 for two factors, S3 for one factor and N2 for no factor. Figures 6.7a and 6.7b illustrate the results for two land utilization types for part of the study area.

6.5 Prediction of land properties and qualities from soil surveys

As Bouma (1989) states, some soil surveys have reached a crucial stage given the completion or near completion of field mapping in such countries as The Netherlands or Scotland. In countries where soil survey is incomplete, questions are increasingly being asked about the usefulness and cost-effectiveness of continuing with such research. Justification is provided by stressing the increased need for soil survey results given the requirements for environmental management or environmental

impact assessment. In other words soil survey interpretation continues to fulfil a crucial role. As demonstrated in the earlier sections of this chapter, the traditional emphasis has been on grading or assessing the suitability of soil conditions for specific land uses. Bouma (1989) notes a change in types of questions being asked by soil map users with an emphasis now on more specific and quantitative queries. In addition some users are now requiring a quantitative listing of available options rather than generalized statements of land suitability. Increasing use has to be made of computer simulation techniques to predict land qualities under different climatic and land management scenarios. As the results from environmental impact assessment become more open to public scrutiny, then the basis to such predictions needs to be made absolutely clear. This involves making the database and models explicit, a process known as parameter audit which will

(a)

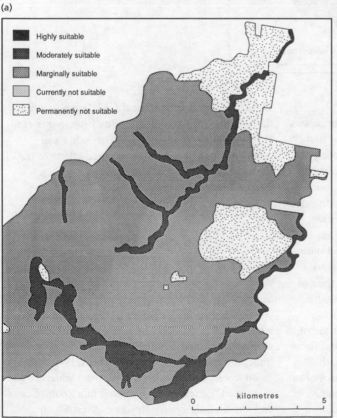

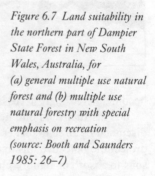

Figure 6.7 Land suitability in the northern part of Dampier State Forest in New South Wales, Australia, for (a) general multiple use natural forest and (b) multiple use natural forestry with special emphasis on recreation (source: Booth and Saunders 1985: 26–7)

(b)

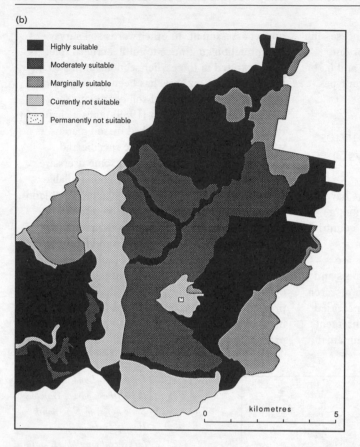

Highly suitable
Moderately suitable
Marginally suitable
Currently not suitable
Permanently not suitable

0   kilometres   5

Figure 6.7 Land suitability in the northern part of Dampier State Forest in New South Wales, Australia, for (a) general multiple use natural forest and (b) multiple use natural forestry with special emphasis on recreation (source: Booth and Saunders 1985: 26–7)

become increasingly necessary.

It is instructive to outline two Dutch examples as discussed by Breeuwsma et al (1986). In the first project the objective was to evaluate the capacity of soils to absorb or remove phosphate and nitrate derived from the application of farmyard manure. The aim was to produce maximum application rates for different soils ensuring that groundwater was not polluted. The authors based their study on a standard 1:50,000 soil survey with associated data. From such information, they derived three land qualities of the unsaturated zone: (1) travel time of water (T) from the soil surface to the water-table, (2) cation exchange capacity (CEC), and (3) phosphate sorption capacity (PSC). Travel time of water was of importance in assessing potential for groundwater pollution. CEC was relevant with respect to cation transport while PSC has proved to be an important land quality in The Netherlands in areas of high rates of liquid manure application.

Direct measures of PSC and CEC are possible though time-consuming and thus Breeuwsma et al (1986) predict these qualities from other soil properties as will be explained; predictions of travel time (T) cannot be made directly and require various modelling components.

Travel time (T) was calculated from the following equation:

$$T = (D \times \theta)/N$$

where T is the travel time of water from the soil surface to the water-table (days), D is the thickness of the unsaturated zone (metres), θ is the average volumetric moisture content of the unsaturated zone and N is the average yearly precipitation surplus expressed as a daily rate. Dutch soil maps indicate mean highest water level (MHW) and mean lowest water level (MLW) from which D was calculated. Estimates of θ proved more complicated and a modelling approach was evolved which required data on hydraulic conductivity, moisture retention, moisture flux rate and D. As a result Bouma et al (1986) were able to produce a map showing travel-time classes according to both the mean highest water level (MHW) and mean lowest water level (MLW). They note the large range of values, but the most frequent times vary from 0.5 to 1.5 years. Particular stress is given to the role of water-table levels in controlling travel times.

Cation exchange capacity (CEC) was found to correlate well with clay and organic contents and was thus estimated from linear regression models. In turn cumulative CEC was calculated for the unsaturated zone through taking into account thickness and bulk density of horizons. It was then possible to map CEC classes as expressed in terms of cumulative CEC in relation to MHW and MLW. Again using transfer functions, phosphate sorption capacity (PSC) was estimated from measures of oxalate-extractable aluminium and iron. A cumulative estimate of PSC was made for the unsaturated zone, using thickness and bulk density data. A map was then provided showing the PSC classes of the unsaturated zone for both MHW and MLW. The overall flexibility of this type of approach is noteworthy. Results can quickly be produced for different water-table conditions, fluxes can be varied and Breeuwsma et al (1986) point out the possibilites for using dynamic models of travel time and adsorption and exchange for predicting outcomes from different waste management schemes.

The second Dutch example illustrates a quantitative land evaluation approach designed to answer a 'what if' question. In this instance, what is the effect of water supply on crop yield if there is a reduction in the water-table level as a result of enhanced groundwater extraction? Prediction of impacts on crop yields are essential if farmers are to be compensated for loss in production. With this type of study in soil survey interpretation, emphasis is placed upon the determination of soil use-potentials rather than upon use-limitations as in capability or suitability assessments. Availability of water in the root zone is obviously not a static property but varies according rainfall, flux conditions and evapotranspiration. It is thus

possible to develop models to predict potential moisture conditions under differing scenarios. The study as described by Bouma et al (1980) is based on the simulation of water regimes in order to estimate soil moisture deficits during the growing season. Critical input data were hydraulic conductivity curves, moisture retention curves and rooting depth. Values of P, relative fractional production of a grass crop, were predicted for a range of soils using the following equation:

$$P = (\Sigma \, E_{act} \, / \, \Sigma \, E_{pot})^2$$

where E_{act} is the actual evaporation rate and E_{pot} is the potential evapotranspiration rate. This simulation model was applied using different boundary conditions and different frequencies of occurrence of dry years. The simulations were repeated for different depths of water-table lowering to produce results as shown in Figure 6.8. As can be seen from these curves, soils vary in their response to water-table lowering. For example, there is little impact on a typic udipsamment formed on recent aeolian sand. This is because there is already little upward flow to a shallow root zone. The typic haplaquept which has a fine loam over sandy-skeletal material shows the most marked drop in relative production of a grass crop. The studied soils thus vary in their response to water-table lowering and Bouma et al (1980) derive indices to express relative sensitivities to such changes. As a result they are able to input the results to a mapping program as an efficient way of plotting spatial variability in crop yield responses to water-table lowering. Bouma et al (1980) stress the merits of this type of approach to soil survey interpretation given the flexibility to vary differentiating criteria and compare results. As they express it, 'the user is given a choice rather than a judgement' as is the case with the more traditional approach to soil survey interpretation.

As increasing use is made of quantitative land evaluation procedures in soil survey interpretation, problems associated with availability and quality of data assume critical importance. In the already quoted study by Bouma et al (1980), calculations of evapotranspiration and equivalent relative production were based on data derived from

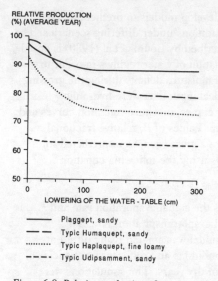

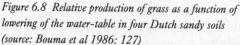

Figure 6.8 Relative production of grass as a function of lowering of the water-table in four Dutch sandy soils (source: Bouma et al 1986: 127)

pedons considered to be representative of mapping units. Information on mapping unit variability is not normally provided as part of standard soil survey. Another important data issue is the point that conventional soil maps are based on pedological criteria. This means that emphasis is given to the identification and mapping of soils according to diagnostic attributes of soils as specified in soil classification systems. The problem is whether it is valid to assume that the spatial units obtained using pedological criteria can also be applied to other soil properties such as saturated hydraulic conductivity and soil moisture retention. This is a topic which has been investigated by McKeague and Topp (1986) with reference to soil drainage properties. They selected soils in the Ottawa area of Canada for which there was a good database on such properties as saturated hydraulic conductivity, particle size distribution and soil structure. Their particular interest lay in comparing such measures of soil physical properties with soil drainage determined by routine soil survey. They concluded that saturated hydraulic conductivity values were incompatible with drainage classes as given for at least four out of the nine studied soils; this led them to propose that 'interpretations of the

drainage characteristics of soil series have serious limitations'. They propose that interpretations would be improved if better methods of assessing soil morphology were adopted along with routine measures of such key properties as saturated hydraulic conductivity.

In all projects concerned with soil survey interpretation, it needs to be remembered that the prime objective is the generation of results relevant to the issue or problem. Soil survey interpretation is an applied science and the application must dictate to large measure the adopted methodology. Thus it is not a question of qualitative interpretation being replaced by such quantitative procedures as illustrated in this section. For example, at the regional or national planning levels, broad interpretations of soil and climatic conditions may be all that is required for strategic land use purposes as with identifying areas which have potential for afforestation. If more specific questions about potential yields or financial returns are required, then quantitative land evaluation incorporating simulation techniques becomes necessary. A frequent assumption is that the greater use of quantitative land evaluation techniques will necessitate more detailed field survey data. This need not be the case as discussed by Bouma (1989). The costs associated with obtaining additional data may not be justifiable on the basis of associated increased accuracy in predictions. Once again, the key issue is the nature of the problem being tackled.

What is the future for soil survey interpretation? There is no doubt about the continuing importance of such assessments to aid land use planning and management from scales ranging from the global to the individual farm. The questions being posed in the western world are very different in the 1990s to those being addressed in the 1960s and 1970s when optimization of output was the prime objective. As discussed earlier in this chapter, emphasis in land evaluation in Europe is now towards agricultural diversification. For example, in The Netherlands there is a plan to withdraw 150,000 ha from agriculture over the period 1990 to 2005 and to give greater priority to nature conservation. At the same time as discussed in

Chapter 1, there is the continuing need to enhance agricultural output from countries in the developing world. In the past it has been possible to store and present results only on the basis of soil mapping units which in turn have depended upon taxonomic units. Classification is a means of compressing vast quantities of survey data derived from sample points. Now it is possible to achieve such data storage with computer-based system. This means that it will become increasingly possible to carry out soil survey interpretations for point rather than areal units. The use of geographical information systems, spatial interpolation and simulation modelling as discussed in Chapters 7 and 8 provide such opportunities. In addition, data are increasingly being obtained from remote sensing techniques as well as by monitoring sensors in situ. Such data provide the means both for simulation and calibration in order to be able to predict land potentials under different management or environmental conditions.

7

Land Resource Information Systems

Since the first edition of this book, there has been considerable scientific and commercial development of geographical information systems (GIS). The prime advantages of GIS are their capability to permit easy update of information and to present results in forms required by users. It must be stressed that such systems have to be driven by user requirements. A high level of activity is possible only through the increasing availability of cheaper GIS software which can run on microcomputers. It is now possible to buy hardware and software for a complete GIS for about £5,000 though the more professional systems are considerably more expensive than this. Of course GIS are applicable to a wide variety of situations such as the management of utilities (eg gas, electricity and water supplies), maintenance of land registers and military uses; the increase in GIS applications to land evaluation is thus part of a broader development.

7.1 Nature of geographical information systems

What is a GIS? Inevitably there is diversity of opinion, for example diagnostic features might be the ability to overlay a variety of distributions and produce new ones, or the integration of a relational database with computer mapping capabilities. In many ways it is better to consider a GIS as a set of tools to permit the collection, storage, retrieval, transformation and display of spatially referenced data. Burrough (1986) stresses that GIS are more than the sum of these tools in that they are models of the real world. This means that it is possible to explore within GIS a wide variety of 'what if' type questions using different scenarios. It is this modelling and thus predictive capacity of GIS which is of paramount importance with reference to environmental planning and management.

A fundamental distinction arises between vector-based and raster-based data structures. A vector has magnitude and direction, thus a line when digitized consists of a sequence of points with x–y coordinates; a feature representation code will be attached to the line to indicate that it corresponds say to a river and in addition, information must be stored in order to express the connectivity or structure of the river network. In addition to lines, points and polygons are also represented as vectors. Vector data structures provide efficient storage of data and also provide the most acceptable results in terms of digital cartography. Operations such as map overlay or processing of spatially referenced data are easier using raster or grid cell data structures. By this approach the values for specific variables are specified for each component cell; data on different variables for the same area can be stored using a range of layers. Editing or updating raster data is easier than with vectors since with the latter, the data require to be re-structured in order to maintain information on connectivity. Vector data when displayed provide more aesthetically pleasing results while with raster displays, the values of component cells are indicated in different colours or shades. The quality of raster displays is controlled by the resolution of the grid and the selection of cell size is a crucial decision. Data

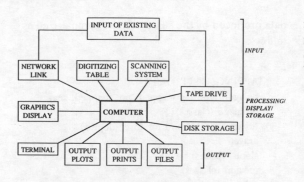

Figure 7.1 Hardware components of a GIS

input time and required disk storage markedly increase if a small cell size is selected. Also relevant to the choice of cell size is the smallest decision-making spatial unit, in other words the actual use of the output has to be considered. Errors associated with the source maps as well as the area of the smallest mapping units also need to be borne in mind. Many modern GIS have the capability to operate in both vector and raster modes, thus the advantages of both approaches can be obtained. Such flexibility is particularly important if raster data from satellite imagery or scanning maps or aerial photographs require to be inputted. Such integration of image analysis capabilities with GIS is becoming increasingly common.

The hardware components in a GIS are summarized in Figure 7.1. Three possibilites of data input are shown. Features on maps can be traced with a cursor over a digitizing table in order to produce digital data. Such data have four attributes, location within a coordinate system, codes to indicate feature type (eg a feature code for a road), one or more associated values (eg a height linked with a contour), and information on the linkage or topology of features. For the second method of data input, maps can be scanned automatically and then features coded according to type, value and topology. The third method of input utilizes the growing availability of data from other sources, for example from remote sensing and organizations which sell digitized data (eg Ordnance Survey). Such data can be obtained on tapes which can be read into the GIS using a tape drive; alternately data may be acquired from some remote source and transferred within a computer network. The processing, display and storage components of a GIS are self-explanatory; it has been the outstanding increase in processing and storage capacities which has led to the growth of GIS. The idea of GIS being a set of tools has already been introduced and it is inevitable that the quality of the tools will be judged by the final products. Output can range from very cheap prints on dot matrix printers to large plots using high cost plotters or colour thermal printers. Also important is the capability to produce output files which can be imported into other systems for further processing.

The applicability of GIS to land resource issues is best summarized by consideration of a range of processing capabilities: first, map input, editing, polygon processing and output, and second, digital terrain models.

Map input, editing, polygon processing and output

Information on maps exists in the form of point, line, area and text data. These data can be input to a GIS by digitizing features on a digitizing table, data capture through automated scanning of the original maps or through the purchase of data in digital form as provided by the Ordnance Survey. At present most data capture is by digitizing, a time-consuming and tedious task. The importance of good quality digitizing cannot be under-emphasized since subsequent difficulties in data processing are minimized. A critical test for any digitizing module in a GIS is the ease with which errors can be identified and corrected. Once input, the digitized data can be updated very easily. All input data have to be coded so that features such as spot heights, roads and lakes have characteristic numbers. A zoom and window facility exists to permit detailed consideration of any sub-area. To point, lines, areas and text can be added data on one or more variables. This is tackled in different ways dependent upon the particular system. One method involves the assignment of attribute codes, for example the height value for a contour line. Another and more refined technique is the input of such data to an integrated relational database system.

The actual use of a GIS in a land resource project is best illustrated by way of a particular example. The author has been involved with a collaborative project with the Soil Science Institute of Athens in Greece. The project area is Viotia to the north-west of Athens and the objective is to develop a land resource information system for a Mediterranean environment using GIS technology. The aims are to produce single factor and land capability maps, but the main research emphasis is to develop techniques for assessing land suitability for specific crops. Viotia is typical of many basins in Greece – an extensive plainland mantled with Pleistocene and Holocene sediments and surrounded by uplands and mountains formed of Tertiary and Cretaceous flysch and limestones. An outstanding feature of the plain is the reclaimed Lake Kopias. Before reclamation early in the twentieth century, Kopias was a vast reedy lake in winter while in summer it became a marshy plain. Former areas of peat have disappeared through cultivation, fire and shrinkage; an overall lowering of 3.50 m has been estimated on the former lake bed between 1882 and the present. Entisols and gleys occur on the former lake, while inceptisols and vertisols are associated with the fringing terraces and fans. Alfisols are found higher, either on the upper stable terraces or on the upland plateau areas while entisols are dominant on the colluvial areas and steeper slopes.

The soils of Viotia were mapped by the free soil survey approach with emphasis being given to aerial photo interpretation and subsequent field checks and sampling. Such an approach proved particularly suitable in Viotia given the clarity of soil-landform assemblages, for example the former lake area and the sequence of coalescing alluvial fans round the perimeter of the plain are very distinct. Mapping was also restricted to lowland areas of agricultural value. Within each mapping unit, at least one full soil profile description was obtained as well as subsequent analytical data. Sites of brief inspection using an auger were also recorded. In summary, the data produced by the survey can be summarized as follows:

MAPPING UNIT DATA
polygon type (eg mapped, not mapped, sea)
drainage (classes)
texture (classes and for three depths)
gravel
slope (classes)
erosion (classes)
calcium carbonate (classes)
soil order, suborder and great group
irrigability
variability class and limitations
rainfall

SITE DATA
profile descriptions
analytical data for different horizons
sand, silt and clay
electrical conductivity
salt content
calcium carbonate
organic matter
cation exchange capacity

For input and processing of the Viotia data, use is made of Laser-Scan software running on a microVAX II with a Sigmex 6000 graphics terminal. In the digitizing module, line segments are digitized for mapping units, contours and coastline; attribute codes for the variables listed above are added to each seed point within each mapping unit. A similar approach is also adopted for the input of attribute codes for sampling points (soil analytical data). Following digitizing of mapping unit segments, the vector 'spaghetti' requires to be put through geometry idealization and structure formation; this involves amalgamation of coincident lines, extension or truncation of line ends to meet at T junctions, the formation of unique junction points at line ends, the breaking of crossing lines and the generation of link/node junction structure. Polygons corresponding to soil mapping units can then be generated using another module and polygon labels are taken from seed point data.

With soil mapping data in this form, tremendous

flexibility then exists in terms of selecting polygons according to one or more attribute codes to generate as many maps as required. Data on such polygons can be stored in the form of attribute codes associated with the perimeter lines, as seed points or in an integrated database system. It is the flexibility of map presentation which is the outstanding characteristic of geographical information systems. Such flexibility is particularly important in land resource mapping and land evaluation when the need is to produce maps in forms determined by user requirements. Styles of lines, symbols, shading and text can be easily changed by manual means or through the use of macro routines. The final maps can be displayed in a very impressive manner on high resolution graphic screens, but of greater relevance is the ability to obtain good quality hard copies through the use of plotters or colour thermal printers. In summary the mapping unit data can be retrieved,

combined or modified using Boolean algebra of union, intersection or negation; such processing and map display is aided by the provision of purpose-written macro routines. Figure 7.2a illustrates the capability of selecting one attribute of a mapping unit, in this instance soil erosion class, and plotting the results. In Figure 7.2b mapping units have been coded according to soil order, but in addition, the pH of topsoil as measured at sampling points, is indicated. With the type of database described earlier for the project in Viotia, Greece, there is an almost infinite possibility of selecting and displaying attribute values for mapping units or sampling points. Furthermore, particular combinations of crop growing requirements can be specified so that land suitability can be assessed.

A more complicated type of processing is required when the need is to overlay different polygons to meet specific requirements. Again this

(a)

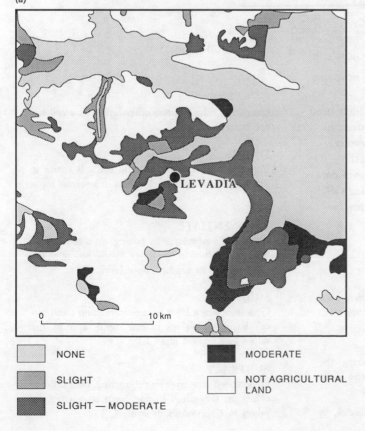

Figure 7.2 Examples of GIS capability for selecting and plotting attributes of areas and points; in (a) soil erosion classes are plotted for the area round Levadia, Greece; in (b) pH values at sampled points and soil orders are shown for mapping units

NONE

SLIGHT

SLIGHT — MODERATE

MODERATE

NOT AGRICULTURAL LAND

(b)

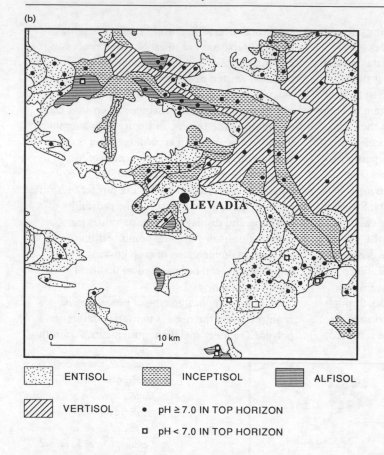

Figure 7.2 Examples of GIS capability for selecting and plotting attributes of areas and points; in (a) soil erosion classes are plotted for the area round Levadia, Greece; in (b) pH values at sampled points and soil orders are shown for mapping units

LEVADIA

0   10 km

| ENTISOL | INCEPTISOL | ALFISOL |

VERTISOL   • pH ≥ 7.0 IN TOP HORIZON

□ pH < 7.0 IN TOP HORIZON

is a fundamental GIS operation and is widely used in land evaluation. Processing is usually done in raster mode. An indication of such processing capabilities can be given by summarizing the commands which perform different forms of data analysis available within a raster GIS called OSU MAP-for-the-PC (Geographic Information Systems Laboratory 1989).

Local operations

ADD

Generates a new layer by adding together, on a cell-by-cell basis, the values in two or more input layers

COVER

Forms a new layer for display by 'covering' the cells in one layer with the cells in a second layer

CROSS

Forms a new layer, using user-defined codes, by comparing values in two other layers on a cell-by-cell basis

DIVIDE

Forms a new layer by dividing the cell values in one input layer by the cell values in a second input layer

EXPONENTIATE

Generates a new layer by raising, on a cell-by-cell basis, the values in one layer to the power of the values found in another input layer

MULTIPLY

Generates a new layer by multiplying, on a cell-by-cell basis, the values in one input layer by the values in a second input layer

SUBTRACT

Generates a new layer by subtracting, on a cell-by-cell basis, the values in one input layer from the values in a second input layer.

Reclassification

AVERAGE
Creates a new layer the values of which are the average of the values of the input layers

FILTER
Creates a new layer whose values are a function of the values in the input layer and filters are applied to result in smoothing of values or the addition of contrast between borders so that regions are sharpened

MAXIMIZE
Creates a new layer the values of which are the maximum values of the specified existing layers

MINIMIZE
Creates a new layer the values of which are the minimum values of the specified existing layers

RENUMBER
Creates a new layer in the database, the reassigned values and categories of which replace the values and categories of the existing layer

SLICE
Generates a new layer in the database, the categories of which are established at N equal intervals

SORT
Creates a new layer of increasing ordinal values

Distance analysis

DRAIN
Defines a downhill path over a surface from a specified starting-point

RADIATE
Generates a new layer in the database to indicate whether specified points are visible from other points

SPREAD
Measures the shortest distance between a specified region and any cell that falls within a given radius of that region

Shape analysis

CLUMP
Generates a new layer the values of which define regions consisting of cells with the same value derived from the original map

EULER
Generates a new layer in the database, the values of which characterize the categories of the original map by 'Euler Number' as used for shape analysis. (A Euler Number indicates the solidness of an area; its value reflects the degree to which an area is fragmented and punctured.)

SIZE
Generates a new layer in the database, the values of which indicate the size of areas of the original map occupied by cells of the same value

SURVEY
Generates a new layer, the values of which indicate the overall convexity of the categories of the original layer

Statistical analysis

DESCRIBE
Provides a summary of the specified layer and a count of the number of cells in each category

SCAN
Summarizes the cell values within a local neighbourhood by calculating a descriptive statistic about the neighbourhood and assigning that value to the neighbourhood's central cell

SCORE
Compiles a number of summaries and statistics about the relationships between the cells in two layers

Terrain analysis

DIFFERENTIATE
Generates a new layer, the values of which are the slopes (derivatives) of the cells on the input layer

ORIENT
Generates a new layer, the values of which indicate the aspect or direction in which the surface of the cell faces downhill

PROFILE
Generates a new layer in the database, the values of which characterize the local area about each cell on the original map. The characterization generated represents the vertical silhouette of three adjacent cells.

(source: Geographic Information Systems Laboratory 1989)

The availability of powerful and low cost raster based GIS software such as OSU MAP-for-the-PC or IDRISI (Eastman 1990) means that there is no need for computer programming to be undertaken for routine GIS operations. An obvious analogy is with statistical packages; again nobody today needs to write programs for standard statistical analysis. The availability of powerful GIS packages has markedly increased because of the power and low cost of PC computers. Prior to such availability, special purpose programs had to be written to analyse and present raster data. As an example, Davidson and Jones (1988) describe a project in central Scotland designed to help with the identification of prime agricultural land and land suited to forestry. Information on elevation, slope, aspect, soils, land capability, vegetation, land type, and tree species and yield class were coded for a total of 7300 cells, each measuring 100 by 100 m. Information could then be selectively extracted from the data array, processed and presented. An example of the output is shown in Figure 7.3; in this instance, the results from two different definitions of prime agricultural land are shown. For definition 1, cells in order to be classified as prime agricultural land had to meet the following criteria:

elevation: <150 m
slope: <3 degrees

soil drainage: free or imperfect
maximum rooting depth: usually >40 cm

As can be seen, few cells round the village of Gargunnock meet these requirements. The outstanding advantage of this approach is that results can be quickly compared when selection criteria are varied. Thus for definition 2 in Figure 7.3, cells were plotted as indicating prime agricultural land if they met the following conditions:

elevation: <300 m
slope: <11 degrees
soil drainage: free or imperfect

As can be seen, prime agricultural land is far more extensive with using this second definition. This key GIS attribute of flexibility is again emphasized. Furthermore, as the trend towards parameter audit continues as part of environmental impact assessment, the importance of quoting in full selection rules concerning land quality will become apparent.

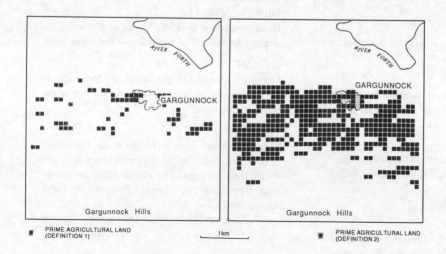

PRIME AGRICULTURAL LAND
(DEFINITION 1)

1km

PRIME AGRICULTURAL LAND
(DEFINITION 2)

Figure 7.3 The distribution of prime agricultural land round the village of Gargunnock in central Scotland according to two definitions (see text for details); each symbol corresponds to an area of 100 × 100 m (source: Davidson and Jones 1988: 89)

Digital terrain models

Digital terrain models (DTMs) are increasingly being used as an effective way of portraying landscape form and pattern. The starting-point is digitizing of contours and then a spatial structure generation program has to be used. Thiessen neighbours are determined for each point and then a system of triangles is constructed which uniquely segment the map area (Delaunay triangulation). An option may exist for constrained Delaunay triangulation so that the connectivity of original data strings (eg rivers, ridgelines) is honoured. Further data processing is then necessary to translate the triangulation data to a regular grid. Heights for the cells require to be determined by an interpolation procedure and two methods of interpolating the height values are common: (1) a linear facet option whereby the interior triangular surface is assumed to be smooth and (2) a smooth patch option whereby a smooth surface is fitted to the vertices of the triangles. The first option proves quite acceptable if the data density is high in relation to the grid size. It is important to check the results from interpolation of heights. As an example problems are associated with flat bottomed valleys where there is a dearth of contours. The interpolation procedure leads to the downward extension of valleysides to give false height values to the valley floor. These have to be corrected by using an editing facility.

After such data preparation which has involved a change from vector to raster data structures, the images of the landscape can be generated. These images can be rotated, tilted, viewed from different heights and positions and vertical exaggeration changed. Of particular practical value is the overlay capability whereby any digitized information in the original digitized files can be draped over the DTM. This information can be in the form of point symbols, lines, fill-in patterns or fill-in symbols.

The first reaction to the striking images of DTMs may be that they are fun but of little practical value. Such was the initial opinion of the author! However, there are many potential areas of application in dealing with rural land use matters.

As an example, views from particular points in a landscape can be generated and then the results compared using different afforestation policies. Figure 7.4 illustrates the results of draping part of the Tinto Hills in south central Scotland with a forestry pattern which was proposed but not implemented. The advantage of such simulated images is their reality compared to conventional maps. An immediate impression of landscape impact can be achieved with the use of such simulations. An example of using a DTM as a means of illustrating a skiing development is given in Figure 7.5; again, such an image provides members of planning committees with a realistic impression of the development within the landscape. The example of forestry simulation in Figure 7.4 is limited in two ways. First, the simulation gives no impression of particular landscape textures as created by different tree species though some software packages are available which have this capability. Second, a static image is simulated while landscape planning of forestry necessitates evaluating both the growth and harvesting of trees. Kellomaki and Pukkala (1989) describe a technique for simulating changing forested landscapes. For individual forest stands or plots, stem volume, sawlog volume and pulp wood volume are calculated. Predictions can then be made about various future volumes under different management strategies. Results are presented in tabular as well as in landscape simulation form for future years using different management strategies.

Visibility analysis becomes possible once DTMs have been created – areas within which one or more features are visible can be determined and plotted. The area visible from a popular tourist spot known as the Commando Memorial near Spean Bridge is shown in Figure 7.6. Visibility analysis can be along particular line of sights, within defined arcs, up to defined distance limits and be calculated taking into account the height of surface features. Figure 7.6a demonstrates the impact of forestry on visibility. Besides mapping visible areas from points in the landscape, it is also possible to map the number of features such as individual electricity pylons which are visible (Figure 7.7). Account must be taken of the height of the pylons. Results can be

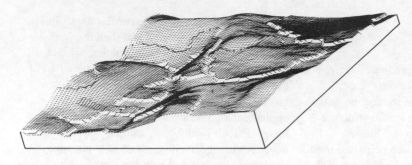

Figure 7.4 *A digital terrain model of part of the Tinto Hills to the south of Glasgow showing a proposed forestry pattern which was not established*

plotted for different proposed routes for powerlines in order to determine which one causes least visual intrusion. Figure 7.8 shows how areas within which at most five pylons are visible can be draped over a DTM. Again, such simulations assist with the evaluation of alternative routes and assessment of impact within landscapes of outstanding scenic quality. High cost GIS software is not necessary in order to perform such visibility analyses; Hadrian et al (1988) demonstrate how they adapted the Map Analysis Package (MAP), the forerunner of OSU MAP-for-the-PC, in order to map automatically visibility along transmission line corridors.

7.2 Objectives of geographical information systems

The value of a GIS, like any other information

system, stems from the usefulness of the results. Thus a GIS has this applied focus of storing, processing and presenting spatially referenced data important to managerial functions. In a review of these general issues, de Man (1988) identifies such functions as planning, decision making, maintaining an inventory, research and monitoring. The objective in providing information towards these activities is to reduce uncertainty in decision making. The provision of information costs money, and thus the reduction in uncertainty over decision making must warrant the expenditure. Thus the key point is that a GIS has to justify itself in terms of efficiency of operation, quality of output, but most important of all, in provision of results helpful to decisions. Any organization considering the purchase of a GIS has to identify the types of decisions which will benefit from such a system. The whole approach must be dictated by the management issues.

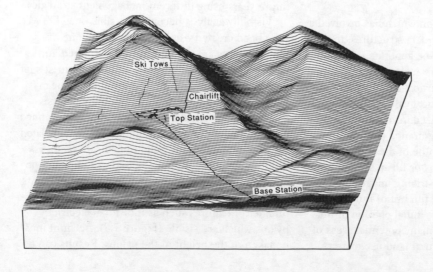

Figure 7.5 *A digital terrain model of Aonach Mor near Fort William showing the main features associated with the ski development*

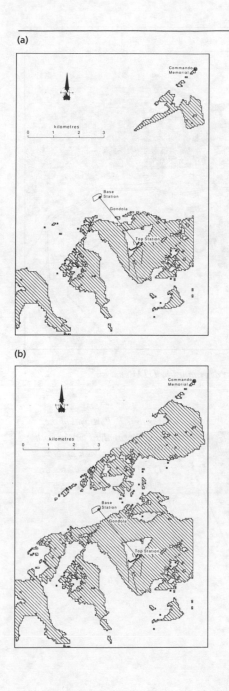

(a)

(b)

Figure 7.6 Visible areas from the Commando monument near Spean Bridge are indicated by shading; such mapping is done automatically using DTM data; in (a) account is made for the effect of existing forestry on visibility; in (b) no such account is made

Anyone who becomes proficient in a particular GIS will quickly be impressed by the considerable scope for different forms of information presentation. This is a great strength of GIS, but also a potential weakness. The danger is that decision makers will be swamped by the information possibilities meaning that they cannot assimilate it all. In the mid-1980s, the author began to be involved with regional planners in trying to demonstrate the potential assistance of GIS to strategic planning. His approach was to input all available information and then to produce many different forms of output which, in some way, might prove to be of assistance. The end result was that much of the output was ignored, first because there was far too much of it, and second, because it was not shaped to the issues confronting the planners. Of course, there is a chicken and egg problem in that decision makers cannot formulate specific questions which can be addressed by GIS until they have acquired some experience of GIS capabilities. This is now becoming less and less of a problem given the accelerating rate at which commercial and public bodies are purchasing geographical information systems.

An evaluation of GIS output can be done by assessing the extent to which decisions can benefit from the availability of such information. Benefit can be in the form of better decisions through the provision of more relevant information. In addition there may be benefits of speed of information provision as well as ease by which databases can be maintained and updated. It is instructive to summarize some of the results from a study designed to evaluate the extent to which a GIS could assist with the provision of information for rural environmental planning (Davidson et al 1991). In this project, four contrasting case studies were selected; a skiing development, an overhead powerline development, a forestry scheme and an open-cast coal-mine proposal. Output from some of these case studies has already been demonstrated in Figures 7.4 to 7.8. For these case studies, selection of input data, processing and forms of ultimate output were driven by the issues defined by the planners involved. A key component was a workshop held towards the end of the project when

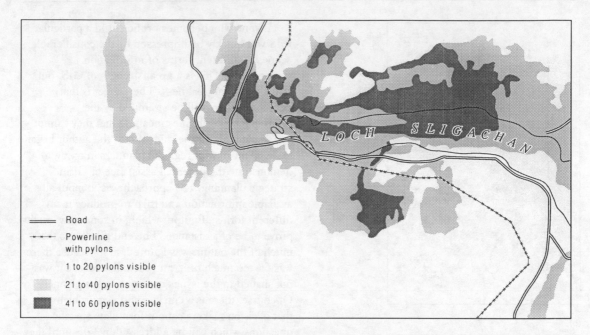

Figure 7.7 The visibility of electricity pylons in the Loch Sligachan area of Skye as determined by DTM analysis

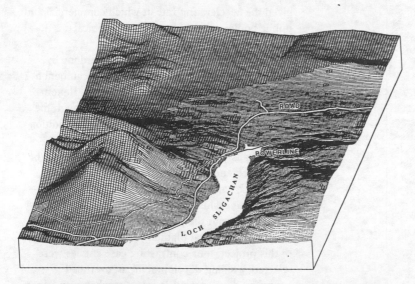

Figure 7.8 Portrayal of the visibility analysis for the Loch Sligachan area as a draped DTM; in the shaped area, five pylons at most can be seen

the output from the case studies was presented to the planners. Their task was to assess the extent to which the results were cost-effective and helpful with respect to the defined planning issues.

The use of DTMs with draped overlays as well as visibility analysis were most favoured by the planners. The merits of DTMs in presenting

realistic landscape simulation were stressed, not so much in terms of assisting with detailed planning or design, but rather with obtaining overall impressions of development proposals. Thus GIS processing, mainly in terms of landscape modelling and visibility determinations, was highlighted for the case studies dealing with development proposals for skiing, forestry and an overhead powerline; the use of GIS for the open-cast coal-mine proposal did not prove justified. The major criticism from the planners centred on the database in terms of time of input and lack of information on certain topics deemed important. For example, a total of 104 hours were spent inputting the information for the Aonach Mor skiing development; the area covered 56 km^2 and necessitated digitizing contours, the skiing development, forestry, vegetation, footpaths and streams. Contour digitizing took the greatest time, not surprising given the location adjacent to Ben Nevis! In total, 59 out of the 104 hours were devoted to digitizing information from topographic maps and the planners felt that such time when translated into cost would be excessive, especially if the planning authority had to pay. Ventura et al (1988) consider the cost of data input as a major constraint to the adoption of GIS technology. For Wisconsin, they quote a price of $12 per square kilometre for digitizing soils in 1985; this is reduced to $5 per square kilometre when a scanner is used though there is the inevitable degradation in data quality with a raster system. On the other hand, if GIS is being used as an aid to environmental impact assessment as in a skiing proposal, the cost of data input in relation to the cost of the development is minute. Also, it needs to be noted that data in digital form are increasingly being provided by such bodies as the Ordnance Survey and this should increase speed and reduce cost of data input. In many ways the most interesting aspect of the evaluation for Aonach Mor was that more specific and analytical questions began to be asked. For example, could the impact on vegetation of summer visitors be predicted? Could landscape simulations be provided to indicate the results for different forest felling schemes? What will the impact on drainage be of the development? Thus the use of a GIS should not be seen as the end point in information provision, but also as a stimulus to the formulation of further questions, some of which may be amenable to solution by making further use of the system.

7.3 Applications of geographical information systems

In this section emphasis is given to summarizing a range of case studies which apply GIS to land resource questions. The intention is to give the reader an impression of the diversity of GIS applications. The approach is to select GIS applications according to scale and purpose.

Continental land resources

The Australian Resources Information System (ARIS) as described by Cocks et al (1988) is designed to assist with decisions regarding small-scale problems of resource utilization. ARIS began in the mid-1970s as a means of displaying population characteristics according to enumeration districts as well as utility data, for example electricity consumption. This digital map base provided the foundation for a continental scale GIS which was established during 1979–82. This had as one of its aims, the creation of a spatially co-ordinated resource database which could be used to provide continental perspectives for regional land use studies. In the first instance, basic mapping units were derived from local government areas, the larger of which were subdivided into smaller cells or watersheds. Data on such variables as soils, natural vegetation, climate, lithology, land cover, population and census data, coastal land use, water usage, transport statistics and terrain were stored for each basic mapping unit. Particular problems were encountered with changes in administrative units since alterations were also required in the databases. As a result, subsequent development of ARIS has been based on a grid cell framework, 3000 half by half degree latitude-longitude cells and 11,000 quarter by quarter latitude-longitude cells. The following databases were established: GAZETTEER (names and features from national topographic maps), LGA81 (the 1981 census statistics), AGSTATS (data on agricultural enterprises), ARDB (bio-physical data), ELECT81 (maps based of electoral divisions and associated data), NATPK (register of conservation reserves), COAST (bio-physical and socio-economic data for 10 km sections of the Australian coastline). A suite of GIS processing modules was then established in order to perform such operations as classification, land use allocation, identification of regions, and raster processing (using the Map Analysis Package discussed in section 7.1).

In the latter part of their paper, Cocks et al (1988) outline fourteen projects which have utilized the capabilities of ARIS. An early study was concerned with evaluating the suitability of mapping units for the location of a new city. A similar analysis investigated rangeland resources in terms of suitability for grazing. A later project studied the viability of pastoralism through the identification of areas currently ungrazed, but having good viability prospects and areas currently grazed which might be withdrawn given their poor viability prospects. A different study focused on recognizing localities in Australia distinguished by unusual combinations of soil and vegetation, areas which merit consideration for future national parks status. A GIS such as ARIS is ideal for locating areas with defined characteristics; Cocks et al (1988) quote the Cobar project which had the aims first of assembling soil, vegetation, topography and climate data for a proposed army training area at Cobar in New South Wales, and then to find other areas with a similar mix of bio-physical attributes. Other uses of ARIS were for the location and mapping of rainforests and for the characterization of national parks in terms of bio-geographical province and bio-climate. Such a brief outline is sufficient to demonstrate the potential of a GIS at the continental scale as a means of assisting with land resource evaluation and management.

The continent of Australia has the merit of coinciding with one political unit, a situation which eases questions of data availability and compatibility for a GIS. In the European Community, the need for an information system on the environment to assist with policy formulation is expressed in the CORINE programme which was established in 1985. This programme is not so far advanced as ARIS and has taken a rather different development route. Three principles underlie the CORINE programme: existing data are to be input, collaboration between member states is emphasized, and the system must be capable of providing output at scales ranging from the Community level down to 1 km^2. In a preliminary report, Wiggins et al (1986; 1987) describe progress in inputting data on soils, climate, biotopes and topography. In contrast to the Australian approach, use is being made of a large commercial GIS, ARC/INFO, which, while located in London, can be accessed via computer network from remote nodes within the EC. This necessitates that users at different localities will require experience of the particular system. Wiggins et al (1986; 1987) describe an acute need for training and education of the users as to what a GIS is and what it should be able to do. Demonstration packages along with the provision of user friendly menus should help, but such menus cannot be designed until user requirements are clear. In an initial project dealing with soil erosion risk in the Mediterranean region, Briggs et al (1989) describe considerable problems associated with integrating soil map data in the CORINE database. Soil data were obtained by scanning and manual digitizing of the European Community 1:1,000,000 soil map, but difficulties arose as a result of projection conversion and detailed fitting by which the coverage was registered to the reference geographic base as used in the CORINE project. For example, when the soil coverage was overlaid on the CORINE base, coastline displacements of up to 50 km became apparent. Investigations into the map projection details and cartographic history revealed that the original soil map had been arranged in latitudinal zones, each on a different projection. Considerable effort had to be spent on converting the projection of these zones and in addition edge matching was necessary to recombine them. The experience from this project provides a salutory lesson in the difficulties associated with combining data from different sources into one GIS.

National land resources

National geographical information systems can deal with such tasks as providing resource inventories, for example managing and retrieving soil or geological information, maintaining cartographic and statistical cover, or performing a range of land evaluation analyses to predict land productivity in biological or economic terms under a variety of scenarios. An indication of such diversity in objectives can be obtained by summarizing some examples.

In developing a national information system for Japan, the first step involved the computerization of soil survey data in order to give the flexibility of database management and presentation (Kosaki et al 1981). This provided the basis for developing a soil information system which is part of a larger agricultural land resource information system (Kato 1984). Besides soil information, this agricultural land resource information system has files on crop performance and management, agrometeorology, geomorphology and geology, water resources and land use. The soil information system stores soil mapping information at different scales as well as all the descriptive and analytical data derived from point sampling. Kato (1984) identifies the ability to interpret soil mapping units for defined purposes as one of the most important attributes of the system. Emphasis is also given to the input of soil monitoring data, for example soil temperature and moisture, so that prediction of future conditions may be possible. Such capabilities are possible only through the availability of relevant data and national agencies have key responsibilities for this. As an example of what is required, the US Soil Conservation Service has developed a State Soil Geographic Data Base. Such data can be linked with information on topography, land use and land cover data to provide an infinite number of interpretive maps at the regional, state and national scales (Bliss and Reybold 1989).

Examples from Sri Lanka and Jamaica are selected to illustrate more specific systems for evaluating land resources at the national level. In Sri Lanka the Land Use Policy Planning Division of the Ministry of Lands and Land Development use a land information system (Dent and Ridgway 1986; Ridgway and Jayasinghe 1986). The system was designed to answer questions of the following type. Within Sri Lanka, how extensive are areas with a broad potential for sugar cane? Where are these areas and what proportion of these areas is available for further development? Where are the areas with the highest soil erosion hazard?

Priority was given to developing a low cost system which would ensure easy access. A grid system was adopted with varying cell sizes according to scale of application. At the national scale, a map at 1:500,000 proved convenient and a cell size of 25 km^2 was adopted; corresponding cell sizes for the district and local scales were 1 km^2 and 1 ha. For land evaluation at the national scale, data on geology, landforms, climate, hydrology, soil, vegetation and land use were coded for component cells and input to a database system. Prediction was then possible for certain other variables, for example soil erosion hazard on the basis of slope, rainfall erosivity and soil type codes. Land evaluation was achieved by grading relevant land properties such as drainage, slope or depth. Then an overall suitability class was determined on the basis of the most limiting property. The results were printed out using a low cost dot matrix printer. The Sri Lankan system is noteworthy in that it started with the types of question which required to be answered; also, priority was given to the use of low cost hardware and software.

The Jamaica Resource Assessment Project was initiated in 1981, the main aim being to improve agricultural development through the use of a Comprehensive Resource Inventory and Evaluation System (CRIES). Agriculture provides employment for about one-third of Jamaica's workforce, and with the decline of the bauxite industry, the Jamaican government realized the importance of stimulating the agricultural sector. The essential approach was to use the methodology of CRIES as originally developed in Michigan State University (Schultink 1986; Schultink and Amaral 1987) in order to devise the Jamaica Physical Land Evaluation System (JAMPLES).

The three objectives of CRIES are to present a

consistent approach to land resource assessment which can be applied to many different countries, to assist with integrated surveys through the provision of a computer-based system which can analyse development options, and to provide training and assistance for local staff. It is a raster based system whereby a range of environmental, land use and crop response data are referenced per individual cell. Considerable flexibility exists in terms of defining and delimiting agro-ecological production zones, also called resource planning units. Data input and processing is achieved by a GIS menu within CRIES. Input, editing, provision of statistics, and output are fairly obvious component functions; also of interest is the capability within an analysis module to calculate soil loss using the universal soil loss equation. Another menu available within CRIES is an agro-economic information system; other modules provide scope for predicting water balance and yield and appraising land use options.

Information on topography, agro-climatology, soils and land use constitute the database for the Jamaica Physical Land Evaluation System (Batjes et al 1987). The FAO *Framework for Land Evaluation* (FAO 1976) is the basis of the physical assessment procedure. Before the matching of land use requirements with land qualities is undertaken, a check is first made that the particular crop is feasible on agro-climatic requirements, and also that the predicted erosion rate is acceptable in relation to the tolerable rate. These two preliminary operations require the use of models to predict soil moisture balance and erosion rates. For the former, crop water requirements for the growing period are compared with estimates of soil moisture availability; the differences are correlated with yield response in order to provide agro-climatic zoning. The soil erosion model uses data on rainfall erosivity, and slope value and length. After such preliminary analysis, the soil requirements of crops are matched with land qualities; these are soil reaction in the topsoil, nutrient retention, nutrient availability, calcium carbonate content, salinity and sodicity hazards, oxygen availability, soil depth and workability. The intention is that suitability assessments for fifty different crops will be possible.

As Batjes et al (1987) report, JAMPLES is envisaged as providing a powerful tool in planning studies designed to determine the location and extent of land most suitable for particular uses.

Regional and local land resources

Review of the literature on GIS applications to subnational administrative units indicates that such systems have often been developed for more specific purposes. This is not to deny that some states or regions within particular countries have developed multipurpose geographical information systems. For example, Treworgy (1984) reports early progress on a GIS by the Illinois Department of Energy and Natural Resources. The need in Illinois was a corporate system to serve the needs of component divisions, natural history, geology, water survey, state museum and energy and environmental affairs. The overall aim was to provide major files of general interest which could be shared between divisions, while leaving each division free to develop files of specific interest to their own needs. An example of a state GIS dedicated to land resource data is given by Nielson et al (1990) for Montana. The data are grid based with component cells measuring 5.6 by 3.8 km. For each cell, about 200 environmental attributes are coded; these can be summarized under such headings as precipitation means, growing season means, temperature means, evaporation and potential evapotranspiration, soils, land use, physiography and land use. Climatic measures for component cells were predicted from regression analysis. The result is a considerable database for Montana. Nielson et al (1990) give a brief indication of the use of the system which has been in operation since 1987. It has been used to identify agricultural areas where there is a potential for nonpoint-source pollution of groundwater through percolation. The system has also been used to help with assessing land suitability for alternative crops. This necessitated the specification of requirements for these crops and then the interrogation of the

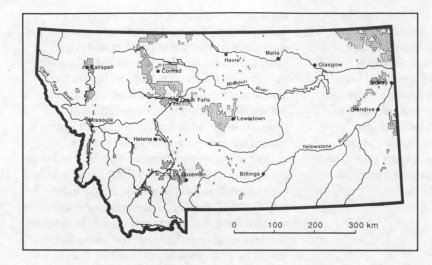

Figure 7.9 Potential for spring canola production in Montana based on length of frost-free season, irrigation capability, annual and growing season precipitation, and ambient temperature during peak flowering
(source: Nielson et al 1990: 453)

database to determine which cells met the conditions. Figure 7.9 illustrates the results for spring canola while similar analyses have been done for safflower and amaranth production. One particularly innovative capability of the Montana system is to be able to match any farm with the most similar research farm in terms of environmental attributes; this means that farmers can be given advice on crop variety and performance based on environments similar to their own. Such prediction also makes use of research farm data from other states.

As an example of a GIS implemented in response to a specific land management need, reference is made to Dane County in south central Wisconsin (Ventura et al 1988). A county conservation committee was charged with the responsibility of devising soil erosion control plans. In detail the requirements were to specify maximum acceptable rates of erosion, locate where erosion standards were not being met and determine land ownership, identify land use or management changes which would result in acceptable soil erosion rates, advise on suitable measures for controlling soil erosion and establish priorities for controlling soil erosion. Clearly a GIS could help with some of these tasks. A raster database was established, incorporating information on soils, soil erosion attributes (soil erodibility, slope length, steepness, tolerable soil loss, wind

erodibility), land ownership, and agricultural land cover from Landsat TM imagery. After local calibration, the universal soil loss equation was used to estimate erosion rates and it was then possible to map automatically soil loss for each quarter section (about 65 hectares). The ratio of predicted erosion rate to tolerable rate was calculated and mapped to indicate the varying need for the adoption of conservation measures. Also calculated was the combined cropping and conservation practice factor, as in the universal soil loss equation, in order to achieve a tolerable soil erosion rate. Again the results were mapped in order to highlight areas requiring the adoption of soil control measures.

Another example from the USA serves to illustrate how a GIS can be used as an aid to environmental management at the local level. In this instance reference is made to a designated wilderness area called the Hercules Glades Wilderness Area, part of the Mark Twain National Park in southern Missouri (Lowell and Astroth 1989). The key question was the selection of a management strategy for such an area; evidence exists to indicate that the area had been burned in the past to aid hunting and to keep the glades open for cattle grazing. The glades are essentially rocky barrens dominated by herbaceous flora with sparse woody vegetation. One view was that the glades were a fire-dependent ecotype and the prohibition of burning as a result of wilderness designation, would lead to their loss. Nevertheless the Forest Service has had to carry out some burning, primarily to limit the wildfire hazard. Before such burning is permitted, the Forest Service is required to evaluate the impact of such controlled fires. The use of a GIS as described by Lowell and Astroth (1989) has proved invaluable with reference to studying the changing nature of the glades, investigating the physiographic factors which influence ecological succession in the glades, and predicting likely impacts of proposed burns in particular areas.

The use of GIS for monitoring

There is an obvious need at the local planning level to try to ensure that loss of agricultural land to urbanization takes place with minimum impact. Geographical information systems can be of considerable assistance with such planning as can be demonstrated by examples from Florida and Massachusetts. Tan and Shih (1988) summarize the considerable pressure which has occurred in Florida since the early 1960s, epitomized in the 45 per cent increase in population in the ten years prior to 1988. They stress the merits in adopting a GIS as a means of storing historical data on agricultural land use, monitoring land use change, and identifying changing spatial patterns in agricultural activities. A preliminary investigation is conducted in the coastal area of St Lucie County, Florida. Historical patterns of land use were obtained from analysis of aerial photographs whilst more recent data were extracted from Landsat imagery. Tabular information on land use change was produced from processing within the database system, and the integrated GIS capability meant that spatial patterns of change could also be displayed. The basic premise is that knowledge and understanding of such patterns and magnitude of change should lead to better planning control for the future.

Loss of agricultural land has consequences not only for the agricultural economy, but also with respect to the loss of open space and cultural

heritage. In response to such pressures in Massachusetts, the legislature there has invested money in the purchase of developments rights on agricultural land (Lindhult et al 1988). Another strategy under discussion there is the creation of land banks, funded by a surcharge on real estate transactions. Decisions on the selection of strategies designed to protect farmland require information on land resources as well as upon an analysis of any conflict between farmland and urban development. Lindhult et al (1988) describe how the Metropolitan Landscape Planning Model (METLAND) provides a comprehensive approach to landscape and planning assessment. In detail it has three components, assessment of landscape resources, generation of land use plans, and evaluation of these plans. Such analysis is very much enhanced in terms of speed and level of detail by the adoption of a GIS. The result has been the implementation of a low cost, vector based GIS. Importance was attached to a low cost system to ensure implementation at the local planning level; furthermore a polygon based system was necessary given the required level of accuracy in recording land ownership patterns. Lindhult et al (1988) provide a detailed case study dealing with the city of Westfield in Massachusetts, the aim being to determine the extent and location of conflict between urban development and the city's farmland. This involved the input of data on farm boundaries, soils, land use, areas liable to flood, surface drainage, roads and railways, slope, and sewers. In order to assess conflict between agriculture and urban development, five evaluation procedures were used, agricultural productivity potential, municipal or administrative forces, commitment to agriculture, physical development suitability, and flood plain hazard areas. The methodology is demonstrated with respect to identifying and mapping those farms which meet the criteria of the Massachusetts Agricultural Restriction Program; these farms are under the greatest development pressure and if they meet the criteria for this program, are eligible for preferential protection. Lindhult et al (1988) thus argue on the basis of their case study that a GIS can be of great assistance with the evolution of policies designed to protect farmland within a comprehensive planning process.

These examples from Florida and Massachusetts demonstrate how land use monitoring is aided by the use of geographical information systems. The monitoring and prediction of surface water acidity is another type of investigation which can benefit from the application of GIS technology. Such a study is reported by Campbell et al (1989) who describe the Direct/Delayed Response Project implemented by the US Environmental Protection Agency. The prime scientific questions in this project are to determine whether 'additional effects of acidic deposition might be immediate or immediately proportional to the levels of deposition (direct) or whether there are lags in time (delayed) related to important edaphic characteristics' (Campbell et al 1989: 350–1). The project has three study regions in the eastern USA where extensive data were assembled on surface water chemistry, soils, geology, vegetation, soil depth and soil drainage. Integral to the approach is the use of models at different levels, for example input-output budget estimates, models of processes regulating the supply of base cations and retention of atmospherically deposited sulphur, and integrated drainage basin models for predicting future effects of atmospheric sulphur on surface water chemistry (Robbins Church 1989). A GIS is used to assist with data collection and verification, analysis of spatial data, and communication of scientific results through the provision of mapped information. As one example, the GIS is used to demonstrate there is a relationship between the deposition of atmospheric sulphur and concentrations of surface water sulphate. Campbell et al (1989: 355) stress that the particular merit of using a GIS in the Direct/Delayed Response Project is the ability to 'interpret interactively the spatial trends of the results of modelling for alternative scenarios of atmospheric deposition'.

Geotechnical applications

Land use planners are faced with issues other than the protection of farmland in dealing with urban expansion. A consequence of directing urban expansion away from the better agricultural lands may be having to use areas with particular geotechnical difficulties or hazards. Soils may contain a high amount of expansive clay, thus special measures need to be taken to ensure structural stability. Areas of high water-table or peat also pose problems. In some cities such as Glasgow, certain areas are liable to subsidence as a result of the collapse of old mine workings; such information is relevant not only to planners, but also to land developers, estate agents, property valuers as well as to potential house purchasers. It can be readily appreciated that geotechnical information is of importance to any GIS designed to assist with land use planning and the identification of hazards to proposed development. For example, information can be extracted from geomorphological maps on the occurrence of landslides, slope instability, gullies and other forms of erosion. As discussed in Chapter 5, some soil surveys include geotechnical data on soil mapping units. Such data again can be included within a GIS in order to provide hazard predictions, for example for the stability of excavation trenches or septic tank operation; an additional capability would be to locate resources of sands or gravel. Another source of geotechnical data is from geological surveys. As an example, the British Geological Survey have provided reports dealing with geology for land use planning in the Clyde valley (Browne and McMillan 1989). Maps at a scale of 1:50,000 provide detail on the nature and thickness of drift deposits. Knowledge of the occurrence of sands, gravels, clays, silts, organic deposits, peat and landslips is of particular importance at an early stage of project design.

The advantages of a GIS for maintaining an inventory of geotechnical data should thus be apparent and can be illustrated by an example from Hong Kong. Styles et al (1986) explain how a computer-based terrain inventory has proved of value within the Geotechnical Control Office. Considerable pressure exists in Hong Kong for development, but there are also substantial geotechnical constraints. Information on slope, landform and morphology, erosion and instability, and geology (solid and drift) from a geotechnical survey at 1:20,000 has been input to a GIS using a raster approach with component cells measuring 2.04 ha. Additional information on aspect, relief, land use, vegetation, and average annual rainfall were also entered for each cell. Using this information, cells were automatically assigned to one of four geotechnical classes which express geotechnical limitations, suitability for development, engineering costs for development, intensity of site investigation required, and typical terrain characteristics. The GIS has the capability of mapping such classes as well as computing statistics. Of particular interest in the Hong Kong study is the determination of undeveloped land which poses no major geotechnical constraint. The resultant maps show the potential areas for development and are of particular assistance to land use planners.

7.4 Quality of GIS results

To conclude a chapter on geographical information systems, it is very relevant to discuss the issue of quality of output. As already explained, GIS are used as a means of providing information for a wide range of decisions. It is inevitable that there is a certain degree of uncertainty with any decision; the role of supportive information is to reduce such uncertainty, but this can never be eliminated. Ideally decisions should be made with the knowledge of this uncertainty, though in practice this seldom takes place. The degree of uncertainty which is acceptable in any particular GIS output should be considered at the start of any project; such considerations have a strong influence on selection of source data, cell grid if a raster approach is adopted, methods of GIS processing and resolution of map output.

Broad issues associated with the quality of GIS results can be introduced by considering a hypothetical example, digitizing the outline of the British Isles from a source map at 1:1,000,000. If digitizing is being done manually, the operator has to follow the coastline and every few moments, the button on the cursor is pressed. A highly irregular coastline is transformed into a large number of straight lines. A more sophisticated form of digitizing would include the fitting of smooth curves between digitized points, though this results in a considerable increase in the number of stored points. Clearly the operator plays a crucial role in controlling how close the digitized outline corresponds to the source map. The results from different operators or from the same operator repeating the process can be compared with the source map; the deviations between the digitized results and the source map are an expression of the digitizing *precision*. In order to assess *accuracy* in contrast to *precision*, the digitized outline has to be compared with the true or actual coastline of the British Isles. This involves concern with the level of detail on the coastline as portrayed on the 1:1,000,000 source map, potential accuracy, and errors associated with the map projection. GIS processing may necessitate transforming the vector coastline data into raster format. A crucial decision is the size of the component cells; if a large cell size is selected and the digitized coastline is converted into raster form, then if the raster data are re-converted to vector form a substantial loss in coastal detail will be evident. This example is used to illustrate how data degradation can result from GIS processing and may well be hidden in any ultimate output. Another related problem arises if the mapping units on the source map are about the same size as the cells. As Wehde (1982) shows, mapping errors can vary from 0 per cent to 100 per cent according to the position of grid cells with respect to mapping units.

From this introduction, what then is meant by quality of GIS results, either in map or statistical forms? In essence this is expressed in variation between output and source information (precision), and between output and truth or reality (accuracy). To understand such variation it is necessary to review possible sources of errors associated with geographical information systems, a topic comprehensively discussed by Burrough (1986). Three broad categories of possible error sources are described by him: obvious sources of error (for example, intensity of original survey and scale of published map), errors resulting from natural variations or from original measurements (for example, variability within mapping units), and errors arising through processing (for example, errors propagated by the overlay of maps or vector-raster transformations). To this list has to be added errors associated with data input to the GIS. Vitek et al (1984) who also plead for greater attention being given to the quality of GIS output, group the first two error sources of Burrough (1986) under the heading of inherent errors with the third corresponding to operational errors. It is relevant to summarize some of these errors, but particular emphasis is given to issues of natural variability and GIS processing given their importance to land resource assessment.

Any map is a model or generalization of reality; the degree of generalization is dependent upon such obvious factors as scale of original survey, density of field observations or measurements, methods used to predict properties in space, and publication scale of the map. A landscape is analogous to looking at a thin section of rock under a microscope; quite contrasting patterns are evident at different magnifications. Exactly the same applies with landscape patterns. There is a very real danger that in compiling data in a GIS for a particular area, maps of different scales are combined and treated as though they are of equivalent qualities. Errors are inevitable with data aggregated by mapping unit (polygon) or grid cell. The problems associated with categorizing soil mapping units according to defined properties have already been discussed in section 3.3. There is also the danger of accepting satellite data as providing truly representative values for average reflectance per pixel. Variation in ground surface conditions within such pixels can result in biased reflectance figures.

The hypothetical example of digitizing the coastline of the British Isles introduced the types of errors associated with operators as well as with the source map. Anyone who has done much digitizing knows the tedious nature of the task and errors are inevitable. In the transformation of segment to structured polygon data, again errors are likely. In large GIS projects it is essential to introduce quality control guidelines as in the already mentioned Direct/Delayed Response Project (Campbell and Mortenson 1989). According to these guidelines, quality control is applied at three stages, before, during and after digitization. At the first stage, source maps are checked for consistency, accuracy and completeness. Particular attention is paid in this project to the delineation of drainage basins. At the second stage, quality control checks during digitizing are concerned with consistency of digitization, line segment accuracy and attribute accuracy. At the third post-digitization stage, the focus is on coverage accuracy and ground registration. Particular attention is given to quality control procedures in the Direct/Delayed Response Project because the results are anticipated to have a significant influence on 'acid rain' legislation (Campbell and Mortenson 1989). In this study quality control is achieved by formalized log sheets giving details on what was done to validate the digitized data; in addition the accuracy and precision of the data at various entry stages are evaluated.

The nature of the earth's surface is such that spatial units of distinctive land resource value do not occur as discrete and homogeneous entities. Consider the deceptively simple problem of mapping areas of forest in an area of natural regeneration. What density of trees is necessary in order to define an area of forest? How tall do trees need to be before they constitute a forest? What are acceptable proportions of young and older trees for a forest? What is the minimum size of mapping area? The same type of problems of mapping unit definition, delineation and mapping purity apply to soils as discussed in Chapter 3. The underlying problem is the representation in chloropleth form of distributions which are continuous. Burrough (1986) explains how boundaries on maps of natural phenomenon can be drawn on the basis of an abrupt change, for example the junction of estuarine deposits with adjacent hillslopes, an ordered trend in properties, for example downslope, or just from the vagaries of sampling which happen wrongly to suggest a change. Two responses are possible to the problems associated with dealing with mapping purity. One approach is to use spatial interpolation techniques such as geostatistics. With these methods, data from individual points are retained and used to establish spatial dependency by means of deriving semi-variograms. The other response is to use the information on variability per mapping unit or grid cell in order to compute errors associated with GIS processing such as overlay analysis. The remainder of this section is devoted to issues of output quality as influenced by GIS processing.

In section 7.1 the processing capabilities of a raster GIS are illustrated by quoting the commands available in OSU Map-for-the-PC (Geographic Information Systems Laboratory 1989). As explained, a database is constructed through recording for each cell, a numerical value for specific variables; data on different variables are thus stored in a three-dimensional array. With such values, it is then possible to generate new layers through a large number of arithmetic operations; the simplest is to use the ADD command which generates a new layer by adding together, on a cell-by-cell basis, the values in two or more input layers. With any component number there is an associated error and thus any calculated number will also have an error. The calculation of errors resultant upon the use of formulae is standard practice in the physical sciences, but is far less common in the environmental sciences; introductions are provided by Davidson (1978) and Burrough (1986). With the simple case of adding two numbers and assuming these two variables are uncorrelated, the fractional error associated with the result is equal to the square root of the sum of the squares of the fractional errors of the terms being added. It should be explained that the fractional error is the ratio of total error to the true value. With multiplication of uncorrelated variables, fractional errors are cumulative. Burrough (1986) takes the example of the Universal Soil Loss Equation which predicts soil loss by multiplying measures of rainfall

erosivity, soil erodibility, slope value and length, and measures of cultivation and protection techniques. He estimates errors with each of these component factors and then determines the error associated with the erosion prediction, 23 +/− 14.8 tonne yr⁻. This considerable error reflects the large uncertainties associated with the constituent measures in the equation and the fact that these measures are multiplied together. The dangers of simply incorporating the Universal Soil Loss Equation into a GIS and then plotting the results without assessment of errors are thus very obvious. The theory of error propagation and its application to models and map overlays is discussed by Heuvelink et al (1989); in one of their case studies, they demonstrate error calculations in the mapping of lead and cadmium in a floodplain. Interpolation using point kriging allows the prediction and thus mapping on a regular grid of lead and calcium levels as well as relative errors. An overall assessment of health risk (R) as posed by lead and cadmium is determined from the equation:

$$R = Pb + 13Cd$$

The reason for the large cadmium weighting is the health risk from that element compared to lead. Through taking into account the correlation between lead and cadmium, Heuvelink et al (1989) map the risk factor (R) and its relative error. It is argued that such maps provide a more informed basis for judging where vegetables can best be grown taking into account health safety considerations.

Inexactness also has implications in terms of land evaluation operations, for example finding areas which meet defined conditions. As an illustration, suppose cells in an area have been coded according to mean angle of slope. A new combine harvester has a safe operational limit of 12° and the need is to determine in which cells this machine can be used. The simplest operation would be to locate those cells with values less than 12°, but there is a chance that even in slopes deemed safe by this process, there may be instances of slopes in excess of 12° as a result of data errors or variability within cells. For the same reason, safe slopes may occur within the areas considered unsafe. This example demonstrates the distinction between *crisp sets* and *fuzzy sets*. With the former, it is a question of a definitive yes or no to membership of the set while with the latter, there is the possibility of one set containing elements of another. Thus even in cells classified as having an angle of slope greater than 12°, this may not always be the case. The application of fuzzy mathematics to land evaluation questions has been pioneered by Burrough (1989) who describes it as a generalization of set theory known as Boolean algebra. As already stated, inexactness in slope data results from measurement errors and spatial variability. Inexactness can also be the consequence of a certain vagueness of definition. An obvious example is the categorization of soils according to whether they are well, imperfectly or poorly drained. Although detailed guidance is usually given on such drainage classes, judgement by individual soil surveyors is inevitable.

Following Burrough's (1989: 480) approach, the fuzzy set A in X is the set of ordered pairs

A = {x, μ_A(x)} with x belonging to set X

where μ_A(x) is termed the grade of membership of x in A. This can vary from 0 indicating non-membership to 1, full membership. With crisp sets, only two grades of membership exist, yes or no to a defined criteria such as soil drainage class. With fuzzy sets, the grade of membership provides a graded answer to the question as to whether a soil exposure is well drained or not. Burrough (1989) presents two forms of membership function, a symmetrical and an asymmetrical one; the latter is illustrated in Figure 7.10. Symmetrical functions are applied when a particular range in a property, for example soil pH, is considered optimal for crop growth with increasing nutritional constraints being exerted in pH values on either side of the optimal range. With an asymmetrical function such as dealing with membership grade of soil depth, constraints to a particular crop will apply up to a certain limit such as 80 cm as in Figure 7.10, but beyond that depth, differences in soil depth are

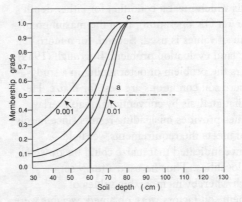

Figure 7.10 Four curves illustrating the variation in membership grade of a fuzzy set according to soil depth; the parameter 'a' controls the shape of the curves and examples are given for values of 0.01, 0.006, 0.003 and 0.1; the bold vertical line indicates a crisp set boundary between shallow and deep soils (division at 60 cm)
(source: Burrough 1989: 483)

irrelevant. The following asymmetric functions are given by Burrough (1989: 482):

$$\mu_A(x) = 1 \qquad\qquad \text{for } x \geqslant c$$
$$\mu_A(x) = (1 + a(x - c)^2)^{-1} \text{ for } x < c$$

where a is a parameter controlling the shape of the curves, and c is the value beyond which variations in the property are irrelevant, 80 cm in the case of Figure 7.10. The membership grade as indicated on the y-axis expresses the possibility of a given value of x being a member of the set. As can be seen from Figure 7.10, the possibility of a soil being considered deep (over 60 cm) gradually increases according to the selected curve until at values over 80 cm, a certainty prevails.

The application of fuzzy set theory to land evaluation questions is illustrated by Burrough (1989), first with reference to simple questions such as finding areas with defined properties. From the soil depth example above, values could be plotted ranging from 0.0 to 1.0 to indicate the possibility of membership. If the task is to plot membership values for cells according to depth and slope, then the minimum membership values for these two properties is selected. In contrast, if the need is to find cells which meet a condition for either depth or slope (an OR operation), then the maximum of each pair of values is used. Second, for a more realistic land evaluation problem, Burrough (1989) considers the problem of determining in a study area where soil conditions are best for maize. He shows that analysis by conventional map overlay techniques provides misleading results since hardly any land meets the requirements, yet field experience indicated that maize could be grown in certain localities. Thus he used a fuzzy set approach whereby membership values of component soil factors were obtained, weights were selected for these ensuring that the weights summed to 1.0, and then overall membership values were determined by summing the results from multiplying the weights with the corresponding component membership values. Wang et al (1990) provide another case study which compares land evaluation results using the conventional limiting factors approach with that using the fuzzy set technique. For the Cimanuk watershed area on the north coast of west Java, Indonesia, they define seven land qualities relevant to determining suitability for agricultural crops. These qualities are temperature regime, water availability, rooting conditions, nutrient retention, nutrient availability, toxicity and terrain. Following the FAO (1976) *Framework for Land Evaluation,*

particular land characteristics are defined in order to assess these qualities. The first part of their study follows the limiting factors approach in order to determine suitability classes of mapping units. The second part of their analysis presents suitability rating methods using fuzzy set theory and the analysis is integrated within a geographical information system. Wang et al (1990) conclude that the use of fuzzy techniques reduces information loss through the determination of membership grades for each land suitability class. In addition they demonstrate how relative suitability can be assessed for individual crops.

It can be concluded that the application of fuzzy set theory is an important development in land evaluation. The use of fuzzy set theory can very much improve both the quantity and quality of information in land resource evaluation. In no sense must the use of GIS be viewed merely as an easy way of performing well established, but rather tedious operations; instead GIS open up considerable scope for the refinement of land resource assessment procedures. Although the importance of source data quality has always been realized in land evaluation, the actual incorporation of quantitative measures of data quality is only now possible through the use of GIS and associated database management systems.

8

Modelling of Land Resources

Models are a simplified representation of the real world and they are expressed in a wide variety of forms such as maps, geographical information systems, three-dimensional diagrams, conceptual diagrams showing the linkage between system components, classification systems, deterministic and probabilistic mathematical models and simulation models. In land evaluation, modelling provides a means of collecting, processing and evaluating land resource data and predicting land performance in biological or financial terms. In land evaluation a distinction can be made between qualitative and quantitative approaches; the latter predicts output such as crop yields in quantitative terms (van Lanen 1991). Such a division provides a useful framework for models in land evaluation. Although this chapter has the title of modelling of land resources, all the previous ones with the exception of the first have dealt in different ways with modelling. Thus consideration has already been given to models of qualitative land evaluation based on expert judgement, for example, land

capability schemes, application of the FAO (1976) *Framework for Land Evaluation*, soil survey interpretation, and parametric indices of land quality. In practice the distinction between qualitative and quantitative land evaluation is often indistinct since it may well be possible to make predictions about yields from suitability classes or parametric indices.

In this chapter, particular emphasis is given to three groups of modelling approaches as used in quantitative land evaluation. First, an overview of spatial interpolation techniques is presented. Any land evaluation analysis deals with spatial variability in land characteristics, thus the prediction of these properties for unsampled points or areas is a fundamental requirement. Second, methods for predicting crop yield using process-orientated models are illustrated. During the 1980s there was a considerable rise in interest in models which simulate crop growth; such models are deterministic and are based on an understanding of the actual mechanisms of plant growth. Third, approaches to integrated land evaluation models are described and explained. Such models are integrated in the sense that they combine the results of physical land evaluation with a range of alternative goals such as maximizing economic return or maximizing landscape or habitat conservation. The integrated approach to land evaluation is an example of spatial allocation models, many of which use linear programming techniques. The objective of integrated land evaluation models using linear programming techniques is to predict land use alternatives by means of maximizing, or minimizing, stated objectives under defined constraints.

8.1 Spatial prediction of land characteristics

Land characteristics as determined by field measurement, monitoring or sampling are site specific. Thus depth to gleying is measured at specific sites with other examples provided by the monitoring of precipitation or the determination of cation exchange capacity from topsoil samples.

There is clearly the need to be able to interpolate such results to other points, for example to predict values on a regular grid framework, to draw isolines or to predict average values for cells. Such interpolation is possible only as a result of an analysis to determine spatial variability and spatial dependence.

Variation in land resource properties is to be expected within any study area, be it 100 m^2 or 10,000 km^2. Discerned patterns in variability will necessarily depend upon the scale of investigation. For land evaluation purposes, it is necessary to produce valid generalizations about areas relevant to particular land use issues. In turn this means that the nature, magnitude and scales of variability in land resource properties have to be assessed. It is not just a question of producing the best estimate of say soil drainage in an area, but the magnitude of variability in itself may be of direct relevance to the land user. For example, farmers find it more efficient to apply the same management technique to individual fields and this is possible only if their fields do not suffer from marked internal variability.

When an area is bounded by a line and assigned to a soil mapping unit such as a soil series, the implied assumption according to classical statistics is that the sampling mean is the expected value throughout the mapping unit. The differences between the population mean and actual values at different points are considered to be normally distributed. The usual approach is to use mean values of soil properties as estimates at unsampled points with precision being indicated by such statistics as coefficients of variation or standard deviation. With increases in these statistics, larger samples are necessary in order to estimate the mean with a given level of confidence. The major limitation in using this statistical procedure for estimating values at points in space is that variation is assumed to be random within the sampling unit. This is unlikely to be the case given the degree of spatial order or pattern which is usually evident in soil landscapes.

A regionalized variable is one which assumes different values according to location within a region. Suppose a region is defined as the middle and lower part of a particular hillslope. Over such

a region, drainage conditions could be expected to vary from free in the mid-slope position to poor in the lower slope. Thus if soil organic matter was being investigated, an increase would be anticipated from the well drained to poorly drained slope positions. Soil organic matter in such an example demonstrates the nature of a regionalized variable. However, despite a clear downslope trend in organic matter, random fluctuations will also occur. A measure known as the *semi-variance* is used to express the spatially dependent component in the measurement or prediction of a soil property at a point in space. A crucial issue to emphasize is that the semi-variance depends upon the distance apart and direction of sampling points and not on specific locations. This can be illustrated by considering the variation in organic matter on the imaginary hillslope. Suppose that a transect line is located along the maximum line of slope and that sampling points are selected at 5 m intervals (Figure 8.1). It is possible to work out the differences in values between sampling points at different distances apart or lag. For example, to determine the differences at lag 5 m, the following subtractions are made:

lag 5 m
  (value at point 2) − (value at point 1)
  (value at point 3) − (value at point 2)
  etc

lag 10 m
  (value at point 3) − (value at point 1)
  (value at point 4) − (value at point 2)
  etc

lag 20 m
  (value at point 5) − (value at point 1)
  (value at point 6) − (value at point 2)
  etc

The semi-variance can be calculated for each of these lags according to the equation:

$$\gamma(h) = \frac{1}{2n} \sum_{i=1}^{n} \{z(x_i) - z(x_i + h)\}^2$$

where $\gamma(h)$ is the semi-variance at lag h, n the number of sampling pairs separated by distance h, $z(x_i)$ is the value of variable z at position x_i and

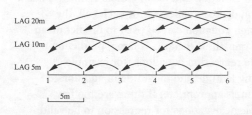

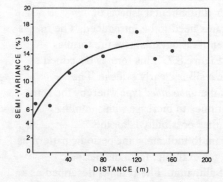

Figure 8.1 Illustration of determining differences in values at different lags between sample points

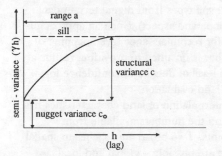

Figure 8.2 Theoretical semi-variogram to illustrate the following properties: range, sill, structural and nugget variance

$z(x_i + h)$ is the value of variable z at the next sampling point. In essence, the semi-variance is the sum of the squares of the differences between successive sampling points divided by twice the number of sampled pairs.

A plot of semi-variance against sampling distance is called a semi-variogram which reveals the nature of the geographic variation in the soil property and is also required to provide kriged estimates for unsampled points. An idealized semi-variogram is shown in Figure 8.2. In this case, the best fit line through the scatter of points levels off

Figure 8.3 An example of a bounded semi-variogram using topsoil clay values from an area of carse soils near Stirling University, Scotland

at a horizon distance known as the range. The corresponding semi-variance value once this levelling off has occurred is known as the sill. When the lag is zero ($h = 0$), the semi-variance also ought to equal zero to mean that the curve should pass through the origin. This is often not the case and instead the curve intersects the semi-variance axis at a point to give the nugget variance (c_o) as shown in Figure 8.2. As Burgess and Webster (1980) explain, the nugget variance embraces variation in soil properties over distances much shorter than the sampling interval and the effect is to limit the precision of interpolation. The magnitude of the structural variance (c) indicates the impact of spatial dependence on the range of variance. It is common for the nugget variance to be given as a percentage of the sill value; this has the merit of permitting comparison between different soil properties. Trangmar et al (1985) quote nugget variances ranging from 0 to 100 per cent of sill values. A result of 0 per cent indicates there is no measurement error or variation over distances less than the smallest sampling interval; in contrast a value of 100 per cent indicates a total lack of spatial correlation based on the sampling approach.

Two other fundamental aspects of semi-variograms need to be introduced. The first is that not all semi-variograms have the form as exhibited in Figure 8.2. This form is described as *bounded* since a sill is clearly evident. The alternative is the *unbounded* type whereby the semi-variance continues to increase with sampling interval. Another possibility is for the semi-variogram to indicate some periodic pattern as could result, for example, from the periodic deposition of alluvium. The result is described as a 'hole-effect' semi-variogram which has a wave form of decreasing amplitude with increasing distance (Trangmer et al 1985). An example of an actual semi-variogram is given in Figure 8.3. In this case, clay values for topsoil were determined on a nested sampling frame for an area of carseland near Stirling University, Scotland.

The second aspect of semi-variograms which requires mention is that their form may vary according to direction of sampling. If the spatial dependence is equal in all directions, then the pattern is described as isotropic. This can be confirmed by constructing semi-variograms for transects orientated in different directions and getting virtually the same results. In contrast, if soil properties vary more in one direction than another, the pattern is described as anisotropic. Such a situation would exist with the example of variation in organic matter over a hillslope. Greater variation would be expected downslope than across the slope. Semi-variograms can be drawn for different directions and the degree of anisotropy will be expressed in the magnitude of the envelope between these semi-variograms. Anisotropy ratios can be constructed to express the extent of directionality in soil variation (Burgess and Webster 1980).

The easiest form of spatial interpolation is prediction based on a statistical relationship between data collected from specific points and the values of variables which are available for any point. This can be understood by considering the prediction of mean annual rainfall for component

cells in an area; for the inevitably few climatological stations in the area, a strong correlation is likely between elevation and mean annual rainfall. Thus if elevation data are collected for each cell, the regression equation can be used to predict mean annual rainfall. If the area is large, prediction using multiple regression equations, for example including latitude and longitude in addition to elevation, is appropriate. If there are too few climatological stations for regression to be valid, then use can be made for an analogous area of an established lapse rate, for example the decrease in mean annual temperature with elevation. Predictions of variables other than climatic ones on the basis of statistical relationships are few. Reference was made in Chapter 3 to broad prediction of soil types from digital terrain data (elevation, slope and aspect). Such an approach is appropriate for reconnaissance level mapping of large areas, but is unsuited to providing results at the required level of detail and confidence for quantitative land evaluation.

Spatial interpolation of land characteristics has to be based on the numbers available from sampling points. Two broad approaches to spatial interpolation are possible – global and local methods. With global methods, prediction is based on a model based on all the available data. Trend surface analysis is the best known global method; in summary the mathematical function which provides the best fit through the scatter of points is determined on the basis of least squares. The method can be considered as the three-dimensional equivalent of regression analysis. It works well if the trend is clear and can be well approximated by low order polynomial equations. With land resource data, this is not usual. If determined, a trend surface function smoothes a distribution so that predicted and measured values at sampling points are not the same. Burrough (1986), in a comprehensive review of spatial interpolation methods, comments that the main value of trend surface analysis is the ability to determine where in a study region there is the greatest deviation from an established pattern. There may well be some spatial pattern to such deviancy.

With local methods, the prediction of a property

value at a point in space is based on one or more of the sampling points which occur in the vicinity of the unknown point. The simplest approach is just to use the value from the nearest sampling point as the estimate. A slightly more satisfactory approach is to centre a window over the unknown point and to take the arithmetical mean of the values from sampling points within the window as the estimate. Such an approach takes no account of spatial pattern or trend within the window, and of course, the results are highly dependent upon the selected size of window. A more refined approach is to calculate a weighted mean whereby sampling points near to the unknown point are given greater weighting than more distant points. This can be expressed as an equation:

$$z(x_0) = \sum_{i=1}^{n} \lambda_i \, z(x_i)$$

where $\Sigma\lambda_i = 1$, $z(x_0)$ is the predicted value of variable z at location x_0, n is the number of neighbouring samples $z(x_i)$ and $\lambda_i(x_i)$ are the weights assigned to each $z(x_i)$. Such an equation can be used for predicting values at specific points and for defined areas or blocks. Key problems are posed in determining the set of sample values in the neighbourhood and also by making best estimates of the weights. Such difficulties are overcome if use is made of a technique known as *kriging*. The method was originally devised by D. G. Krige as a means of estimating gold content in South African goldfields and is based on the theory of regionalized variables. Webster and Oliver (1990) state that kriging in its simplest is a way of weighted averaging of observed values in order to predict point values (punctual kriging), or for areas (block kriging). It is possible to present only the barest outline of the methodology along with reference to selected examples; readers wishing more detailed guidance are referred to reviews by Burrough (1986), Oliver et al (1989a; 1989b), Trangmar et al (1985), Webster (1985) and Webster and Oliver (1990).

If measured properties at points in space varied in a statistical sense according to a normal distribution, then such values could be characterized by the mean and variance. Thus the expected value of a property at a point z(x) within the sampling frame is given by:

$$z(x) = \mu + \epsilon(x)$$

where μ is the mean and $\epsilon(x)$ indicates a spatially uncorrelated random value about the mean. In a situation where there is no trend in spatial variation, the expected difference between any two predicted points is zero. With many land resource characteristics, it is to be expected that predicted values at one point should be different from values at another because of some spatial pattern or interdependence. This concept is integral to regionalized variable theory whereby values at points in space depend upon their location within a region as well as a random component.

Spatial dependence is investigated by comparing pairs of values and is expressed in the form of semi-variograms. According to one of the conditions in the intrinsic hypothesis of regionalized variable theory, the differences between pairs of points depends only on the lag and not upon location. The critical part of the semi-variogram is the section of the scatter with increasing semi-variance according to increasing lag. Spherical, exponential or linear models are commonly used as best-fit functions through the scatter of points in the semi-variogram. The importance of these functions is that they are used in the determination of weights as required for interpolation. Two principles govern the computation of such weights; first, the estimate of a property at a point does not incorporate any bias (the expected difference between the predicted and true values is zero), and second, the estimation variance is minimized. Variances are determined from solution of the best-fit function for the semi-variogram. A set of simultaneous equations require solution in order to determine the weights (λ) and there is a growing number of geostatistical computer packages which perform such operations. Readers requiring details of the mathematical procedures are referred to Webster and Oliver (1990). Thus the value of a property can be predicted at any unsampled location and furthermore, the estimation variance can be provided. A map of estimation error can be provided alongside the interpolated distribution to indicate reliability. The principle that no difference is to be expected between predicted and true values has the important consequence that kriging gives exact predictions for sampled points. The merit of kriging is that, unlike other spatial interpolation procedures, it has the optimality attributes of unbiasedness and minimum variance (Trangmar et al 1985).

It needs to be stressed that kriging encompasses a range of methods. Discussion in this section has focused on punctual kriging – the prediction of values at specific points such as on a grid frame from which an isoline map can be drawn. Predictions can also be made on an area basis – block kriging, the advantage being that some of the irregularities in the spatial distribution are smoothed. The technique of co-kriging is used when where there are two or more spatially correlated variables; spatial interpolation of one makes use of information on the variability of the other(s). As an example, Stein et al (1988) use co-kriging to provide predictions of thirty-year average moisture deficits in a Dutch study area. Co-kriging was used because of the correlation between soil moisture deficit and the height of mean highest water-table. They compared the results of spatial interpolation with and without stratifying their sample according to mean highest water class. Their conclusion was that co-kriging generally resulted in more precise predictions than did kriging. Their study is of general importance since it shows how soil survey data can be incorporated into geostatistical procedures with a corresponding enhancement of precision in spatial prediction. Disjunctive kriging is another method which merits mention given its potential application to land evaluation issues. With this method it is possible to calculate the conditional probabilities of true values being greater or less than defined thresholds. Webster and Oliver (1989a; 1989b) demonstrate the application of calculating these probabilities to soil nutrient and salt thresholds. For example, they produce a map for south-east Scotland showing where the estimated cobalt content is less than 0.25 mg/kg; superimposed upon this are the isarithms of conditional probability. Such results

make it much easier for farmers or agricultural advisers to assess the risk of soils falling below, or above, critical thresholds. The final kriging method which requires mention is universal kriging. The basis of ordinary or simple kriging is the intrinsic hypothesis, one condition being that the difference in values between any two points the same distance apart should be the same. If there is a spatial trend or drift in variation, this condition does not apply and universal kriging has been developed for this situation. The methods must incorporate an estimate of the drift.

In summary, the following steps are required in order to predict spatial patterns using simple kriging:

1   check data for normality

2   compute and plot semi-variogram

3   if appropriate, select and fit a suitable function to the scatter of points on the semi-variogram

4   use the kriging method in order to predict values for points or blocks

5   plot distributions of predicted values and estimation errors; if required, input data to a GIS for further processing.

As Webster and McBratney (1987) explain, step number 3 is the most difficult and controversial. An understanding of soil variability and the applicability of different functions for expressing the form of the semi-variogram is required. In practice, the investigator has to determine the results on a trial and error basis until an acceptable function is determined. The other steps can largely be carried out automatically within software packages. The increasing availability of geostatistical packages should encourage the use of such methods with users being pleasantly unaware of the solution of simultaneous equations or the use of a Lagrange multiplier as is needed for minimization operations! As one example of a geostatistics software package, the US Environmental Protection Agency has developed GEOPACK (Yates and Yates 1990). This package has the capability to plot semi-variograms, fit mathematical models (for example gaussian, exponential, linear, spherical or power) using the nonlinear least squares minimization technique, perform kriging, co-kriging or disjunctive kriging, and cross-validation (a check to test if the covariance function is appropriate for the experimental data).

To conclude this section on the spatial prediction of land characteristics, it is instructive to compare the results from different methods. Particular emphasis has been given to kriging given its advantages in terms of permitting exact predictions for sampled points and for providing estimates of error. There has been a tendency for kriging to be applied mainly at the very detailed scale, for example, individual fields or experimental plots. For instance, Munoz-Pardo et al (1990) determine semi-variograms for selected soil and crop yield attributes within a 1.21 ha field. However, there are many instances in the literature of geostatistical investigations in much larger areas. Xu and Webster (1984) analysed selected topsoil characteristics as determined from 102 sites within Zhangwu county in China, an area of 3635 km^2. Of the various properties investigated, soil pH exhibited the strongest spatial dependence. An isarithmic map of soil pH was thus produced by contouring estimates over 1 km × 1 km blocks. Such a map was paralleled by one showing the estimation variance which is large. One merit of the approach is that guidance can be given on further sampling; from the semi-variograms, Xu and Webster (1984) recommend further sampling for lags in the range 0.5 km to 5 km. Another study which demonstrates the use of geostatistical methods at the regional level is by Ovalles and Collins (1988). The aims of this study in north-west Florida were to investigate spatial variability, determine if such variability could be related to physiographic regions, and to identify areas in need of more intensive sampling. Parameters for semi-variograms were computed for different orientations; then spatial predictions and error estimates determined from universal kriging were displayed as three-dimensional diagrams. Thus it was possible to compare these diagrams with the nature of the physiographic regions. As with the Chinese study, guidance was provided on where

further sampling would be most efficient.

Two investigations in The Netherlands provide interesting comparisons of predictions from different interpolation techniques with those on the basis of soil mapping units. In the first, van Kuilenburg et al (1982) selected a very small study area (2 km × 2 km) in Gelderland, and produced a conventional soil survey map at a scale of 1:10,000 with site data collected at 530 random survey borings and 661 test borings. Interpolation of values was done using proximal, weighted average and kriging techniques. By the proximal method, the value from the nearest sample site was selected. Comparison of the root mean squared errors indicated that the weighted average and kriging technique produced very similar results, and furthermore these results were better than those from the proximal method. The results of prediction using the soil map are of particular interest. The authors conclude that with a small increase in sampling intensity, the root mean squared error of moisture supply capacity would be only 10 per cent higher than that from the weighted average and kriging techniques. The results from the study confirm the validity of a soil map as a basis for spatial prediction. Also, soil survey maps can be used for predicting patterns in a wide range of variables. In the second Dutch study, Bregt et al (1987) compare a conventional soil map with a thematic map produced on the basis of kriging. The soils in a study area of 125 ha near Groenlo in the eastern Netherlands were mapped at 1:5,000 with mapping units delineated in the field by the interpretation of landscape patterns and information from field borings. Emphasis was given to producing a soil map designed to provide information on soil hydrological behaviour. Interpolation using universal kriging was carried out on three soil properties with the results being predicted on a regular grid of 20 by 25 points. After combination of the data for each interpolated point, the grid map was transformed into a polygon map. The quality of the conventionally produced soil map could then be compared with the polygons derived from spatial interpolation. Both maps exhibited an average purity of 77 per cent indicating no difference. Thus Bregt et al (1987) comment that the good results which they obtained by interpreting soil maps should encourage the use of such maps given their wide availability.

The inference from these examples might be that kriging, despite its mathematical elegance, does not yield markedly better results of spatial prediction than conventional soil survey. However, it would not be correct to propose this in general since the two quoted case studies are from very small areas where intensive soil surveys were carried out. There are strong advantages in determining semi-variograms since these demonstrate the degree of spatial dependence within areas. Furthermore, kriging, as already explained, involves the calculation of estimation variances. Also, it should not be a case of comparing prediction from soil maps as against using a geostatistical approach; the investigation by Stein et al (1988) showed that the best of both approaches can be achieved by the incorporation of soil survey data into geostatistical analysis.

8.2 Modelling of land use response

The importance of being able to predict yields of crops needs no emphasis though there are considerable modelling difficulties given the potential influence of environmental, management, economic and social conditions. The most straightforward approach is to make predictions on the basis of monitoring yields for a number of years. As one example, Dumanski et al (1986) analysed maize yield data for Ontario over the period 1961–82. By statistical analysis, the influence of weather on yield was removed; it was then shown that the rates of increase of yield resultant upon technological improvements varied according to land suitability with the best land giving the greatest response. In practice, it is unlikely that there will often be comparable yield data over an adequate time period and use will have to be made of other methods. One solution is to utilize productivity ratings as discussed in section 5.3 though some yield data will still be required for

calibration purposes. An alternative approach is to apply models which simulate the nature and success of crop growth processes. These process-orientated models, also called 'mechanistic' models, simulate the physiological, physical and chemical processes governing crop yield (Dumanski and Onofrei 1989). Such models are the subject of this section.

The Agro-Ecological Zones Project, already introduced in Chapters 1 and 2, was one of the first to use a simulation approach for predicting biomass production (FAO 1978a). The essence of the approach is first to estimate the net biomass yield assuming there are no constraints to production other than crop physiological response to received radiation, the temperature regime during the growing period and the length of the growing period. At the second stage, an expected yield is predicted by assessing the degree of constraint resultant upon, for example, moisture stress or soil workability. These two stages require some explanation and the FAO (1978a) methodology is summarized below.

The net rate of biomass production (b_n) equals the rate of gross biomass production (b_g) less the respiration rate (r). The rate of crop growth, if plotted against time, follows a bell-shaped curve, rising from zero to a maximum (b_{nm}) when the crop first fully covers the ground and then declining ultimately to zero. The seasonal average rate of crop production is taken as half the maximum rate ($0.5\ b_{nm}$). Thus the net biomass production for a crop over N days (B_n), is obtained by multiplying the average rate by the growth duration.

$$B_n = 0.5\ b_{nm} \times N$$

To calculate net biomass production (B_n), the maximum rate (b_{nm}) has to be determined. This is done by finding the difference between the maximum rate of gross biomass production (b_{gm}) and the respiration rate (r_m) at that time. The maximum rate of gross biomass production (b_{gm}) is determined from the following equation

$$b_{gn} = F \times b_o \times (1 - F)b_c$$

where b_o and b_c represent total number of overcast and clear days respectively and F is calculated as follows:

$$F = (A_c - 0.5\ R_g)/0.8\ A_c$$

where A_c is photosynthetically active radiation on a clear day and R_g is total short-wave global radiation. The respiration rate (r_m) is easier to calculate in that it is a linear function of the rate of gross biomass production. The result is the ability to predict net biomass production (B_n) from the following equation

$$B_n = 0.36 \, b_{gm} / (1/N + 0.25 \, c_t)$$

where b_{gm} is the maximum rate of biomass production, N is the number of growing days, and c_t is a temperature and crop dependent respiration coefficient. This equation applies when the leaf area index (the ratio of leaf to ground area) at the time of maximum gross biomass production is 5; adjustments have to be made to the value of b_{gm} when this index is less than 5. Of course the whole of crop biomass is not harvested, thus the yield biomass, B_y, is determined as follows:

$$B_y = B_n \times H_i$$

where H_i is the harvest index or the fraction of the net biomass that is economically useful. Readers requiring further details as well as a worked example of this procedure should consult the original source (FAO 1978a: 62–71).

The calculation of the yield biomass, B_y, completes the first stage; in the second, account has to be taken of such constraints as moisture stress, pests, diseases and weeds and climatic factors which influence yield, quality of produce, farming operations and cost of production. In the Agro-Ecological Zones Project, percentage scores are assigned according to a qualitative assessment of the degree of constraint. In a Canadian case study, changes in the methodology were necessary in order to define crop growing periods on the basis of temperature rather than moisture regimes; the other modification was the quantification of factors which reduce yields (Dumanski and Stewart 1983; Stewart 1983). Expected yield (B_{ya}) is predicted according to

$$B_{ya} = B_y \times MSF \times WF \times SI$$

where B_y is yield biomass of crop, MSF moisture stress factor, WF workability factor and SI soil index. In an overview of the Canadian project, Dumanski and Onofrei (1989) consider that the

database scale of 1:5,000,000 is too small for anything other than analysis at the national scale. They point out that the structure of the model cannot easily be altered and that the prediction accuracy of $+/-$ 20 per cent is inadequate.

The adoption of modelling crop growth is very much eased as there is available a fully tested and user friendly software package. As an example, the Comprehensive Resource Inventory and Evaluation System (CRIES), developed at Michigan State University, incorporates a module for predicting yield using the same methodology as in the Agro-Ecological Zones Project. In CRIES, there are two main menus, a geographical information system and an agro-economic information system (Schultink 1987). The merit of a package which integrates GIS capabilities with modelling should be immediately obvious. Consideration here is limited to outlining the yield module within the agro-economic information system (Schultink and Amaral 1987). Five phases are necessary to estimate yields:

1 calculation of maximum yield of a standard crop

2 determination of maximum evapotranspiration

3 determination of actual evapotranspiration

4 calculation of estimated yields

5 adjustment of estimated yields according to fertilizer availability, soil salinity and moisture content.

Use of the yield module within CRIES allows prediction for thirty different crops. Data requirements include temperature, precipitation, relative humidity, wind velocity, solar radiation, sowing dates, crop selection, length of growing stages, soil texture and slope gradient, soil moisture characteristics in the root zone, and root development over various growing stages. In addition, there is the option to include data on farm management, soil moisture conservation, salinity and nutrient availability. Schultink and Amaral (1987) provide initial validation for the model through comparing actual and predicted yields for sugar cane in Jamaica; they invite research collaboration to test the model in other situations.

One key characteristic of dynamic modelling in land evaluation is the ability to make predictions of yield estimates for crops which have not been grown in particular localities. As explained above, this is achieved by simulating the responses of crop growth and development to such factors as temperature, moisture and nutrient regimes. The use of simulation models is central to the IBSNAT Project (International Benchmark Sites Network for Agrotechnology Transfer), based at the University of Hawaii. IBSNAT is an international effort to use simulation models for assessing crop performance in new areas. Since 1989, IBSNAT has been making available a software package called Decision Support System for Agrotechnology Transfer (DSSAT). The package comes with a database on soils, weather and crops so that users can run models which simulate the outcomes of alternative management practices. In addition the models within DSSAT are being used to predict agricultural yields according to different climatic change scenarios. Models for predicting yields of maize, peanuts, soybean and wheat are available in early versions of DSSAT. As an example, the CERES-Rice model simulates the development, growth and yield of rice under upland and lowland conditions. The model permits simulation of the effects of cultivar, planting density, weather, soil water balance and nitrogen dynamics on crop growth (Singh et al 1990). Validation of the results has been done on the basis of experimental data from Thailand, the Philippines and Hawaii. Of particular interest is the capability within the model to identify cultivars which match the length of growing season, or have the ability to reach critical growth stages before there is an outbreak of pests or diseases. Cultivars can be further evaluated according to yield potential. In a case study in Thailand, Singh et al (1990) tested the CERES-Rice model to predict yields of rice grown on soils varying in pH and treated with different levels of nitrogen. They also predicted the impact of climatic change on rice yields in this locality. Lower yields were generally predicted as a consequence of shorter growing seasons and more frequent instances of water and nitrogen stress. Thus the

applications of DSSAT are not limited to crop yield prediction, but can be used for impact assessment of environmental change. Other possibilities in using the DSSAT package are to explore yield outcomes from intercropping of different crops using varying management strategies and also to translate yield figures into economic terms for individual farms. This latter topic necessitates the simulation of farming systems with yield predictions as one important input.

The crop models within DSSAT utilize an integral minimum dataset on soils, crops, weather, management and yields as supplied by contributing institutions to the project. Such information is stored within a relational database which is accessed by the particular models. The important consequence is that models can be run and validated using the minimum dataset for one or more areas and then applied to other analogous areas. Transfer of agro-technology, fundamental to the IBSNAT project, is thus achieved. Most simulation models of crop yield do not have such ready access to data for validation. As examples, reference is made to two simulation models, ALMANAC and WOFOST.

Crop simulation involves predicting and validating the effects of soils, weather, management and crop genotype on crops growth, development, yield and economic return. ALMANAC is a model, developed at the Grassland Soil and Water Research Laboratory at Temple, Texas, which simulates such processes as soil temperature regime, hydrology, erosion, nutrient cycling, and crop growth and yields. The overall package is designed to assist with general agricultural management, but for present purposes, consideration is limited to summarizing the methodology for simulating crop growth (Allan Jones and O'Toole 1987). The growth model is based on genotype-specific coefficients which describe differences in growth of various crops and crop cultivars. Allan Jones and O'Toole (1987) explain that these coefficients control the simulation of development and senescence of leaf area, conversion of intercepted photosynthetically active radiation to biomass, growth of the root system, nutrient composition of tissues, development of economic yield, and sensitivity of the crop to temperature, water and nutrient stresses. Rice is selected as the case study crop and the coefficients were calibrated on the basis of experimental data. The model was used to simulate rainfed rice production for four production situations:

1   Plant nutrients and water are amply supplied, and only crop genotype, temperature, and irradiance limit crop growth.

2   Plant nutrition is adequate, but soil water may limit crop growth.

3   Both nutrition and water may be limiting factors.

4   Few or no external inputs are used. Yields are limited by the soil's capacity to recycle nutrients, often nitrogen.

In a case study in the Ganga Plains, India, Allan Jones and O'Toole (1987) applied the ALMANAC model to simulate rice production for these four production situations. As an example, under situation 1, the yields for twenty consecutive years were simulated using generated daily weather data. Applied amounts of fertilizer and irrigated water were sufficient to ensure minimal nutrient or water stress. The results from the twenty simulated yields were then ranked from lowest to highest and plotted against the probability of years having equal or lower yields. To exemplify this, consider the graph for traditional rice (Figure 8.4); there is a probability of 50 per cent that the yield of this crop will be equal to 3.0 Mg/ha or less. The differences in yield response between long season cultivars of high yielding semi-dwarf, intermediate and traditional plant types are very clear. In particular there is a consistent and better response of high yielding semi-dwarf plant types compared to tall traditional cultivars when plant nutrients and water are in abundance. The investigation simulated yields not only for different plant types, but also for varying maturity periods. Allan Jones and O'Toole (1987) found that the risk of very small rainfed rice yields was less for short-season than for long-season cultivars. The study highlighted the importance of being able to estimate weather parameters from readily available monthly data.

There is considerable scope for research to investigate methods for interpolating daily weather parameters from weekly or monthly measures; geostatistics offer one approach in a similar manner to spatial interpolation from sample point data.

The final simulation model for crop production to be mentioned is WOFOST, an acronym for World Food Studies. This model has been developed at the Centre for World Food Studies in Wageningen, The Netherlands (van Diepen et al 1989). It is similar to ALMANAC in that it models the growth and production of annual crops according to crop species, soil type, hydrologic conditions and weather during the growing season from emergence to maturity. Crop growth and soil water balance are modelled at a daily scale while nutrient balance is analysed for the growing season as an entity. Three situations of growth constraints are defined: potential production (optimum nutrient and water supply), water-limited production (nutrient supply is optimum), and nutrient limited production. Simulation based on the first predicts maximum yield under a particular climatic regime with irrigation if necessary. The net daily increase in dry matter as a result of assimilation and respiration is calculated. Rates of such processes are determined by environmental conditions and crop status, the latter expressed in green leaf area, biomass and stage of phenological development. In

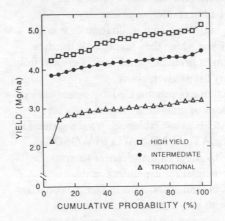

Figure 8.4 Effect of plant type on cumulative yield probabilities for well irrigated and well fertilized 140 day rice cultivars (source: Allan Jones and O'Toole 1987: 204)

order to run WOFOST, data on the following are required:

1   selection of crop species, climate and soil type (the package comes with data from certain weather stations, and on particular soils and crops)

2   site information (eg initial moisture status, depth to groundwater, nature of soil surface and soil fertility)

3   climate data (conversion of monthly data from files to daily values or input of new data on such parameters as minimum and maximum temperature, humidity and wind speed)

4   soil physical data (eg soil moisture retention and soil hydraulic conductivity)

5   soil fertility data (eg uptake rates of nitrogen, phosphorus and potassium from unfertilized soils)

6   crop data (eg initial dry weight, properties determining assimilation and respiration rates, rate of phenological development).

Results from the simulation, such as for total above ground biomass, are given for each tenth day of the growth cycle. Finally, yield predictions are made for the three different situations of growth constraint. Without doubt, WOFOST is a scientifically elegant crop simulation model. In evaluating their model, van Diepen et al (1989) point out the limitations of the assumptions and simulation procedure, for example the time resolution of one day is inadequate in dealing with infiltration or runoff. The other issue which they highlight is the data requirements, a problem which is very evident from the summary list as given above.

This section has summarized the potentialities and limitations of crop simulation models for predicting yields as available within such systems as CRIES, DSSAT, ALMANAC and WOFOST. Varcoe (1990) suggests that there is almost unlimited potential for expanding simulation approaches to land evaluation. In fact, he considers there has been very limited advance in land evaluation since the 1960s, a view which seems unduly pessimistic given the methodological and technological developments during the 1970s and 1980s. The outstanding feature of a simulation

approach is that it is dynamic, yields through time can be predicted and for different constraint conditions. The integration of such models within a geographical information system allows display and further processing of spatially referenced data. Limitations of simulating crop production centre upon over-simplification of crop growth processes, data availability and quality, and verification of models.

8.3   Integrated land use models

The underlying assumption throughout this book is that information on land resources will be incorporated into land use management or planning decisions. In practice, managers or planners have to make decisions on the basis of a wider range of considerations. Suppose a farmer with land of the highest agricultural quality, located on the outskirts of an urban area, submits a planning application for housing development. The decision on the application is not made solely on the presence of high quality land; in addition consideration needs to be given to such issues as need for new housing, impact on existing infra-structure, loss of agricultural landscape, urban spread and wildlife impact. Thus it has been argued for some time that techniques need to be developed to ensure that land use planning integrates all relevant information.

Smit et al (1984) use the phrase *integral land evaluation* to refer to a comparison of the physical suitability or yield of land with alternative societal goals as expressed in priorities such as those given to economic returns, amenity provision and landscape or habitat conservation. According to this view, integral land evaluation involves the synthesis of land resource information with goals and objectives for land use. The result is the identification of land use options for each land unit and the extent to which such uses are critical in the land units. A variety of approaches as discussed by Compagnoni (1986) have been adopted to cope with the integration of diverse goals within environmental planning. A longstanding approach is cost-benefit analysis which requires cost estimation and then comparison of resources to be used and resultant benefits. The use of planning balance sheets means that such intangible costs as social or environmental benefit can be included. Methodological problems led in the 1960s to alternative approaches to the evaluation and selection of plans as illustrated by the rank-based expected value method and the goals-achievement matrix method. The former requires the ranking of plan objectives, ranking of plans under each objective and the estimation of probabilities of implemention. The goals-achievement matrix method provides a comparative evaluation of alternative courses of action and the resultant selection of the best strategy. Such a methodology can be described by summarizing a modelling system called LUPLAN as developed in Australia by the Division of Wildlife and Ecology, CSIRO (Ive and Cocks 1983; Ive et al 1985).

Application of the LUPLAN package requires three major components. First, the study area is subdivided into mapping units or planning zones and information is assembled on these. Second, mapping units are rated in terms of their attractiveness for a range of land uses on the basis of different policy guidelines. These ratings express the relative contribution which each mapping unit can make to the achievement of each specified policy. Third, the relative importance of the different policy guidelines is assessed. This requires stating a relative preference for each policy to ensure that those considered more important are given higher votes than those deemed of less importance. The LUPLAN package has the capabilities of inventory (database on the mapping units), evaluation (ability to provide attractiveness ratings for each potential land use), and allocation (on the basis of the ratings, determining the most attractive land uses for each mapping unit). Output from LUPLAN is in the form of percentages which express the extent to which individual land use plans achieved the guiding policy. A review of the results then follows and assigned votes to policies may be changed. Further runs of LUPLAN are then necessary until acceptable results are achieved.

In Australia, LUPLAN has been used as an aid to rural and conservation planning. As one example, Cocks and Ive (1988) describe its use as an aid to land use planning of Crown Lands in New South Wales. The LUPLAN approach has the merit of being able to assess the extent to which particular land use plans meet policy objectives.

The approach in LUPLAN conforms to the objectives of integrated land evaluation which is designed to assess the range of land use options and to determine the effects of policies on outcomes. In essence, this integrated approach is a methodological development of the FAO *Framework for Land Evaluation* which stresses the importance of comparing alternative land uses for mapping units. In Canada, development of the integrated land evaluation methodology has been by the Land Evaluation Group of the University of Guelph. This group has designed a land evaluation system called LEM 2 and applied it to Ontario (Smit 1981). The aim is to link inventories of land capability and productivity with land use decisions or policies. As an example, LEM 2 could help with identifying which areas in Ontario are crucial for certain uses if provincial needs and objectives are to be achieved. The land resource base of Ontario was characterized according to climatic zones, proximity to urban areas and land type, defined on the basis of soil quality relevant to productivity and input requirements. The model evaluated land resource areas for twenty different uses. Necessarily a range of assumptions had to be made, for example, product quality was uniform, not varying within and between land resource areas. A set of resource, agricultural land use, urban land use and forestry land use constraints had to be defined. For example, restrictions had to be placed on the frequency with which certain soil depleting land uses could occur on particular land resource areas. The aim of land evaluation is to determine the degree of land use flexibility which exists under specified constraints. In LEM 2 this required for linear programming the specification of an objective function in order to select the minimum possible allocations of each land use to each land resource area. Smit (1981) reports the availability of four objective functions in the LEM 2 demonstration system. As examples, one objective function minimizes the total area of land allocated to uses across the whole of Ontario. Another minimizes the sum of squared proportions (PSQ) of each land unit allocated to each use. This can be expressed as follows:

$$\text{Minimum PSQ} = \sum_c \sum_p \sum_t \sum_u p_{cptu}^2$$

subject to the specified contraints where p_{cptu} is the proportion of the area of climate zone c, urban proximity zone p, land type t that is allocated to use u (Smit 1981: 18). The sum of the evaluation measures and individual evaluation measures tend to zero as constraints are relaxed. This objective function is·of particular importance in land evaluation. If, for example, the value of p_{cptu} is close to 0, there is great flexibility concerning the use of that area of land. In contrast, a value near 1 indicates very little flexibility. This is because $\text{Min}(p_{cptu}^2)$ tries to allocate uses to areas in equal proportions approaching zero, as far as constraints permit. Thus the critical importance of particular areas for specified uses is identified. The LEM 2 system has five major components: data management, generation of scenarios, solution algorithms, generation of evaluation measures and map production. Data are required on the parameters of the model for specifying scenarios. These data include crop yields as estimated from a soil moisture based regression model, forest yields, input requirements in terms of fuel and nitrogen, nutrient content of crops used for animal feed, nutrient units per unit of livestock, livestock feed intake restrictions, livestock product yield, land availability, commodity demands, available fuel and nitrogen, import restrictions, and urban land requirements.

The overall objective in using LEM 2 in Ontario was to determine the extent to which it was necessary to retain areas for particular land uses in the future; results are provided by Smit (1981) and Smit et al (1984). Increases in agricultural output under different scenarios were investigated ranging from the situation as existing in 1976 to one of substantial growth. The results indicated that there is considerable flexibility in land use under the

1976 scenario; any policy of retaining all land for agriculture would be needlessly restrictive with only lands in critical areas requiring selected protection. In contrast, for scenarios of modest and substantial agricultural growth, there is a much clearer need for the preservation of land for agriculture. Other reports from the Ontario project predict the impact of environmental change on agricultural production. In one study, estimates of the long-term impact of soil erosion on agricultural productivity are made followed by an assessment of the physical opportunities for sustainable agricultural production (Land Evaluation Project 1983). The results indicate the extent to which the physical production of selected crops in certain areas could be increased without a lowering in soil quality. The impact of climatic change on agricultural resource potential is a topic of increasing concern; Brklacich and Smit (1986) use the LEM 2 system to investigate this topic for Ontario. Two scenarios of climatic change are stated with estimates generated for monthly norms of mean daily temperature and total precipitation. Spatial interpolation techniques had to be used to provide data on a regional basis for Ontario. Data transformations were also necessary to estimate a wider range of agro-climatic parameters such as length of growing season, mean daytime temperature and potential evapotranspiration. It was then possible to predict yield responses under these two climatic scenarios. Increases in length of growing season and in temperature in northern Ontario would enhance crop growing potential, but such benefits are in part offset by increases in moisture stress. For south central, western and south-western Ontario, Brklacich and Smit (1986) predict that yields for most major crops would be expected to decline, with yields for small grains, oilseeds and potatoes suffering most. Areas with an economic potential for expanding grain corn in northern and eastern Ontario are shown to have an enhanced potential as a result of climatic warming. In another study, Brklacich et al (1987) discuss the effect of agricultural land drainage on the long-term prospects for food production using five scenarios. One of the criteria used to define these scenarios is the extent of agricultural land drainage.

Under a scenario which assumes drainage of 267,000 ha of imperfectly to poorly drained land in northern and eastern Ontario along with general increases in crop yields, the overall production from Ontario would exceed projected targets by 11 per cent. In summary, the research by the Land Evaluation Group of the University of Guelph demonstrates how an integrated approach can determine the production sensitivities to changes in environmental and socio-economic conditions.

The integrated approach to land evaluation as devised by the Guelph team is based on a land use allocation model. According to Tercafs (1986: 357), such a model is based on the following three principles:

1 The variables are the possible land uses that could occur in the defined mapping units.

2 All known information about productivities or input utilization for each mapping unit is incorporated in the constraints of the allocation model.

3 The constraints specify the known limitations, resources and requirements for crops.

In essence, the allocation which indicates the minimum specialization or maximum flexibility of land uses within mapping units is chosen. A different type of approach is given by Aspinall (1990) who applies an inductive spatial model in order to predict the distribution of a particular habitat in north-east Scotland. The problem which he addresses is assessing the conservation significance of large areas beyond nature reserves. His model is based on a process of inductive learning from pattern in spatial data and he applies it to a case study dealing with predicting habitat suitability for red deer. Sample survey data on the occurrence of red deer as well as upon the relevant habitat attributes of altitude, land use cover and accumulated frost, were available for 1 km^2 cells. Thus the frequencies with which specified habitat attributes occurred according to the presence or absence of red deer could be calculated. From such frequencies, conditional probabilities were derived and then combined to provide a single probability

indicative of habitat suitability for red deer. The benefit of such results mean that it was then possible to predict suitability for localities for which there were no data on deer occurrence. The result is a probability map of red deer occurrence as well as one of uncertainty associated with the prediction. Aspinall (1990) compared his predicted distribution of deer with that of a regional forestry indicative plan, the aim being to identify areas where deer may come into conflict with forestry or where forestry may influence deer habitat.

This example from north-east Scotland illustrates the contribution which modelling when linked to a geographical information system can make to predicting the distribution of wildlife resources. For another example of a modelling approach to natural area management, reference is made to the study of Kessell (1990) in Australia. He describes a suite of geographical information and modelling systems (GIMS) developed to meet natural area and rural management. GIMS is used to assist with management of 6×10^6 ha of fire-prone rural land in eastern Australia where the needs are to model vegetation and fuel dynamics, fire behaviour and its environmental effects. Prediction of vegetation in grid cells is based on functions derived from easily obtained parameters, such as elevation, topographic position, aspect, slope value and soil type. GIMS has the capability of predicting change in vegetation, either through natural or disturbance-induced succession, using a deterministic or conditional probability approach. To model the spread of fire, predictions are necessary on the availability of dead fine organic matter which is inflammable. Two modelling approaches are available within GIMS in order to predict the fire's rate of spread and direction. With such results it is then possible to predict how fire area and perimeter change through time, information of critical importance for input to an allocation and optimization module within GIMS for fire control resources. Kessell (1990) explains that the modules necessary to support such resource allocation and optimization procedures have been mounted on pocket computers in order to assist with actual fire control situations. Other capabilities of the GIMS system are modelling the changes in animal habitats following fires and subsequent regeneration, and the prediction of fire hazard as an aid to land use planning. One of the key aspects of the GIMS system as noted by Kessell (1990) is that it presents research results in forms of direct relevance to operational decision making. Despite high costs of implementing GIMS, considerable cost-effectiveness is achieved even with one large fire. Kessell (1990) envisages considerable scope for developing GIMS for real-time emergency management.

9

Conclusion

The aim of the first edition of this book, published in 1980, was to demonstrate the advantages of utilizing land resource information as an aid to land use planning. This remains a major concern in this edition, but since 1980 there has been a substantial change in the technology, methodology and types of land resource question posed by land planners and managers.

Technological change is reflected in the increasing use of modelling procedures linked with geographical information systems. The evaluation of land resources, using whatever technique, necessitates the modelling and prediction of land value and potential. The increasing integration of geographical information systems with modelling offers exciting possibilities in the evaluation of land resources. The central role of a GIS in land evaluation is illustrated in Figure 9.1. As shown, data sources for this information system can be field sampling and monitoring, land resource survey, results from spatial interpolation, and the analysis of remote sensing imagery. Another key

input is the selection of land utilization types so that an expert system can be created within the GIS based on the methodology of the FAO (1976) *Framework for Land Evaluation*.

Within geographical information systems there is much merit in the integration of models which are based on knowledge of fundamental environmental processes. Particular emphasis has been given to simulating crop growth using such models. As another example, the use of soil for cropping depends on such land qualities as soil-water deficit, soil aeration and workability which are influenced by soil-water flow. Thus in the prediction of these land qualities, acceptable models of soil-water movement are essential. For example, van Stiphout et al (1987) modify a conventional soil-water flow model by taking into account the role of macropores caused by cracks and worm channels and thus are able to provide better estimates of soil moisture deficits for a clay loam grassland soil. Research into soil-water movement is also of importance to the modelling of pollutant dispersal in soils. Thus the incorporation of appropriate physically based models into land evaluation procedures depends upon the refinement and testing of models which predict environmental processes.

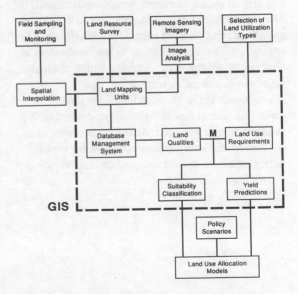

Figure 9.1 A system for the evaluation of land resources; the key role of a GIS is indicated; the process of matching land use requirements with land qualities is represented by M

Land planners and managers, in order to formulate strategy, are now posing far more challenging land resource questions; they are faced with having to evaluate a wide range of considerations from physical to economic and social. The need for integrated land evaluation will thus become more pressing. As explained in section 8.3, the use of spatial allocation models which use linear programming techniques, means that land uses can be predicted which maximize or minimize defined objectives such as crop yield or nutrient leaching. Results from such analyses can be much better incorporated into policy formulation. Land evaluation using integrated techniques is a major advance on the older approach whereby guidance was given on land suitability only for specific crops.

It must never be forgotten that modelling in land evaluation is dependent upon the availability of land resource data. A serious problem is that government funding for soil survey or meteorological monitoring is often inadequate or being reduced. As examples, the Soil Surveys of England and Wales and of Scotland have been substantially cut in recent years. In many countries, even within the European Community, there is still a dearth of detailed or semi-detailed soil maps. The other data issue is that of quality with variability in space and time being of particular importance. The application of fuzzy set theory to land evaluation as a means of dealing with variability within mapping units was discussed in section 7.4; one consequence is the increased need for data on variability so that functions expressing membership grade can be determined. Analytical procedures such as spatial interpolation now exist for making better estimates of land resource characteristics at unsampled locations. In addition, statements can be made on the reliability of such estimates. Research requires to be done to quantify temporal variability in climatic parameters so that risk analysis can be incorporated into land evaluation. Decisions about land use would benefit from such risk prediction. Another avenue for research in land evaluation is the application of artificial neural networks which can deal with incomplete or inadequate data. These networks do not use any classification or rule-based approach, but instead learn from a range of examples. When faced with an unknown dataset, the approach is to find the best fit pattern to the learned examples.

The conclusion to the first edition of this book was the prime need in soils and land use planning for the application of known techniques rather than further methodological development. The basis to this statement was the view that sufficient consideration was not given in land use planning to basic land resource issues. One reason for this could be the quality of the results from land evaluation analysis. Land use planners and managers now require far more information on the reliability of predictions as well as the findings from integrated land evaluation analyses. Thus the conclusion to this book is different from that of the first edition in that major research challenges in land evaluation are identified for the next decade. These are model validation and linkage to expert and geographical information systems, and the further development of integrated approaches to land use issues. It is to be hoped that with such scientific advances, land evaluation can play a key role in fostering a more sensitive approach to the use of land resources in the twenty-first century.

Appendix 1

Glossary of soil science terms

(Note that this is not a full list since only terms used in the text are included.)

argillic horizon: an illuvial horizon characterized by an accumulation of clays.

Atterberg limits: a soil can exist in a liquid, plastic or solid state, depending upon its moisture content; Atterberg limits refer to the boundary values of these states (see **liquid** and **plastic limit**).

base saturation: the extent to which exchange sites in a soil are saturated with exchangeable cations other than hydrogen and aluminium.

caliche: a near-surface layer cemented by secondary calcium or magnesium carbonate.

cation exchange: the exchange between cations in solution and cations held on the surfaces of soil colloids (clays and organic matter).

cation exchange capacity: the total amount of exchangeable cations that a soil can absorb expressed in milliequivalents per 100 g of soil (meq/100 g).

coat, soil: the lining or coating of a natural interface with such soil constituents as clays, sesquioxides or coarser material (through the removal of finer material).

colour, soil: the colour of soil horizons is described by using a Munsell Soil Colour Chart; information is collected not only about dominant and subdominant colours in horizons but also about the moisture status, since this influences colour.

concretion, soil: see **nodule**.

consistence, soil: this property results from the kind of cohesion and adhesion; it is described according to strength (resistance of soil to crushing), type of failure, cementation, maximum stickiness and maximum plasticity (see **plasticity**).

dispersal index: the ratio between the total amount of very fine particles obtained by chemical and mechanical dispersion and the amount of the same material obtained by mechanical dispersion.

electrical conductivity, soil: measured to indicate the salt concentration in soil; measures are made in units of milli-reciprocal ohms per centimetre (mmhos/cm); values less than 4 mmhos/cm (approximately equivalent to less than 3000 ppm salts in solution) suggest that most crops should not suffer from salinity conditions.

erodibility: the resistance of soil particles to detachment and transportation; it depends upon soil properties such as texture, aggregate stability, and organic content as well as upon topographic position and slope value.

fragment, soil: a soil aggregate, like a clod, less permanent than a ped; fragments occur at or near the surface and result from cultivation or frost action.

gilgai: microrelief of soils produced by expansion and contraction resultant upon moisture changes; gilgai is associated with expansive clays.

gleyed soil: a soil developed under poor drainage conditions, indicated by the reduction of iron and other elements, grey colours and mottles.

horizon, soil: a layer of soil approximately parallel to the soil surface; it differs from adjacent layers in terms of colour, and often also structure, texture, consistence, and chemical, biological and mineralogical composition.

horizon boundary: a description of the boundary between soil horizons; such terms as sharp, clear, gradual or diffuse are used to indicate the clarity of the boundary while the form of the boundary is also described by such terms as smooth, wavy, irregular or broken.

horizon notation: horizons are designated by the use of letters to permit the comparison and classification of profiles; examples are L for a fresh litter horizon, F a partly decomposed litter horizon, H a well-decomposed organic layer, A an upper mineral horizon which also includes organic matter, E (or A_2) a subsurface horizon which is lighter in colour and contains less organic matter, iron, aluminium or clay than the immediately underlying horizon, B a subsurface mineral horizon with the illuvial concentration of clay, iron, aluminium or humus, and C the parent material from which the soil has developed.

hydraulic conductivity: the rate at which water can move through soil; one experimental technique for determining its value is to drill a hole to below the water-table; the water is then pumped out of the hole, and from measurements of the rate of rise of water, the value of hydraulic conductivity can be calculated.

infiltration rate: the maximum rate at which water can enter a soil under specified conditions.

leaching: the transfer of material within the soil by solution.

liquid limit: the moisture content at which a soil changes from a plastic to a liquid state.

mottle: a spot of colour or shade interspersed with, and different from, the dominant colour of a soil horizon; mottles are distinct from colour variation associated with ped surfaces, worm holes, concretions or nodules.

nodule, soil: a unit within soil, different from the surrounding material because of the concentration of some constituent (for example calcium carbonate); usually nodules are cemented and hard; concretions are nodules which are more symmetrical owing to a more concentric accumulation process.

numerical taxonomy: the use of statistical techniques in order to classify soils.

particle size class: size ranges of particle size are labelled by such terms as clay, fine silt, medium silt, coarse silt, fine sand, medium sand and coarse sand.

ped: relatively permanent soil aggregate, separated by voids or natural surfaces of weakness.

pedalfer: a soil in which iron and aluminium sesquioxides increase relative to silica during soil development; an example is a podzol.

pedocal: a soil in which calcium carbonate accumulates during soil development; an example is a chernozem.

pedon: the smallest three-dimensional unit of soil which can be examined.

pH, soil: a measure of the hydrogen ion concentration in soils; values below 7 indicate acid conditions while values above 7 indicate alkalinity.

phase, soil: a subdivision of a soil series according to variations in such properties as depth of horizons or stoniness.

plasticity: the ability of soil to change shape constantly when stress is applied and to retain the new shape after the stress is removed.

plasticity index: the difference between the plastic and liquid limits.

plastic limit: the moisture content at which a soil changes from a solid to a plastic state.

salinity: see **electrical conductivity**.

series, soil: a grouping of soil profiles to permit the mapping of soils; each series, named after a locality where it is well represented, is characterized by a similar sequence of horizons developed on uniform parent materials and under similar drainage conditions.

sierozem: (obsolete term) a soil type found in arid and semi-arid areas and characterized by a low organic content, a lack of leaching and an accumulation of calcium carbonate in middle and lower horizons.

solod: a soil which develops from the leaching of a solonetz with the formation of a bleach E horizon which, as in a podzol, is deficient in iron and aluminium, has a sandy texture and is acid; the underlying B horizon is gleyed and has a columnar structure developed in clays.

solonchak: a light-coloured soil with a high concentration of soluble salts (sodium chloride and sodium sulphate).

solonetz: a dark-coloured soil which develops from a solonchak by leaching of some of the sodium which has the effect of deflocculating the soil mass; the soil develops a characteristic columnar structure when dry and is highly alkaline.

structure, soil: the shape, size and degree of development of the aggregation of primary soil particles into naturally or artificially formed structural units called peds, clods or fragments (see **fragment**); terms such as 'platy', 'prismatic', 'blocky', 'crumb' and 'granular' are used to describe the shape of peds and fragments.

texture, soil: the relative proportions of sand, silt and clay defining soil textural classes such as sandy clay, clay loam, sandy clay loam, silty clay loam, etc.

Unified Soil Classification System: a classification based on certain engineering properties of soils: optimum moisture content, permeability, compressibility and shear strength.

void: a space in soil not occupied by solid matter; this space can be occupied by soil water, or the soil atmosphere.

void ratio: a ratio of the volume of void space to the volume of solid matter in a soil mass.

warp soil: a soil developed from alluvial or estuarine deposits, artificially raised by controlled sedimentation above the level of normal alluvial soils; warp soils are usually 50–75 cm thick and frequently show the original laminae laid down in the process of accumulation; these soils are often neutral or slightly alkaline in reaction.

References

Adams, J A and Wilde, R H (1980) Comparison of the variability in a soil taxonomic unit with that of the associated soil mapping unit. *Australian Journal of Soil Research* 18: 285–97

Agricultural Development and Advisory Service (1976) Agricultural land classification of England and Wales. The definition and identification of sub-grades within grade 3. Technical Report 11/1

Agricultural Development and Advisory Service (1980) The classification of land in the hills and uplands of England and Wales. Ministry of Agriculture, Fisheries and Food, Booklet 2358

Alexandratos, N (ed) (1988) *World Agriculture: Toward 2000*. An FAO study. Belhaven Press, London

Allan Jones, C and O'Toole, J C (1987) Application of crop production models in agro-ecological characterization: simulation models for specific crops. In Bunting, A H (ed) *Agricultural Environments*. CAB International, Farnborough, pp 199–209

Ameyan, O (1986a) Quality of land facets as soil mapping units in an area of northern Nigeria. *Geoforum* 17: 97–107

Ameyan, O (1986b) Surface soil variability of a map unit on Niger River alluvium. *Journal of the Soil Science Society of America* 50: 1289–93

Anderson, J L and Robert, P C (1987) PRODEX: productivity ratings for land parcels using a microcomputer. *Applied Agricultural Research* 2: 248–51

Areola, O (1982) Soil variability within land facets in areas of low, smooth relief: a case study on the Gwagwa Plains, Nigeria. *Soil Survey and Land Evaluation* 2: 9–13

Aspinall, R (1990) An integrated approach to land evaluation: Grampian region. In Bibby, J S and Thomas, M F (eds) *Evaluation of Land Resource in Scotland*. Macaulay Land Use Research Institute, Aberdeen, pp 45–56

Avery, B W (1980) Soil classification for England and Wales. Technical Monograph No 14, Soil Survey, Harpenden

Bartelli, L J (1962) Use of soils information in urban-fringe areas. *Journal of Soil and Water Conservation* 17: 99–103

Bartelli, L J (1978) Technical classification system for soil survey interpretation. *Advances in Agronomy* 30: 247–89

Batjes, N H and Bouwman, A F (1988) JAMPLES: a computerized land evaluation system for Jamaica. Paper presented at the Symposium Land Qualities in Space and Time, held at Wageningen, The Netherlands, 22–6 August 1988

Batjes, N H, Bouwman, A F and Sinclair, K M (1987) Jamaica physical land evaluation system. In Beek, K J, Burrough, P A and McCormack, D E (eds) *Quantified Land Evaluation Procedures*. ITC Publication No 6, Enschede, The Netherlands, pp 39–43

Baumgardner, M F and van de Weg, R F (1988) Space and time: dimensions of a world soils and terrain digital database. Paper presented at the Symposium Land Qualities in Space and Time, held at Wageningen, The Netherlands, 22–6 August 1988

Bawden, M G and Carroll, D M 1968 The land resources of Lesotho. Land Resource Study No 7, Land Resources Development Centre, Ministry of Overseas Development, Surbiton, England

Bawden, M G, Carroll, D M and Tuley, P (1972) The land resources of north east Nigeria. Volume 3, the land systems. Land Resource Study No 9 Land Resources Development Centre, Ministry of Overseas Development, Surbiton, England

Beckett, P H T (1978) The rate of soil survey in Britain. *Journal of Soil Science* **29**: 95–101

Beckett, P H T (1981) The cost–benefit relationships of soil surveys. Soil Resource Inventories and Development Planning, Tech Mono No 1, Soil Management Support Services, Soil Conservation Service, USDA, 289–311

Beckett, P H T and Bie, S W (1978) Use of soil and land-system maps to provide soil information in Australia. Division of Soils Technical Paper No 33, CSIRO

Beckett, P H T and Webster, R (1971) Soil variability: a review. *Soils and Fertilizers* **34**: 1–15

Beek, K J (1975) Land utilization types in land evaluation. In *Land Evaluation in Europe*, FAO Soils Bulletin No 29, Rome, pp 87–106

Beek, K J (1977) The selection of soil properties and land qualities relevant to specific land uses in developing countries. In *Soil Resource Inventories*, Agronomy Mimeo No 77-23, Cornell University, Ithaca, New York, pp 143–62

Beek, K J (1978) Land evaluation for agricultural development. Publication No 23, International Institute for Land Reclamation and Improvement, Wageningen, The Netherlands

Beek, K J and Bennema, J (1972) Land evaluation for agricultural land use planning: an ecological methodology. Department of Soil Science and Geology, Agricultural University, Wageningen, The Netherlands

Bellocchio, M M and Magaldi, D (1987) Agroclimatic mapping in Mediterranean regions. *Soil Survey and Land Evaluation* **7**: 43–6

Bergmann, H and Boussard, J (1976) *Guide to the Economic Evaluation of Irrigation Projects*, OECD, Paris

Best, R H (1973) Land conversions to urban use. *SSRC Newsletter* **19**: 11–13

Bibby, J S (1990) Land evaluation: progress in Scotland (1980)–(1989). In Bibby, J S and Thomas, M F (eds) *Evaluation of Land Resource in Scotland*. Macaulay Land Use Research Institute, Aberdeen, pp 17–23

Bibby, J S and Mackney, D (1969) Land use capability classification. Soil Survey Technical Monograph No 1

Bibby, J S, Douglas, H A, Thomasson, A J and Robertson, J S (1982) Land capability classification for agriculture. Monograph of the Soil Survey of Scotland, Macaulay Institute for Soil Research, Aberdeen

Bibby, J S, Heslop, R E F and Hartnup, R (1988) Land capability classification for forestry in Britain. Soil Survey Monograph, Macaulay Land Use Research Institute, Aberdeen

Bie, S W and Beckett, P H T (1971) Quality control in soil survey. Introduction: I. The choice of mapping unit. *Journal of Soil Science* 22: 32–49

Bie, S W and Beckett, P H T (1973) Comparison of four independent soil surveys by air-photo interpretation, Paphos area (Cyprus). *Photogrammetria* 29: 189–202

Billingsley, F C and Urena, J L (1984) Concepts for a global information system. In *Spatial Information Technologies for Remote Sensing Today and Tomorrow, Proceedings Pecora meeting*, IEEE Computer Society, 123–31

Birkeland, P W (1984) *Soils and Geomorphology*. Oxford University Press, New York

Birse, E L and Dry, F T (1970) Assessment of climatic conditions in Scotland. 1 Based on accumulated temperature and potential water deficit. Soil Survey of Scotland, Aberdeen

Birse, E L and Robertson, L (1970) Assessment of climatic conditions in Scotland. 2 Based on exposure and accumulated frost. Soil Survey of Scotland, Aberdeen

Bliss, N B and Reybold, W U (1989) Small-scale digital soil maps for interpreting natural resources. *Journal of Soil and Water Conservation* 44: 30–4

Booth, T H and Saunders, J C (1985) A trial application of the FAO 'Guidelines on Land Evaluation for Forestry'. Divisional Report 85/3, Institute of Biological Resources, CSIRO, Canberra.

Bouma, J (1986) Using soil survey information to characterize the soil-water state. *Journal of Soil Science* 37: 1–7

Bouma, J (1989) Using soil survey data for quantitative land evaluation. *Advances in Soil Science* 9: 177–213

Bouma, J and van Lanen, H A J (1987) Transfer functions and threshold values: from soil characteristics to land qualities. In Beek, K J, Burrough, P A and McCormack, D E (eds) *Quantified Land Evaluation Procedures*, ITC Pub No 6, Enschede, The Netherlands, pp 106–10

Bouma, J, de Laat, P J M, van Holst, A F and van de Nes, Th J (1980) Predicting the effects of changing water-table levels and associated soil moisture regimes for soil survey interpretations. *Journal Soil Science Society of America* 44: 797–802

Bouma, J, van Lanen, H A J, Breeuwsma, A, Wosten, H J M and Kooistra, M J (1986) Soil survey data needs when studying modern land use problems. *Soil Use and Management* 2: 125–30

Bowser, W E and Moss, H C (1950) A soil rating and classification for irrigation lands in western Canada. *Scientific Agriculture* **30**: 165–71

Brady, N C (1984) *The Nature and Properties of Soils*. Tenth edition. Macmillan, New York

Breeuwsma, A, Wösten, J H M, Vleeshouwer, J J, Van Slobbe, A M and Bouma J (1986) Derivation of land qualities to assess environmental problems from soil surveys. *Soil Science Society America Journal* **50**: 186–90

Bregt, A K, Bouma, J and Jellinek, M (1987) Comparison of thematic maps derived from a soil map and from kriging of point data. *Geoderma* **39**: 281–91

Breimer, R F, van Kekem, A J and van Reuler, H (1986) Guidelines for soil survey and land evaluation in ecological research. MAB Technical Notes 17, UNESCO, Paris

Briggs, D J and Martin, D M (1988) CORINE: an environmental information system for the European Community. *European Environment Review* **2**: 29–34

Briggs, D J, Brignall, P and Wilkes, A (1989) Assessing soil erosion risk in the Mediterranean region: the CORINE programme of the European Community. In Van Lanen, H A J and Bregt, A K (eds) *Agriculture: Application of Computerized EC Soil Map and Climatic Data*, Commission of the EC

Brinkman, R and Smyth, A J (1973) Land evaluation for rural purposes. Publication No 17, International Institute for Land Reclamation and Improvement, Wageningen, The Netherlands

Brklacich, M and Smit, B (1986) Effects of climatic change on agricultural land resource potential. In Gelinas, R, Bond, D and Smit, B (eds) *Perspectives on Land Modelling*, Polyscience Publications Inc, pp 135–47

Brklacich, M, Smit, B and McBride, R (1987) Land evaluation and environmental change: the case of land drainage and food production. In Cocklin, C, Smit, B and Johnson, T (eds) *Demands on Rural Lands: Planning for Resource Use*. Westview Press, Boulder, Col., pp 179–95

Brown, R B (1985) The need for continuing update of soil surveys. *Proceeding Soil and Crop Society of Florida* **44**: 90–3

Brown, R B (1988) Concerning the quality of soil survey. *Journal of Soil and Water Conservation* **43**: 452–5

Browne, M A E and McMillan, A A (1989) Geology for land use planning: drift deposits of the Clyde valley. 3 volumes, Technical Report WA/89/78, Onshore Geology Series, British Geological Survey, Keyworth, Nottingham

Bunce, R G H, Barr, C J and Whittaker, H A (1981) Land classes of Great Britain: preliminary descriptions for users of the Merlewood method of land classification. *Merlewood Research and Development Paper* No 86, Merlewood, England

Burgess, T M and Webster, R (1980) Optimal interpolation and isarithmic mapping of soil properties. 1: the semi-variogram and punctual kriging. *Journal of Soil Science* **31**: 315–51

Buringh, P (1985) The land resource for agriculture. *Transactions of the Philosophical Society of London* B **310**: 151–9

Burnham, C P and McRae, S G (1974) Land judging. *Area* **6**: 107–11

Burnham, C P, Shinn, A C and Varcoe, V J (1987) Crop yields in relation to classes of soil and agricultural land classification grade in south east England. *Soil Survey and Land Evaluation* **7**: 95–100

Burrough, P A (1986) *Principles of Geographical Information Systems.* Oxford University Press, Oxford

Burrough, P A (1989) Fuzzy mathematical methods for soil survey and land evaluation. *Journal of Soil Science* **40**: 477–92

Butler, B E (1980) *Soil Classification for Soil Survey.* Clarendon Press, Oxford

Campbell, J B (1979) Spatial variability of soils. *Annals Association American Geographers* **69**: 544–56

Campbell, W G and Mortenson, D C (1989) Ensuring the quality of geographic information system data: a practical application of quality control. *Photogrammetric Engineering and Remote Sensing* **55**: 1613–18

Campbell, W G, Robbins Church, M, Bishop, G D, Mortenson, D C and Pierson, S M (1989) The role for a geographical information system in a large environmental project. *International Journal of Geographical Information Systems* **3**: 349–62

Canada Land Inventory (1970) The Canada land inventory: objectives, scope and organization. Report No 1 (second edition), Department of Regional Economic Expansion, Ottawa

Caroll, D M, Evans, R and Bendelow, V C (1977) Air photo-interpretation for soil mapping, Technical Monograph No 8, Soil Survey, Harpenden

Centre for Agricultural Strategy (1976) *Land for Agriculture.* Centre for Agricultural Strategy Report, University of Reading

Chang, L and Burrough, P A (1987) Fuzzy reasoning: a new quantitative aid for land evaluation. *Soil Survey and Land Evaluation* **7**: 69–80

Chinene, V R N (1991) The Zambian Land Evaluation System (ZLES). *Soil Use and Management* **7**: 21–30

Chinene, V R N and Shitumbanuma, V (1988) Land evaluation of the proposed Musaba state farm in Samfya District, Zambia. *Soil Survey and Land Evaluation* **8**: 176–82

Christian, C S and Stewart, G A (1952) Summary of general report on survey of Katherine-Darwin Region, 1946. CSIRO Land Research Series No 1

Christian, C S and Stewart, G A (1968) Methodology of integrated surveys. In *Aerial Surveys and Integrated Studies*, UNESCO, Paris, pp 233–80

Christodoulou, M and Nakos, G (1990) An approach to comprehensive land use planning. *Journal of Environmental Management* **31**: 39–46

Claridge, C J (1988) The approach adopted by Highland Regional Council. In Bunce, R G H and Barr, C J (eds) *Rural Information for Forward Planning*, Institute of Terrestrial Ecology Symposium No 21, 21–8

Clarke, G R (1971) *The Study of Soil in the Field.* Clarendon Press, Oxford

Clarke, S R, Fisher, P F and Ragg, J M (1986) Soil profile recorder: a program to enable the recording of soil profile descriptions in the field. *Computers and Geosciences* **12**: 779–806

Clawson, M (1972) *America's Land and its Uses.* Johns Hopkins Press, Baltimore, Md

Clayden, B and Hollis, J M (1984) Criteria for differentiating soil series, Technical Monograph No 17, Soil Survey, Harpenden, England

Cocks, K D and Ive, J R (1988) Evaluating a computer package for planning public lands in New South Wales. *Journal of Environmental Management* **26**: 249–60

Cocks, K D, Walker, P A and Parvey, C A (1988) Evolution of a continental-scale geographical information system. *International Journal Geographical Information Systems* **2**: 263–80

Compagnoni, P (1986) An environmental planning method for Australian jurisdictions? Comments on the SIRO-PLAN/LUPLAN schema. *Environment and Planning B Planning and Design* **13**: 335-44

Cooke, R U and Doornkamp, J C (1974) *Geomorphology in Environmental Management.* Oxford University Press, London

Coote, D R, Dumanski, J and Ramsey, J F (1981) An assessment of the degradation of agricultural lands in Canada. LRRI Contribution No 118, Research Branch, Agriculture Canada, Ottawa

Cowie, J D and Metcalfe, J (1982) Land classification in the hills and uplands of England and Wales: the system of the Ministry of Agriculture, Fisheries and Food. *Soil Survey and Land Evaluation* **2**: 53–9

Davidson, D A (1978) *Science for Physical Geographers.* Edward Arnold, London

Davidson, D A (1980) *Soils and Land Use Planning.* Longman, London

Davidson, D A (1989) The influence of land capability on rural land sales: a case study in Renfrewshire, Scotland. *Soil Use and Management* **5**: 38–44

Davidson, D A and Jones, G E (1985) The use of a low level data base management system for the analysis of soil survey records. *Soil Survey and Land Evaluation* **5**: 88–92

Davidson, D A and Jones, G E (1988) A land resource information system at the 1:25,000 scale. In Bunce, R G H and Barr, C J (eds) *Rural Information for Forward Planning*, Institute of Terrestrial Ecology Symposium No 21, 85–91

Davidson, D A, Selman, P H, Watson, A I and Winterbottom, S J (1991) The evaluation of a geographical information system. Report to the Natural Environmental Research Council, Swindon, Project GST/02/492

de Bakker, H and Schelling, J (1966) (System for soil classification for The Netherlands: the higher orders) Centre for Agricultural Publications and Documentation, Wageningen, The Netherlands

Dekkers, J T M, Zegers, H J M and Westerfeld, G J W (1972) Deel van de bodemkartering ten behoeve van het structuurplan Helmond e o (gebied Brouwhuis), Stichting voor Bodemkartering, Wageningen, The Netherlands

de Man, W H E (1988) Establishing a geographical information system in relation to its use. A process of strategic choices. *International Journal of Geographical Information Systems* **2**: 245–61

Dent, D and Young, A (1981) *Soil Survey and Land Evaluation*. George Allen and Unwin, London

Dent, D L and Cook, H (1987) Soil water sufficiency: data needs and error bars of a soil water potential model. In Beek, K J, Burrough, P A and McCormack, D E (eds) *Quantified Land Evaluation Procedures*, ITC Pub No 6, Enschede, The Netherlands, pp 111–18

Dent, D L and Ridgway, R B (1986) A land use planning handbook for Sri Lanka FAO, Colombo

Dent, D L and Scammell, R P (1981) Assessment of long-term irrigation need by integration of data for soil and crop characteristics and climate. *Soil Survey and Land Evaluation* **1**: 51–7

van Diepen, C A, Wolf, J, Keulen, H van and Rappoldt, C (1989) WOFOST: a simulation model of crop production. *Soil Use and Management* **5**: 16–24

Doolittle, J A (1987) Using ground-penetrating radar to increase the quality and efficiency of soil surveys. In Reybold, W U and Petersen, G W (eds) *Soil Survey Techniques* SSSA Special Publ No 20, 11–32

Doorenbos, J and Kassam, A H (1979) Yield response to water. *Irrigation and Drainage Paper* No 33, FAO, Rome

Douglas, C L, Rickman, R W, Zuzel, J F and Klepper, B L (1988) Criteria for delineation of agronomic zones in the Pacific Northwest. *Journal of Soil and Water Conservation* **43**: 415–18

Driscoll, R S, Merkel, D, Radloff, D L, Synder, D E and Hagihara, J S (1984) An ecological land classification framework for the United States. Miscellaneous Publication No 1439, Forest Service, USDA

Dudal, R (1978) Land resources for agricultural development. International Society for Soil Science 11th Congress, Plenary Session Papers 2, 314–40

Dudal, R (1987) Land resources for plant production. In McLaren, D J and Skinner, B J (eds) *Resources and World Development*, J. Wiley & Sons, Chichester, pp 659–70

Dumanski, J and Onofrei, C (1989) Techniques of crop yield assessment for agricultural land evaluation. *Soil Use and Management* **5**: 9–16

Dumanski, J and Stewart, R B (1983) Crop production potentials for land evaluation in Canada. Contribution 1983-13E, Research Branch, Agriculture Canada, Ottawa, Canada

Dumanski, J, Bootsma, A and Kirkwood, V (1986) A geographic analysis of grain yield trends in Ontario using a computerized land information base. *Canadian Journal of Soil Science* **66**: 481–97

Dumanski, J, Marshall, I B and Huffman, E C (1979) Soil capability analysis for regional land use planning – study of the Ottawa urban fringe. *Canadian Journal of Soil Science* **59**: 363–79

Eastman, J R (1990) IDRISI: a grid-based geographic analysis system. Graduate School of Geography, Clark University, Worcester, Mass.

Ecoregions Working Group (1989) Ecoclimatic regions of Canada: first approximation. Ecological Land Classification Series, No 23, Environment Canada, Ottawa, Canada

Edelman, C H (1963) Applications of soil survey in land development in Europe. International Institute for Land Reclamation and Improvement Publication No 12, Wageningen, The Netherlands

Environmental Conservation Service Task Force (1981) Ecological land survey guidelines for environmental impact analysis. Ecological Land Classification Series, No 13, Lands Directorate, Environment Canada, Ottawa

Eswaran, H, Forbes, T R and Laker, M C (1977) Soil map parameters and classification. In *Soil Resource Inventories*, Agronomy Mimeo No 77–23, Cornell University, Ithaca, New York, pp. 37–57

Eyles, G O (1985) The New Zealand land resource inventory erosion classification. Water and Soil Miscellaneous Publication No 85, Wellington, New Zealand

Eyles, G O (1986) Recent developments in the New Zealand land resource inventory. *Planning Quarterly* 84: 28–30

FAO (1975) *Land Evaluation in Europe. FAO Soil Bulletin* No 29, Rome

FAO (1976) *A Framework for Land Evaluation. Soils Bulletin* No 32, Rome

FAO (1978a) *Report of the Agro-ecological Zones Project: Volume 1. Methodology and Results for Africa.* World Soils Resources Report 48

FAO (1978b) *Report of the Agro-ecological Zones Project: Volume 2. Results for Southwest Asia.* World Soils Resources Report 48/2

FAO (1980) *Report of the Agro-ecological Zones Project: Volume 4. Results for Southeast Asia.* World Soils Resources Report 48/4

FAO (1981) *Report of the Agro-ecological Zones Project: Volume 3. Methodology and Results for South and Central America.* World Soil Resources Report 48/3

FAO (1984a) *Guidelines: Land Evaluation for Rainfed Agriculture. FAO Soils Bulletin* No 52, Rome

FAO (1984b) *Land Evaluation for Forestry. FAO Forestry Paper* No 48 FAO Rome

FAO (1985) *Guidelines: Land Evaluation for Irrigated Agriculture. FAO Soils Bulletin* No 55

FAO (1987) *FAO Production Yearbook* (1986) Vol 40

FAO (1988) *Land Resources Appraisal of Bangladesh for Agricultural Development.* Seven volumes, FAO, Rome

FAO (1990) *FAO-ISRIC Soil Database (SDB).* World Soil Resources Reports No 64.

Fenton, T E (1975) Use of soil productivity ratings in evaluating Iowa agricultural land. *Journal of Soil and Water Conservation* 30: 237–40

Fenton, T E, Duncan, E R, Shrader, W D and Drumenil, L C (1971) Productivity levels of some Iowa soils, Agriculture and Home Economics Experimental Station, Special Report No 66, Iowa State University of Science and Technology, Ames, Iowa

Ferrari, G A and Magaldi, D (1989) Land suitability evaluation for Mediterranean regions. *Revista di Agricoltura Subtropicale e Tropicale* 83: 109–39.

Finkl, C W (ed) (1982) *Soil Classification*. Hutchinson Ross Publishing Company, Stroudsburg, Pa

Flaherty, M and Smit, B (1982) An assessment of land classification techniques in planning for agricultural land use. *Journal of Environmental Management* **15**: 323–32

Fletcher, J R (1982) Land resources for horticulture New Zealand. *Agricultural Science* **16**: 6–9

Frost, C A and Speirs, R B (1984) Water erosion of soils in south east Scotland–a case study. *Research and Development in Agriculture* **1**: 145–52

Furuseth, O J and Pierce, J T (1982) A comparative analysis of farmland preservation programmes in North America. *Canadian Geographer* **26**: 191–206

Gbadegesin, A (1987) Soil rating for crop production in the savanna belt of south-western Nigeria. *Agricultural Systems* **23**: 27–42

Gbadegesin, S and Areola, O (1987) Soil factors affecting maize yields in the south-western Nigerian savanna and their relation to land suitability assessment. *Soil Survey and Land Evaluation* **7**: 167–75

Geographic Information Systems Laboratory (1989) *OSU MAP-for-the-PC User's Guide*. Version 3.0. Department of Geography, Ohio State University, Columbus, Ohio

Ghazalli, M Z and Nieuwolt, S (1982) The use of an agricultural rainfall index in Malaysia. *International Journal of Biometeorology* **26**: 277–83

Gilbert, G, Helie, R G, Mondoux, J M and Li, L K (1985) Ecosystem sensitivity to acid precipitation for Quebec. Ecological Land Classification Series, No 20, Lands Directorate, Environment Canada, Ottawa

Goldin, A (1988) Statistical comparison of the 1941 and 1983 soil survey maps of Watcom County, Washington, USA. *Soil Survey and Land Evaluation* **8**: 100–10

Grigg, D (1970) *The Harsh Lands: A Study in Agricultural Development*. Macmillan, London

Gynne, M (1990) Global monitoring, data management and assessment within GEMS and GRID. *Proceedings International Conference and Workshop on Global Natural Resource Monitoring and Assessments: Preparing for the 21st Century* Vol 1, pp 87–98, American Society for Photogrammetry and Remote Sensing, Bethesda, Md

Haans, J C F M (1978) Soil survey interpretation in the Netherlands. Paper presented at a symposium between The Netherlands and Romania, September 1978

Haans, J C F M and van Lynden, K R (1978) Assessment factors as an aid for interpreting soil surveys. Paper presented at the International Association for Soil Science Conference, Edmonton

Haans, J C F M and Westerfeld, G J W (1970) The application of soil survey in the Netherlands. *Geoderma* **4**: 279–309

Hadrian, D R, Bishop, I D and Mitcheltree, R (1988) Automated mapping of visual impacts in utility corridors. *Landscape and Urban Planning* **16**: 261–82

Hagan, R M, Haise, R R and Edminster, T W (eds) (1967) *Irrigation of Agricultural Lands*, American Society of Agronomy, Madison, Wis.

Hamilton, G J and Christie, J M (1971) Forest management tables (metric), Forestry Commission Booklet No 34, HMSO, London

Hammond, C M and Walker, B H (1984) A procedure for land capability analysis in southern Africa, based on computer overlay techniques. *Landscape Planning* 11: 269–91

Hargreaves, G H (1985) Crop water requirements. Special communication Washington DC, US Agency for International Development

Harrison, W D, Johnson, M E and Biggam, P F (1987) Video image analysis of large-scale vertical aerial photography to facilitate soil mapping. In Reybold, W U and Petersen, G W (eds) *Soil Survey Techniques* SSSA Special Publication No 20, 1–9

Heuvelink, G B M, Burrough, P A and Stein, A (1989) Propagation of errors in spatial modelling with GIS. *International Journal of Geographical Information Systems* 3: 303–22

Higgins, G M, Kassam, A H, Naiken, L, Fischer, G and Shah, M M (1982) Potential population supporting capacities of lands in the developing world Technical Report of Project INT/75/P13 'Land Resources for Populations of the Future', FAO, Rome

Hirvonen, H E (1984) The Atlantic region of Canada: an ecological perspective Lands and Integrated Programs Directorate, Atlantic Region, Environment Canada

Hockensmith, R D and Steele, J G (1949) Recent trends in the use of the land capability classification. *Proceedings of the Soil Science Society of America* 14: 383–8

Hodgson, J M (1974) Soil survey field handbook. Technical Monograph No 5 Soil Survey, Harpenden

Hodgson, J M (1978) *Soil Sampling and Soil Description*. Clarendon Press, Oxford

Huddleston, J H (1984) Development and use of soil productivity ratings in the US. *Geoderma* 32: 297–317

Ive, J R and Cocks, K D (1983) SIRO-PLAN and LUPLAN: an Australian approach to land use planning. 2 The LUPLAN land-use planning package. *Environment and Planning B: Planning and Design* 10: 347–55

Ive, J R, Davis, J R and Cocks, K D (1985) A computer package to support inventory, evaluation and allocation of land resources. *Soil Survey and Land Evaluation* 5: 77–87.

Jenkin, R N, Rose-Innes, R, Dunsmore, J R, Walker, S H, Birchall, C J and Briggs, J S (1976) The agricultural development potential of the Belize Valley, Belize Land Resource Study No 24, Land Resources Development Centre, Ministry of Overseas Development, Surbiton, England

Jessen, M R (1987) Urban land use capability survey handbook. Water and Soil Miscellaneous Publication No 105, Wellington, New Zealand

Joffe, J S (1949) *Pedology*. Pedology Publications, New Brunswick, NJ

Jones, R J A and Thomasson, A J (1985) An agroclimatic databank for England and Wales. Technical Monograph No 16, Soil Survey, Rothamsted

Joshua, W D (1987) Agro-ecological characterization in Sri Lanka. In Bunting, A H (ed) *Agricultural Environments*. CAB International, Farnborough, pp 289–97

Kalima, C and Veldkamp, W J (1987) Quantified land evaluation in Zambia. In Beek, K J, Burrough, P A and McCormack, D E (eds) *Quantified Land Evaluation Procedures*, ITC Publ No 6, Enschede, The Netherlands, pp 48–52

Kanyanda, C W (1988) Field application of the FAO guidelines for land evaluation for rainfed agriculture in comparison with the national guidelines: criticisms and proposals. *FAO World Soil Resources Reports* No 62, pp 34–44

Kato, Y (1984) A computerized soil information system for arable land in Japan. *Soil Science and Plant Nutrition* **30**: 287–97

Kellogg, C E and Orvedal, A C (1969) Potentially arable soils of the world and critical measures for their use. *Advances in Agronomy* **21**: 109–70

Kellomaki, S and Pukkala, T (1989) Forest landscape: a method of amenity evaluation based on computer simulation. *Landscape and Urban Planning* **18**: 117–25

Kessell, S R (1990) An Australian geographical information and modelling system for natural area management. *International Journal of Geographical Information Systems* **4**: 333–62

King, R B (1970) A parametric approach to land system classification. *Geoderma* **4**: 37–46

King, R B and Birchall, C J (1975) Land systems and soils of the Southern Rift Valley, Ethiopia, Land Resource Report No 5, Land Resources Development Centre, Ministry of Overseas Development, Surbiton, England

Kiome, R and Weeda, A (1988) Rating of land qualities in Kenya. *FAO World Soil Resources Reports* No 62, pp 104–11

Klingebiel, A A (1966) Costs and returns of soil surveys. *Soil Conservation* **32**: 3–6

Klingebiel, A A and Montgomery, P H (1961) Land capability classification. USDA Handbook 210, Washington

Klingebiel, A A, Horvath, E H, Moore, D G and Reybold, W U (1987) Use of slope, aspect, and elevation maps derived from digital elevation model data in making soil surveys. In Reybold, W U and Petersen, G W (eds) *Soil Survey Techniques*, SSSA Special Publ No 20, 77–90

Koreleski, K (1988) Adaptations of the Storie index for land evaluation in Poland. *Soil Survey and Land Evaluation* **8**: 23–9

Kosaki, T, Furukawa, H and Kyuma, K (1981) Computer-based soil data management system (COSMAS). *Soil Science and Plant Nutrition* **27**: 429–41

Krueger, R R (1977) The destruction of a unique renewable resource: the case of the Niagara fruit belt. In Krueger, R R and Mitchell, B (eds) *Managing Canada's Renewable Resources*, Methuen, Toronto, pp 132–48

Krueger, R R and Maguire, N G (1985) Protecting speciality cropland from urban development: the case study of the Okanagan Valley, British Columbia. *Geoforum* **16**: 287–300

van Kuilenburg, J, de Gruijter, J J, Marsman, B A and Bouma, J (1982) Accuracy of spatial interpolation between point data on soil moisture supply capacity, compared with estimates from mapping units. *Geoderma* **27**: 311–25

Kukachka, F R (1987) The microcomputer: a valuable tool for field soil survey. In Reybold, W U and Petersen, G W (eds) *Soil Survey Techniques*, SSSA Special Publ No 20, pp 49–55

Lal, S (1989) Productivity evaluation of some benchmark soils of India. *Journal Indian Society of Soil Science* **37**: 78–86

Land Evaluation Project (1983) Land evaluation under alternative erosion control policies. Report prepared for the Land Resource Research Institute, Agriculture Canada Report 4/81–3 University of Guelph, Ontario

van Lanen, H A J (1991) Qualitative and quantitative physical land evaluation: an operational approach. Doctoral thesis. Agricultural University, Wageningen, The Netherlands

van Lanen, H A J and Wopereis, F A (1991) Computer-captured expert knowledge to evaluate possibilities for injection of slurry from animal manure in The Netherlands. In van Lanen, H A J (1991) Qualitative and quantitative physical land evaluation: an operational approach. Doctoral thesis. Agricultural University, Wageningen, The Netherlands, pp 37–50

Larson, W E (1986) The adequacy of world soil resources. *Agronomy Journal* **78**: 221–5

Larson, W E (1987) An index for assessing the long-term productivity of soil. In Beek, K J, Burrough, P A and McCormack, D E (eds) *Quantified Land Evaluation Procedures*, ITC Publ No 6, Enschede, The Netherlands, 72–5

Lawrance, C J (1972) Terrain evaluation in West Malaysia: Part 1, Terrain classification and survey methods, Transport and Road Research Laboratory Report LR 506

Lawrance, C J (1978) Terrain evaluation in West Malaysia: Part 2, Land systems of south west Malaysia, Transport and Road Research Laboratory Supplementary Report LR·506

Lawrance, C J, Webster, R, Beckett, P H T, Bibby, J S and Hudson, G (1977) The use of air photo interpretation for land evaluation in the western highlands of Scotland. *Catena* **4**: 341–57

Leamy, M L (1974) An improved method of assessing the soil factor in land valuation. New Zealand Soil Bureau Scientific Report 16

Lee, J (1987) European land use and resources. *Land Use Policy* **4**: 179–99

Lee, L K (1984) Land use and soil loss: a 1982 update. *Journal of Soil and Water Conservation* **39**: 226–8 van Liet, L J P, Mackintosh, E E and Hoffman, D W (1979) Effects of land capability on apple production in southern Ontario. *Canadian Journal of Soil Science* 59: 163–75

Lindhult, M S, Fabos, J, Brown, P and Price, N (1988) Using geographic information systems to assess conflicts between agriculture and development. *Landscape and Urban Planning* 16: 333–43

Lindsay, J D, Scheelar, M D and Twardy, A G (1973) Soil survey for urban development. *Geoderma* 10: 35–45

Lowell, K E and Astroth, J H (1989) Vegetative succession and controlled fire in a glades ecosystem: a geographical information system approach. *International Journal of Geographical Information Systems* 3: 69–81

McCormack, D E (1987) Soil potential ratings – a special case of land evaluation. In Beek, K J, Burrough, P A and McCormack, D E (eds) *Quantified Land Evaluation Procedures*, ITC Publ No 6, Enschede, The Netherlands, pp 81–4

McCormack, D E and Johnson, R W (1982) Soil potential for onsite sewage disposal in Leon County, Florida. *Soil Survey and Land Evaluation* 2: 2–8

McCormack, D E and Stocking, M A (1986) Soil potential ratings. 1 An alternative form of land evaluation. *Soil Survey and Land Evaluation* 6: 37–42

McDonald, R C, Isbell, R F, Speight, J G, Walker J and Hopkins, M S (1984) *Australian Soil and Land Survey Field Handbook*. Inkata Press, Melbourne

Mackney, D (1974) Land use capability classification in the United Kingdom. In *Land Capability Classification*, Ministry of Agriculture, Fisheries and Food, Technical Bulletin No 30, HMSO, pp 4–11

McKeague, J A and Topp, G C (1986) Pitfalls in interpretation of soil drainage from soil survey information. *Canadian Journal of Soil Science* 66: 37–44

McRae, S G (1988) *Practical Pedology: Studying Soils in the Field*. Ellis Horwood, Chichester

McRae, S G and Burnham, C P (1981) *Land Evaluation*. Clarendon Press, Oxford

Madsen, H B (1989) Elaboration of a soil profile and analytical database connected to the EC soil map. In van Lanen, H A J and Bregt, A K (eds) *Agriculture: Application of Computerized EC Soil Map and Climatic Data*. Commission of the European Communities, pp 119–32

Maker, H J, Downs, J M and Anderson, J V (1972) Soil associations and land classification for irrigation, Sierra County Agricultural Experiment Station Research Report 233, New Mexico State University

Makin, J and Rose Innes, R (1987) Use of vegetation data in agro-ecological characterization for agricultural potential. In Bunting, A H (ed) *Agricultural Environments*. CAB International, Farnborough, pp 211–19

Makin, M J, Kingham, T J, Waddams, A E, Birchall, C J and Gavin, B W (1976) Prospects for irrigation development around Lake Zwai, Ethiopia Land Resource Study No 26, Land Resources Development Centre, Ministry of Overseas Development, Surbiton, England

Maletic, J T and Hutchings, T B (1967) Selection and classification of irrigable land. In Hagan, R M, Haise, H R and Edminster, T W (eds) *Irrigation of Agricultural Lands*. American Society of Agronomy, Madison, Wis., pp 125–73

Manning, E W (1987) Sustainable use of Canada's rural land resources: relating research to reality. In Cocklin, C, Smit, B and Johnson, T (eds) *Demands on Rural Lands: Planning for Resource Use*. Westview Press, Boulder, Col., pp 23–46

Mansfield, J E, Bennett, J G, King, R B, Lang, D M and Lawton, R M (1975–6) Land resources of the Northern and Luapula Provinces, Zambia–a reconnaissance assessment, six vols, Land Resource Study No 26, Land Resource Study No 19, Land Resources Development Centre, Surbiton, England

Mashimo, Y and Arimitsu, K (1986) A site classification for forest land use in Japan. In Gessel, S P (ed) *Forest Site and Productivity*, Lancaster Nijkoff, Dordrecht, pp 29–41

Mausbach, M J and Reybold, W U (1987) In support of GIS in the SCS: SIS. In Beek, K J, Burrough, P A and McCormack, D E (eds) *Quantified Land Evaluation Procedures*, ITC Publ No 6, Enschede, The Netherlands, pp 77–9

Mausbach, M J and Stubbendieck, G T (1987) Microcomputer processing and analysis of pedon descriptions. In Reybold, W U and Petersen, G W (eds) *Soil Survey Techniques*, SSSA Special Publ No 20, 33–9

Mew, G and Ball, D F (1972) Grid sampling and air photography in upland soil mapping. *Geographical Journal* 138: 8–14

Ministry of Agriculture, Fisheries and Food (1988) Agricultural land classification of England and Wales

Mitchell, A J B (1976) The irrigation potential of soils along the main rivers of eastern Botswana – a reconnaissance assessment. Land Resource Study 7, Land Resources Division, Ministry of Overseas Development

Monteith, J L (1973) *Principles of Environmental Physics*. Edward Arnold, London

Morgan, J P (1974) ADAS (Lands) physical agricultural land classification. In *Land Capability Classification*, Ministry of Agriculture, Fisheries and Food, Technical Bulletin No 30, HMSO, pp 80–9

Moss, G H (1987) Wasting Europe's heritage – the need for soil protection. In Barth, H and L'Hermite, P (eds) *Scientific Basis for Soil Protection in the European Community*. Elsevier Applied Science, Barking, Essex, 17–28

Moss, M R (1985) Land processes and land classification. *Journal of Environmental Management* 20: 295–319

Moss, R P (1978) Concept and theory in land evaluation for rural land use planning. Occasional Publication No 6, Department of Geography, University of Birmingham

Msanya, B M, Langohr, R and Lopulisa, C (1987) Testing and improvement of a questionnaire to users of soil maps. *Soil Survey and Land Evaluation* 7: 33–42

Munoz-Pardo, J, Ruelle, P and Vauclin, M (1990) Spatial variability of an agricultural field: geostatistical analysis of soil texture, soil moisture and yield components of two rainfed crops. *Catena* **17**: 369–81

Murtha, G G and Reid, R (1976) Soils of the Townsville area in relation to urban development. Division of Soils Divisional Report No 11, CSIRO

Nakos, G (1983) The land resource survey of Greece. *Journal of Environmental Management* **17**: 153–69

National Water and Soil Conservation Organisation (1979) Our land resources. Water and Soil Division, Ministry of Works and Development, Wellington, New Zealand

Neimanis, V P (1979) Canada's cities and their surrounding land resource. Report No 15, Canada Land Inventory, Lands Directorate, Environment Canada, Ottawa, Canada

Newsome, P F J (1987) The vegetative cover of New Zealand. Water and Soil Miscellaneous Publication No 112, Wellington, New Zealand

Nielson, G A, Caprio, J M, McDaniel, P A, Snyder, R D and Montagne, C (1990) MAPS: a GIS for land resource management in Montana. *Journal of Soil and Water Conservation* **45**: 450–3

Nowland, J L (1978) Canada's agricultural land resource. Paper presented at the 92nd annual conference Engineering Institute of Canada, St Johns, Newfoundland

Ogunkunle, A O and Izuakor, F O (1988) Impact of differences in profile description and laboratory data on soil classification. *Catena* **15**: 519–28

Oliver, M, Webster, R and Gerrard, J (1989a) Geostatistics in physical geography, Part I: theory. *Transactions of the Institute of British Geographers* **14**: 259–69

Oliver, M, Webster, R and Gerrard, J (1989b) Geostatistics in physical geography, Part II: applications. *Transactions of the Institute of British Geographers* **14**: 270–86

Olson, G W (1981) *Soils and the Environment.* Chapman and Hall, New York

Osunade, M A Adewole (1987) A viable method of land capability classification for small farmers. *Journal of Environmental Management* **25**: 81–94

Ovalles, F A and Collins, M E (1988) Evaluation of soil variability in northwest Florida using geostatistics. *Journal Soil Science Society of America* **52**: 1702–8

Patterson, G T and Wall, G J (1982) Within-pedon variability in soil properties. *Canadian Journal of Soil Science* **62**: 631–9

Pawley, W H (1971) In the year 2070. *Ceres* **4**: 22–7

Penman, H L (1948) Natural evaporation from open water, bare soil and grass. *Proceedings of the Royal Society Series A* **193**: 120–45

Penman, H L (1962) Woburn irrigation (1952–9) II: Results for grass. *Journal of Agricultural Science, Cambridge* **58**: 349–64

Peters, T W (1977) Relationships of yield data to agroclimates, soil capability classification and soils of Alberta. *Canadian Journal of Soil Science* **57**: 341–7

Pettry, D E and Coleman, C S (1973) Two decades of urban soil interpretations in Fairfax County, Virginia. *Geoderma* 10: 27–34

Peyer, K, Frei, E, Jäggli, F and Juhasz, P (1976) Bewasserungsplanung im Val, Mustair (GR) aufgrund von bodenkartering. *Schweizerische landwirtschaftliche Forschung* 15: 361–9

Pleijsier, L K (1988) Variability in soil data. Paper presented at the Symposium *Land Qualities in Space and Time*, held at Wageningen, The Netherlands, 22–26 August 1988

Pohjakas, K (1987) Land irrigability classification in Alberta. In Beek, K J, Burrough, P A and McCormack, D E (eds) *Quantified Land Evaluation Procedures*, ITC Publ No 6, Enschede, The Netherlands, pp 122–6

Purdie, R (1984) Land systems of the Simpson Desert region CSIRO Division of Water and Land Resources, Natural Resources Series No 2

Ragg, J M (1977) The recording and organization of soil field data for computer areal mapping. *Geoderma* 19: 81–9

Ragg, J M and Henderson, R (1980) A reappraisal of soil mapping in an area of southern Scotland. Part I The reliability of four soil mapping units and the morphological variability of their dominant taxa. *Journal of Soil Science* 31: 559–72

Revelle, R (1976) The resources for agriculture. *Scientific American* 235: 164–78

Ridgway, R B and Jayasinghe, G (1986) The Sri Lanka land information system. *Soil Survey and Land Evaluation* 6: 20–5

Rizzo, B (1990) The ecosystems of Canada in 2050: a scenario of change. *State of the Environment, Newsletter* 5: 4–5

Robbins Church, M (1989) Direct/delayed response project: predicting future long-term effects of acidic deposition on surface water chemistry. *Transactions of the American Geophysical Union* 70: 801–3, 812-13

Rossiter, D G (1990) ALES: a framework for land evaluation using a microcomputer. *Soil Use and Management* 6: 7–20

Rossiter, D G and van Wambeke, A R (1989) ALES version 2.2. User's Manual. Department of Agronomy, Cornell University, Ithaca, New York

Rudeforth, C C (1975) Storing and processing data for soil and land use capability surveys. *Journal of Soil Science* 26: 155–68

Rudeforth, C C and Bradley, R I (1972) Soil, land classification and land use of west and central Pembrokeshire, Special Survey No 6, Soil Survey of England and Wales, Harpenden

Sanchez, P A, Couto, W and Buol, S W (1982) The fertility capability soil classification system: interpretation, applicability and modification. *Geoderma* 27: 283–309

Schellentrager, G W, Doolittle, J A, Calhoun, T E and Wettstein, C A (1988) Using ground-penetrating radar to update soil survey information. *Journal of the Soil Science Society of America* 52: 746–52

Scholz, U (1987) Crop geography for agro-ecological characterization in Sumatra and Costa Rica. In Bunting, A H (ed) *Agricultural Environments* CAB International, Farnborough, pp 247–59

Schultink, G (1986) The CRIES resource information system: computer-aided spatial analysis of resource development potential and development policy alternatives. Proceedings 7th ISPRS Commission VII Symposium 933–8

Schultink, G (1987) The CRIES resource information system: computer-aided spatial analysis of resource development potential and development policy alternatives. In Beek, K, Burrough, P A and McCormack, D E *Quantified Land Evaluation Procedures*, ITC Publ No 6, Enschede, The Netherlands, pp 95–9

Schultink, G and Amaral, N C (1987) Assessment of agro-ecosystems production potential in developing countries; the CRIES agro-economic information system yield model. *Soil Survey and Land Evaluation* 7: 187–97

Scott, R M, Healy, P A and Humphreys, G S (1985) Land units of Chimbu Province Papua New Guinea CSIRO Division of Water and Land Resources, Natural Resources Series No 5

Scottish Development Department (1987a) National planning guidelines. National Planning Series

Scottish Development Department (1987b) Land use summary sheet. Agriculture.

Shaw, E M (1988) *Hydrology in Practice*. Van Nostrand Reinhold, London

Singh, U, Tsuji, G Y and Godwin, D C (1990) Planting new ideas in DSSAT: the CERES-Rice model. *Agrotechnology Transfer* 10: 1–6

Smit, B (1981) Procedures for the long-term evaluation of rural land. CRD Publication No 105, University School of Rural Planning and Development, University of Guelph, Ontario

Smit, B, Brklacich, M, Dumanski, J, MacDonald, K B and Miller, M H (1984) Integral land evaluation and its application to policy. *Canadian Journal of Soil Science* 64: 467–79

Smith, R S (1982) The use of land classification in resource assessment and rural planning. Institute of Terrestrial Ecology, Cambridge, England

Soil Conservation Service (1983) National Agricultural Land Evaluation and Site Assessment Handbook, 310-VI, issue 1, US Dept of Agriculture, Washington, DC

Soil Survey of Scotland (1982) 1:250,000 Land Capability for Forestry, Sheet 7, South-East Scotland

Soil Survey Staff (1960) *Soil Survey Manual*. US Department of Agriculture, Agriculture Handbook 18, Washington, DC

Soil Survey Staff (1975) Soil taxonomy – a basic system of soil classification for making and interpreting soil surveys. US Department of Agriculture, Agriculture Handbook 436, Washington, DC

Sombroek, W G and Colenbrander, H J (1990) Importance of global data in monitoring the soil and water resources. *Proceedings International Conference and Workshop on Global Natural Resource Monitoring and Assessments: Preparing for the 21st Century* Vol 1, pp 60–74, American Society for Photogrammetry and Remote Sensing, Bethesda, Md

Sombroek, W G and van de Weg, R F (1980) Some considerations on quality and readability of soil maps and their legends. *Annual Report,*

International Soil Museum, Wageningen, 4–17

Sooryanarayana, V (1985) Agro-ecological zones and agricultural land use in Malaysia: the potential contribution of Soil Taxonomy. *Technical Bulletin Aspac Food and Fertilizer Technology Center* **89**: 1–11

Stamp, L D (1962) *The Land of Britain – its Use and Misuse*, third edition, Longman, London

Stein, A, Hoogerwerf, M and Bouma, J (1988) Use of soil-map delineations to improve (co-)kriging of point data on moisture deficits. *Geoderma* **43**: 163–77

Stewart, R B (1983) Modelling methodology for assessing crop production potentials in Canada. Contribution 1983–12E, Research Branch, Agriculture Canada, Ottawa, Canada

van Stiphout, T P J, van Lanen, H A J, Boersma, O H and Bouma, J (1987) The effect of bypass flow and internal catchment of rain on the water regime in a clay loam grassland soil. *Journal of Hydrology* **95**: 1–11

Stocking, M A and McCormack, D E (1986) Soil potential ratings: 1. A test of the method in Zimbabwe. *Soil Survey and Land Evaluation* **6**: 115–22

Storie, R E (1976) Storie index soil rating (revised) 1978. Special Publication Division of Agricultural Science, University of California, Berkeley, Calif.

Stove, G C and Hulme, P D (1980) Peat resource mapping in Lewis using remote sensing techniques and automated cartography. *International Journal of Remote Sensing* **1**: 319–44

Styles, K A, Hansen, A and Burnett, A D (1986) Use of a computer-based land inventory for delineation of terrain which is geotechnically suitable for development. *Proceedings 5th International Association Engineering Geology Congress* **3**: 1841–8

Swindale, L D (1978) A soil research network through tropical soil families. In Swindale, L D (ed) *Soil-resource Data for Agricultural Development*, Hawaii Agricultural Experiment Station, University of Hawaii, pp 210–18

Sys, C and Verheye, W (1974) Land evaluation for irrigation of arid regions by the use of the parametric method. *Transactions of the 10th International Congress of Soil Science* **5**: 149–55

Tan, Y R and Shih, S F (1988) A geographic information system for study of agricultural land-use changes in St Lucie County, Florida. *Proceedings Soil and Crop Science Society of Florida* **47**: 102–5

Tercafs, R (1986) A computer system to assist optimilization of land management. *Ecological Modelling* **31**: 355–63

Thomas, R G and Thompson, J G (1959) The classification and assessment of soils for irrigation in Southern Rhodesia. *Proceedings 3rd Inter-African Soils Conference* pp 345–50

Thomas, R F, Blakemore, L C and Kinloch, D I (1979) Flow-diagram keys for 'Soil Taxonomy'. New Zealand Soil Bureau, Reports 39A, 39B, 39C, 39D, 39E, 39F, 39G and 39H, Wellington, New Zealand

Thornthwaite, C W (1948) An approach towards a rational classification of climate. *Geographical Review* **38**: 55–94

Trangmar, B B, Yost, R S and Uehara, G (1985) Application of geostatistics to spatial studies of soil properties. *Advances in Agronomy* **38**: 45–93

Treworgy, C G (1984) Design and development of a GIS for Illinois. in *Spatial Information Technologies for Remote Sensing Today and Tomorrow Proceedings Pecora meeting*, IEEE Computer Society, 29–32

UNEP (1990) GRID: Global Resource Information Database. United Nations Environment Programme, Nairobi

USBR (1951) Bureau of Reclamation Manual. Vol V Irrigated land use. Part 2 Land classification Bureau of Reclamation, Department of the Interior, Denver Federal Center, Denver, Col.

USDA (1981) Soil survey of Orange County, New York, USDA, Soil Conservation Service in Cooperation with Cornell University Agricultural Experiment Station

Valentine, K W G (1981) How soil map units and delineations change with survey intensity and map scale. *Canadian Journal of Soil Science* **61**: 535–51

Valentine, K W G (1986) *Soil Resource Surveys for Forestry*. Clarendon Press, Oxford

Varcoe, V J (1990) A note on the computer simulation of crop growth in agricultural land evaluation. *Soil Use and Management* **6**: 157–9

Ventura, S J, Chrisman, N R, Connors, K, Gurda, R F and Martin, R W (1988) A land information system for soil erosion control planning. *Journal of Soil and Water Conservation* **43**: 230–3

Ventura, S J, Niemann, B J and Moyer, D D (1988) A multipurpose land information system for rural resource planning. *Journal of Soil and Water Conservation* **43**: 226–30

Verheye, W H (1986) Principles of land appraisal and land use planning within the European Community. *Soil Use and Management* **2**: 120–4

Vink, A P A (1975) *Land Use in Advancing Agriculture*. Springer-Verlag, Berlin

Vink, A P A and van Zuilen, E J (1974) The suitability of the soils of the Netherlands for arable land and grassland. Soil Survey Papers No 8, Netherland Soil Survey Institute, Wageningen, The Netherlands

Vitek, J D, Walsh, S J and Gregory, M S (1984) Accuracy in GIS: an assessment of inherent and operational errors. In *Spatial Information Technologies for Remote Sensing Today and Tomorrow Proceedings of the Pecora meeting*, IEEE Computer Society, pp 296–302

Volkman, N J (1987) Vanishing lands in the USA: the use of agricultural districts as a method to preserve farm land. *Land Use Policy* **4**: 14–30

Wang, F, Brent Hall, G and Subaryono (1990) Fuzzy information representation and processing in conventional GIS software: database design and application. *International Journal of Geographical Information Systems* **4**: 261–83

Water Development Department, Cyprus and Land Resources Development Centre (1982) Southern Conveyor Project Feasibility Study, WDD, Nicosia and LRDC, Surbiton, Surrey

Water and Soil Division, Ministry of Works and Development (1979) Our land resources: a bulletin to accompany New Zealand Land Resource Inventory Worksheets. Wellington, New Zealand

Webster, R (1977) *Quantitative and Numerical Methods in Soil Classification and Survey*. Clarendon Press, Oxford

Webster, R (1981) Soil survey: its quality and effectiveness. Soil Resource Inventories and Development Planning, Tech Mono No 1, Soil Management Support Services, Soil Conservation Service, USDA, 53–62

Webster, R (1985) Quantitative spatial analysis of soil in the field. *Advances in Soil Science* **3**: 1–69

Webster, R and Beckett, P H T (1970) Terrain classification and evaluation using air photography: a review of recent work at Oxford. *Photogrammetria* **26**: 51–75

Webster, R and McBratney, A B (1987) Mapping soil fertility at Broom's barn by simple kriging. *Journal of the Science of Food and Agriculture* **38**: 97–115

Webster, R and Oliver, M A (1989a) Disjunctive kriging in agriculture. In Armstrong, M (ed) *Geostatistics*, vol 1, 421–32, Kluwer Academic Publishers

Webster, R and Oliver, M A (1989b) Optimal interpolation and isarithmic mapping of soil properties. VI Disjunctive kriging and mapping the conditional probability. *Journal of Soil Science* **40**: 497–512

Webster, R and Oliver, M A (1990) *Statistical Methods in Soil and Land Resource Survey*. Oxford University Press, Oxford

Wehde, M (1982) Grid cell size in relation to errors in maps and inventories produced by computerized map processing. *Photogrammetric Engineering and Remote Sensing* **48**: 1289–98

Weitz, C H (1986) The global context. In Knell, I S and English, J R (eds) *Canadian Agriculture in a Global Context: Opportunities and Obligations*. University of Waterloo Press, 1–16

Western, S (1978) *Soil Survey Contracts and Quality Control*. Clarendon Press, Oxford

White, L P (1977) *Aerial Photography and Remote Sensing for Soil Survey*. Clarendon Press, Oxford

Wiggins, J C, Hartley, R P, Higgins, M J and Whittaker, R J (1986) Computing aspects of a large geographic information system for the EC. Proceedings Auto Carto London Vol 2 Digital Mapping and Spatial Information Systems, Blakemore, M (ed) pp 28–43

Wiggins, J C, Hartley, R P, Higgins, M J and Whittaker, R J (1987) Computing aspects of a large geographical information system for the European Communities. *International Journal of Geographical Information Systems* **1**: 77–87

Wiken, E (1986) Terrestrial ecozones of Canada. Ecological Land Classification Series, No 19, Lands Directorate, Environment

Wilding, L P (1985) Spatial variability: its documentation, accommodation and implications to soil surveys. In Nielson, D R and Bouma, J (eds) *Soil Spatial Variability*. Pudoc, Wageningen, The Netherlands, pp 166–87

Williams, D and Pohl, A (1987) 'Let them eat houses!' The implications of urban expansion onto good farmland. In Cocklin, C, Smit, B and Johnson, T (eds) *Demands on Rural Lands: Planning for Resource Use*. Westview Press, Boulder, Col., pp 85–96

Woode, P R (1981) 'We don't want soil maps. Just give us land capability.' The role of land capability surveys in Zambia. *Soil Survey and Land Evaluation* **1**: 2–5

Worrell, R (1987) Predicting the productivity of sitka spruce on upland sites in northern Britain. Forestry Commission Bulletin 72, HMSO, London

Wright, L E (1984) Agricultural land evaluation and site assessment (LESA): a new agricultural land protection toll in the USA Soil-landscapes, taxonomic units and soil profiles. *Soil Survey and Land Evaluation* **4**: 25–38

Xu, J and Webster, R (1984) A geostatistical study of topsoil properties in Zhangwu County, China. *Catena* **11**: 13–26

Yager, T U, Lee, C A and Perfect, G A (1967) Report on the detailed soil survey and irrigibility classification of the Chalimbana area, Zambia. Soil Survey Report No 1, Ministry of Agriculture, Republic of Zambia

Yates, S R and Yates, M V (1990) Geostatistics for waste management. A user's manual for the GEOPACK (version 1 0) geostatistical software system. US Environmental Protection Agency, Ada, Oklahoma

Young, A (1973) Rural land evaluation. In Dawson, J A and Doornkamp, J C (eds) *Evaluating the Human Environment*. Edward Arnold, London, pp 5–33

Young, A and Goldsmith, P F (1977) Soil survey and land evaluation in developing countries. *Geographical Journal* **143**: 407–31

Zayach, S J (1973) Soil surveys – their value and use to communities in Massachusetts. *Geoderma* **10**: 67–74

Zonn, I (1977) Irrigation of the world's arid lands. *World Crops and Livestock* **29**: 72–3

Index